S0-EGN-066

WITHDRAWN
UTSA LIBRARIES

# Environmental Politics in Egypt

Drawing on extensive fieldwork conducted in Egypt from the late 1990s to 2011, this book shows how experts and activists used distinctive approaches to influence state and firm decision-making in three important environmental policy domains. These include industrial pollution from large-scale industry, the conservation of threatened habitat, and water management of the irrigation system.

These cases show how environmental networks sought to construct legal, discursive, and infrastructural forms of authority within the context of a fragmented state apparatus and a highly centralized political regime. "Managerial networks," composed of environmental scientists, technocrats, and consultants, sought to create new legal regimes for environmental protection and to frame environmental concerns so that they would appeal to central decision-makers. Activist networks, in contrast, emerged where environmental pollution or exclusion from natural resources threatened local livelihoods and public health. These networks publicized their concerns and mobilized broader participation through the creative use of public space, media coverage, and strategic use of existing state-sanctioned organizations.

With the increased popular mobilization of the 2000s, and the mass protests of the 2011 revolution, environmental politics has become highly topical. Expert and activist networks alike have sought to broaden their appeal and diversify their approaches. The result is a more contested, participatory, and dynamic phase in Egyptian environmentalism.

**Jeannie L. Sowers** is an Associate Professor of Political Science at the University of New Hampshire. Her research focuses on the intersections of politics and environmental issues in the Middle East and North Africa. She co-edited *The Journey to Tahrir: Revolution, Protest, and Social Change in Egypt* (2012), and has published articles in *Climatic Change*, the *Journal of Environment and Development*, *Development and Change*, and *Middle East Report*.

# Routledge Studies in Middle Eastern Politics

# Environmental Politics in Egypt

## Activists, experts, and the state

**Jeannie L. Sowers**

Routledge
Taylor & Francis Group

LONDON AND NEW YORK

First published 2013
by Routledge
2 Park Square, Milton Park, Abingdon, Oxon OX14 4RN

Simultaneously published in the USA and Canada
by Routledge
711 Third Avenue, New York, NY 10017

*Routledge is an imprint of the Taylor & Francis Group, an informa business*

© 2013 Jeannie L. Sowers

The right of Jeannie L. Sowers to be identified as author of this work has been
asserted by her in accordance with sections 77 and 78 of the Copyright, Designs
and Patents Act 1988.

All rights reserved. No part of this book may be reprinted or reproduced or
utilised in any form or by any electronic, mechanical, or other means, now
known or hereafter invented, including photocopying and recording, or in any
information storage or retrieval system, without permission in writing from the
publishers.

*Trademark notice*: Product or corporate names may be trademarks or registered
trademarks, and are used only for identification and explanation without intent to
infringe.

*British Library Cataloguing in Publication Data*
A catalogue record for this book is available from the British Library

*Library of Congress Cataloging in Publication Data*
Sowers, Jeannie Lynn, 1967-
Environmental politics in Egypt : activists, experts and the state / Jeannie L.
Sowers.
p. cm. -- (Routledge studies in Middle Eastern politics ; 50)
Includes bibliographical references and index.
1. Environmentalism--Political aspects--Egypt. 2. Environmental protection-
-Political aspects--Egypt. 3. Environmental policy--Egypt. I. Title. II. Series:
Routledge studies in Middle Eastern politics ; 50.
GE199.E9S68 2012
333.720962--dc23
2012023491

ISBN: 978-0-415-78300-2 (hbk)
ISBN: 978-0-203-80897-9 (ebk)

Typeset in Times New Roman
by GreenGate Publishing Services, Tonbridge, Kent

Printed and bound in the United States of America by Publishers Graphics,
LLC on sustainably sourced paper.

Library
University of Texas
at San Antonio

For Ben and Evan

# Contents

# Illustrations

## Maps

## Figures

## Tables

# Acknowledgments

This book would not have been possible without the many people in Egypt who have shared their observations and ideas about environment and politics with me since 1997. Without their contributions, I would have a much-impoverished understanding. Since field interviews were conducted anonymously and confidentially, given the nature of the former political regime and the sensitivity of many environmental issues, these individuals remain unnamed. (A list of organizational affiliations of those interviewed is provided in the appendix.)

For their ongoing help with this project, I would like to thank Ahmed Kamel, Karim Shalaby, the late Mohamed Kassas, John Grainger, Tarek Genena, Khaled Fahmy, Sharif and Mindy Baha Al-Din, and Mary Megalli. Several friends and families in Egypt have sustained me in more ways than they know. For their friendship, regardless of distance and time, I would like to thank Ahmed Kamal and Abeer Kotb, Karim Shalaby and Nariman Sabah, and Halina. I am also grateful for the hospitality and friendship of Boshra Salem, Dina and Samer Shehata, Habib Ayeb, John Sfakianakis, and the late 'Adil Abu Zahra during early fieldwork days in Egypt.

My thanks to Samer Shehata, Joshua Stacher, Amaney Jamal, Waleed Hazbun, Melani Cammett, Stacy VanDeveer, and Erika Weinthal for commenting on various chapters along the way. The group of scholars who work on Middle Eastern environmental politics and history has provided a collegial and exciting forum for the exchange of ideas, and my thanks to Miriam Lowi, Diana Davis, Sharif ElMusa, Neda Zawahri, Murat Arsel, and Jessica Barnes, among others. Participants in panels at the Middle East Studies Association, the European Union Institute's Mediterranean Social and Political Research Meetings, the International Studies Association's Environmental Studies Section, the New England Middle East Politics Workshop, the Harvard University Kennedy School of Government's Dubai Initiative seminars, and the Harvard Middle East Politics Workshop provided helpful comments on various portions of this book.

Fellowships from the Center for Humanities at the University of New Hampshire and the Dubai Initiative at the Harvard University Kennedy School of Government provided me with much-needed time to pursue research and writing. The Graduate School and the College of Liberal Arts at UNH provided summer stipends for research and writing, and the Department of Political Science

kindly provided some funds for travel to Egypt. The Institute for the Study of
World Politics and Princeton University's Center for International Studies funded
the original dissertation research that inspired this project. A Fulbright-funded
Center for Arabic Study Abroad (CASA) III fellowship in Cairo was invaluable.
To all of the above institutions, and the individuals who administer them, I am
most grateful. At UNH, my thanks particularly to Ken Fuld, Marilyn Hoskins,
Burt Feintuch, Claire Malarte-Feldman, Dante Scala, Warren Brown, and Chris
Reardon for their institutional support of this research.

Chris Toensing graciously read and commented upon the entire manuscript.
Denise Powers helped greatly with early versions of the first three chapters.
Hoda Baraka and Safinaz Salah provided excellent research assistance in Cairo
at various times. At the University of New Hampshire, several wonderful students helped track down sources, including Colleen Flaherty, Andrew Smith, and
Trevor Mauck, while Michael Cole helped format the typescript and proofread
with care. Michelle Woodward tracked down photographs for the book, while permission for figures and photographs were graciously supplied by Francis Gilbert
and John Grainger, David Degner, Mohamed Sabry, and Landov. At UNH, I have
been fortunate to have a number of wonderful colleagues who kept up my spir-
its throughout. My gratitude to Sara Wolper, Mary Malone, Stacy VanDeveer,
Alasdair Drysdale, and Roslyn Chavda.

My extended family has graciously helped out, in ways great and small, and
have always been a constant source of encouragement. My very great thanks to
Jean Kennedy and Douglas Archard, Errol Sowers and Meredith Young-Sowers,
Derek and Katia Sowers, Kendra Sowers and Charles Dinklage, Lindsay and
Joerg Waelder, Gillian Charbonneau, Emma and Bryan Hauser, Rabin and Karen
Chandran, and all the children of the next generation.

As is the case for most working parents, the hours I took for solitary research
and writing came out of other important things: childcare and family time, community and school volunteering, and house cleaning, to name but a few. Thanks
to Katia Sowers, Maryna Martin, Jen Lyon, Emily Slama, Hope Flynn, and Sarah
Grandy for helping me out when I most needed it.

For ideas, support, and inspiration from the beginning, I thank Atul Kohli,
Bob Vitalis (what matters is "to get the story right"), and, most importantly, John
Waterbury, who for years had a sign in his Princeton office that read *mamnu'
kalam fadi*. I have tried to live up to this standard.

My husband Ben Chandran unstintingly supported this work in ways both
great and small. I dedicate this book to him and our son, Evan, for their love,
humor, and support throughout.

# Abbreviations

| | |
|---|---|
| AGOSD | Alexandria General Organization for Sanitary Drainage |
| CDM | Camp Dresser & McKee |
| EEAA | Egyptian Environmental Affairs Agency |
| EIA | environmental impact assessment |
| EGPC | Egyptian General Petroleum Corporation |
| EP3 | Environmental Pollution Prevention Project, USAID |
| EPAP (I and II) | Egyptian Pollution Abatement Project I and II, World Bank |
| GEF | Global Environmental Facility |
| HEPCA | Hurghada Environmental Protection and Conservation Association |
| IIP | Irrigation Improvement Project, USAID |
| IUCN | International Union for the Conservation of Nature |
| IWRM | integrated water resource management |
| MOPCO | Misr Fertilizers Production Company |
| NCS | Nature Conservation Sector, EEAA |
| NDP | National Democratic Party |
| NIB | National Investment Bank |
| SCA | Supreme Council on Antiquities |
| SCAF | Supreme Council of the Armed Forces |
| SOE | state-owned enterprise |
| TDA | Tourism Development Authority |
| UNDP | United Nations Development Programme |
| UNEP | United Nations Environmental Programme |
| USAID | United States Agency for International Development |

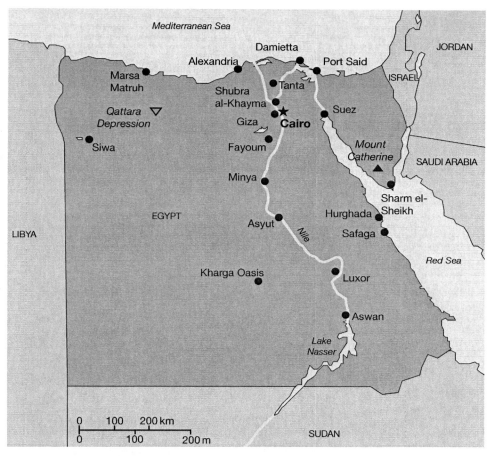

*Frontispiece 1.1* General map of Egypt

*Frontispiece 1.2* Egypt and the Nile River, NASA satellite image, July 19, 2004.
Source: NASA Visible Earth, Jacques Descloitres, MODIS Rapid
Response Team, NASA/GSFC, available at http://visibleearth.nasa.gov

# 1 Networks, authority, and environmental politics in Egypt

In 2008, the Mediterranean port city of Damietta saw escalating environmental protest against plans by the Canadian firm Agrium to build a large fertilizer plant near the popular middle-class tourist resort area of Ras al-Barr. Throughout the spring and summer, as temperatures mounted, thousands of protesters periodically took to the streets, closing workplaces and bringing transport to a standstill (Figure 1.1). From apartment balconies and shop windows, residents hung black banners emblazoned with slogans in Arabic urging: "For the sake of our children's health, no to the project!"; "No to pollution!"; "Respect the will of the people of Damietta!"

In their scale and prominence, the Damietta protests marked a new phase of environmental activism in Egypt. The Damietta campaign was one of the most visible environmental movements to emerge not just in Egypt but in the Arab world. Participants included civil society representatives, parliamentarians, residents, and public-sector employees in a coalition that crossed class and religious lines (Elmusa and Sowers, 2009). A new crop of Egyptian independent newspapers and private TV stations, in addition to such well-known regional satellite channels as *Al Jazeera*, covered the campaign extensively. In the face of sustained popular protest, the Mubarak government cancelled the investment agreement with Agrium, and granted the Canadian firm shares in a nearby state-owned fertilizer plant with guarantees that production would be expanded.

In 2011, after Mubarak had been driven from power by sustained street protest, construction on the expansion of the state-owned fertilizer plant began and popular protest resumed. Groups of villagers from nearby hamlets blocked the main roads leading to Damietta's large industrial port and cut off power to the port from the main power station. The military ordered in soldiers with assault rifles in the early hours of the morning to attack protesters camping out on the road, injuring a number of them and shooting dead a twenty-one-year-old youth. Tens of thousands of residents poured into the streets for the young man's funeral that night.

The protesters in Damietta knew well that protests about environmental issues are also political and social claims about rights, access, livelihoods, and power. In the years before Egypt's January 25 revolution, networks of activists used popular petitions, legal cases, and media coverage to bring environmental problems to

*Figure 1.1* Demonstrators carry banners during a protest against a new fertilizer plant in
Damietta City, June 17, 2008
Asmaa Waguih/Landov, 2008

the attention of decision-makers, to contest air and water pollution, the siting of industrial facilities, water scarcity, and other forms of environmental degradation immediately tangible to ordinary citizens. Frequently, however, activist networks were unable to bring sufficient leverage to bear to change the practices of firms or governmental agencies involved in producing environmental problems.

An extensive array of opaque state institutions has long been tasked with regulating access to resources, such as land and freshwater, in Egypt. Policies enacted by various central ministries in the fields of agriculture, irrigation, land and real estate markets, industry, investment, and military production shape the kinds and distribution of environmental impacts. Thus, the politics of environmental protection in Egypt often centers around the complex re-regulation and restructuring of resources, roles, and authority.

While some environmental issues, such as the salinization of irrigated land, have a long colonial and postcolonial history in Egypt, the identification of "the environment" as a distinct and separate field of policy intervention emerged principally during the 1970s. In the decades that followed, Egypt became a prominent location for policy interventions to "protect the environment" (*himayat al-bi'a*). Expert networks comprised of international and local consultants, environmental professionals, and middle- and upper-level technocrats created new institutions, such as the Ministry of State for Environmental Affairs, and sought to restructure "old" state entities charged with regulating and managing water, agriculture, industry, and investment. I term these actors managerial networks, as they claim authority to manage natural resources on the basis of professional expertise and the authoritative role of governmental institutions.

This book explores the changing contours of Egypt's activist and managerial networks under decades of sustained authoritarian rule and, more recently, revolutionary upheaval. Drawing on extensive interviews and fieldwork conducted in Egypt, I analyze the effectiveness of networks that coalesced around specific environmental policy domains. I analyze the creation of national environmental institutions and trace the evolution of specific efforts to control industrial pollution, establish and manage protected areas, contest urban land use and planning, and restructure water management. I explore under what conditions expert and activist networks mobilized sufficient authority to shape the behavior of firms, governmental agencies, and communities involved in producing pollution and environmental problems. Under what conditions did regulatory initiatives, donor projects, and protest campaigns successfully influence decision-making? How did managerial and activist networks promote new legal frameworks, frame their interventions, and reach constituencies through particular organizational infrastructures? Why did so many environmental projects and campaigns fail to meet their objectives, despite seemingly adequate financing and technical expertise?

To answer these questions, I analyze environmental networks in terms of the kinds of authority that they were able to deploy. I focus on three types of authority—discursive, legal, and infrastructural—to elucidate under what conditions environmental networks influenced policymaking and institutional development.[1] In essence, I argue that networks were more effective when they engaged the rule-making power of the state (legal authority), employed discourses and concepts that resonated with decision-makers and popular constituencies (discursive authority), and could draw upon or create infrastructures and organizations that linked environmental networks with governmental authorities and local communities (infrastructural authority). In the absence of these kinds of authority and linkages, environmental initiatives could quickly become little more than, in the words of one scholar of environmental policy in China, "a paper agreement or a hollow shell with little effect on social action" (Ho, 2005: 3).

Analyzing how networks mobilize authority calls our attention not only to the agency of individuals working together, but also the constraints imposed by institutional contexts, unequal power relations, and conflicting interests. Environmental politics thus serves as a window onto changing state–society relations in Egypt more broadly. Although the country is one of the most extensively studied in the Arab world, relatively few works analyze public policymaking and contestation around issues critical to everyday life. The making of public policies has long been considered "a black box," where the executive "had far-reaching autonomy when choosing policies and making decisions about whom to co-opt and to associate to the exercise of power" (Kienle, 2001: 8). One significant exception was scholarly analyses of political economy and economic reform, which often identified how informal networks of state and business actors influenced the formulation of state policies (Haddad, 2004; Sfakianakis, 2004; Springborg, 1989; Waterbury, 1993).

Scholars of Egypt have long recognized that the autonomy of the executive to take formal decisions, however, simply does not translate into the authority and institutional infrastructures to carry them out effectively (Ayubi, 1995). The reams of legislation, regulations, and administrative decrees issued by ministries in Cairo often bear little resemblance to the localized practices that evolve to access resources or compensate for inadequate public services and public goods. Whole swathes of territory and governance, as Sims notes, "operate largely outside the truncated powers of government or are at best in symbiotic relation with its weakness" (Sims, 2010: 4). Studies of urbanization, particularly focused on Cairo and the rapid spread of informal areas, have analyzed the limits of state action and influence, documenting how extensive, private systems of construction, transport, land conversion, and housing provision have evolved to meet the daily needs of many Egyptians in the absence of adequate public goods and services. The state's approach to much of what is considered the realm of public policy, in both cities and the countryside, has therefore been aptly characterized as the "politics of neglect" (Dorman, 2007).

This book seeks to chart a middle course between analyses that focus primarily on decision-making elites in the capital, and accounts that emphasize the informal, the marginal, and the neglected. For most environmental issues, the "state" is an important arena for contention and influence, but not only in the capital. The deconcentrated personnel and activities undertaken by government ministries in Egypt's governorates (provinces), the professional technocrats and consultants who implement projects, and the centrally appointed governors all play a role that is often understudied. In addition to these manifestations of the local state, analyses of environmental politics must grapple with the less institutionalized but increasingly important role played by expanding public spheres of protest, mobilization, and communication. These shape not only state decision-making but popular discourses about socio-economic and environmental issues.

In the chapters that follow, I thus trace how environmental networks at multiple levels and locations sought to influence formal decision-making, in the context of an expansive, often mistrusted, typically overburdened state apparatus that has long engaged in large-scale structural transformations of the local environment.

## Egypt's puzzle: environmental capacities without performance?

Egypt offers a fascinating case for studying how environmental networks mobilize authority—or fail to do so—because the country cannot be simply dismissed as a "failed" or "weak" state. Development practitioners and scholars alike often argue that developing countries such as Egypt simply lack the resources and expertise to pursue effective environmental interventions or provide adequate public services. Reports by multilateral organizations such as the World Bank (and also the relevant Egyptian state agencies) reiterate these claims, presenting lack of "capacity" as the key factor hindering more adequate action to protect the environment (Tolba and Saab, 2008; Wizarat al-Dawla li-Shu'un al-Bi'a, 2007; World Bank, 2005a). Incapacity is typically defined in terms of inadequate environmental information, scarce financing, and limited technical expertise, combined with weak environmental movements, underinvestment in scientific research, and a general lack of environmental awareness. Bilateral donors similarly emphasize the Egyptian state's lack of environmental capacity—whether in technical know-how or management practices—as a powerful rationale for channeling environmental aid to their own contracting firms.

In a similar vein, local media reporting and environmental experts in Egypt typically focus on the government's lack of enforcement capacity. From the Egyptian press to local officials, many discussions of environmental problems in Egypt return to the lack of *tansiq* (coordination) and *tatbiq* (application) of environmental regulations, particularly within and among different government entities. That is, poor environmental performance is said to flow from lack of political commitment within the regime and duplication and inefficiency of sprawling government bureaucracies.

A related claim, often made by middle- and upper-class Egyptians as well as by outside agencies, is that the public does not care about environmental problems. Therefore, the argument goes, there is little pressure on public authorities to address environmental issues. However, the limited available public opinion data on environmental awareness in Egypt simply does not support this assertion. Hopkins *et al.* conducted surveys focused specifically on perceptions of environmental problems among ordinary, non-elite Egyptians in "popular" neighborhoods (Hopkins *et al.*, 2001). Surveys conducted in 1995 (2,266 respondents) and 1997 (2,307 respondents) in four localities found that 50.4 percent of respondents rated themselves as "very concerned" about environmental pollution, while only 17.3 percent considered themselves "not concerned" (ibid.: 157). Ninety-five percent of all respondents held that pollution was a major problem in their community. When asked to rank environmental problems in their neighborhoods, respondents listed the following: garbage, water quality, and smell of garbage; cement dust; canals and swamps; dust and unpaved roads; sewage; smoke and car exhaust; factories of all types; and factory noise. The relative weights assigned to these categories varied by locality, as proximity to factories and levels of public services differed between urban, semi-urban, and rural areas. When asked to rank the most serious forms of pollution, water pollution came first for rural areas, while urban localities cited air pollution, reflecting both greater urban access to piped water and greater exposure to vehicles and industries. All localities listed garbage collection and disposal as a third priority, an issue not usually considered an environmental one in industrialized countries (ibid.: 161). For ordinary Egyptians, then, "environmental" problems included the provision of clean drinking water, sanitation, and trash collection as well as various kinds of pollution.

These findings make us ask why some environmental issues become political priorities while others, even as they often have more significant public health impacts, receive little external funding and political attention. As importantly, where environmental initiatives emerge, how do we explain variation in outcomes? How are "weak" capacities, under certain conditions, strengthened, while some seemingly robust initiatives fail? And more importantly for the Egyptian case, why are existing regulatory capacities and environmental expertise often under-utilized?

In contrast to many developing countries, we might expect Egypt to exhibit relatively strong environmental capacities as well as strong awareness, if we simply focus on available expertise and resources. With a long tradition of state regulation and intervention, increasingly well-educated if small cadres of environmental professionals, and sizable external resources targeting environmental problems, the country should be relatively well positioned, by conventional accounts, to make significant progress. Egypt was the second largest recipient of international environmental aid during the 1980s, receiving a total of US$2.2 billion (Hicks *et al.*, 2008: 61). During the 1990s, it was the seventh largest recipient of worldwide environmental aid with an inflow of US$3.2 billion (ibid.: 62).

Proliferating state and donor initiatives around environmental issues have indeed boosted the organizational and informational capacities associated with environmental protection in Egypt, particularly during the 1990s and 2000s. Baseline environmental information is more available, governmental and donor resources for environmental protection have increased, and a number of environmental laws and regulations have been promulgated. Thus, at least for the case of Egypt, weak capacity is too over-determined a concept to explain the evolution of environmental initiatives or evaluate variation in the effectiveness. Following Ascher (1999), I suggest that deficiencies in institutional capacity, resources, and lack of political will are not a priori causal factors, but rather outcomes that require explanation.

If we analyze environmental reform efforts in terms of how networks frame environmental problems (discursive authority), enlist the rule-making authority of the state (legal authority), and build linkages to relevant constituencies (infrastructural authority), we can more adequately explain changes in institutional capacity and political will over time and across policy domains.

## Environmental challenges in Egypt and the Middle East

Egypt's environmental challenges exemplify some of the most important environmental issues facing the Middle East and North Africa as a whole. These shared ecological problems include desertification, climate change, diminishing quantities and qualities of water and agricultural land, relatively high population growth rates, hazardous levels of urban air pollution, inadequate sanitation, and inadequate controls on industrial pollution.[2] To these issues we can add water pollution, which holds a particularly prominent place in Egyptian environmentalism given the country's dependence on the Nile River for much of its renewable freshwater supply. The deterioration of water quality from agricultural, industrial, and municipal discharges is linked to many public health effects. The Arabic term for pollution, *talawuth*, as used in the media and in conversation, thus includes public health and behavioral connotations.

Egypt's political economy, and the types of environmental degradation imposed by its development path, also shares some significant structural features with the rest of the Middle East and North Africa. Deposits of fossil fuels such as oil and natural gas, while much less extensive than those of the oil-exporting states of the Persian Gulf, has nevertheless meant the development of capital and pollution-intensive industries relying on fossil fuel inputs, in which state ownership remains extensive.

Egypt's ecology and its pattern of economic development means that many Egyptians face greater exposure to various pollutants—through multiple pathways and in more significant concentrations—than citizens in industrialized countries. International standards for pollutants, toxicity, and exposure may be too lax given patterns of settlement and economic activity. Standards of toxicity and emissions developed in industrialized nations, for instance, were often designed for landscapes in which pesticides were applied to vast mono-cropped tracts, and where industrial facilities had been largely relocated out of urban centers. Neither of these conditions matches those in Egypt.

It is thus not surprising that some environmental problems in Egypt pose significant health risks. For instance, a 2000 World Health Organization/UNICEF study found that child mortality rates in Egypt are significantly higher than average for countries with similar levels of income per capita, particularly in rural areas, due largely to inadequate sanitation. The 2005 Egypt Development Report, written by the United Nations Development Programme and local experts, found that environmental degradation, particularly that associated with air pollution and water quality, was limiting Egypt's development prospects and undermining public health. As the report noted:

Manifestations of a progressive imbalance in the ecosystem in a number of locations in Egypt indicate that Egypt now faces environmental pressures that are likely to impede its social and economic development, and diminish the quality of life of its citizens, in some cases reducing their capacity to contribute productively... Evidence also indicates that the multiplication of environmental hazards to which citizens are exposed in their daily life is progressing at a rate that threatens to outpace restorative action.

> (United Nations Development Programme and Institute of
> National Planning, 2005: 156)

## Environmental networks, activism, and policy change

These kinds of severe environmental problems, combined with the rise of oppositional social movements for indigenous, civil, and human rights, drove the emergence of environmentalism across much of the developing world (Guha, 2000). Environmental movements often emerged as part of broader challenges to authoritarian regimes, corrupt governance, and centralized, statist developmental models. As scholars of development have noted, there has been a historical affinity between durable authoritarian regimes and continued adherence to centralized, technocratic models of development (Khagram, 2004). In the Arab world, authoritarian rule and state-driven development strategies remained tightly coupled until the uprisings of 2011 began to unsettle long-established political orders.

Contentious politics, however, was an increasingly prominent part of political life long before massive street protest challenged incumbent regimes across the region (Beinin and Vairel, 2011; Lust-Okar and Zerhouni, 2008). Some of the elements of this mosaic of contention included Islamic revival movements, labor activism, human rights organizations, and protest around livelihood issues, such as access to farmland and fisheries. In Egypt, intermittent but cumulative economic reform produced a more diversified private sector, a more lively public sphere, and more vibrant forms of associational activity (Lynch, 2006; Rutherford, 2009). Reinvigorated movements by professional associations and unions emerged alongside escalating cycles of street protest (Beinin and Vairel, 2011; Sowers and Toensing, 2012).

These significant structural changes and increased social mobilization stand in stark contrast to decades of half-hearted attempts by incumbent regimes to restructure the administrative apparatus of the state in the name of efficiency. Most regimes in the Arab world have lacked the social bases of information and cooperation necessary to implement institutional reforms, in large part due to their own sustained attempts to disrupt, weaken, and selectively coopt civil society, political parties, and business associations. Public policy has long been marred by the poor performance of government institutions and low levels of civic trust and participation (United Nations Development Programme and Institute of National Planning, 2004). As one excellent survey of globalization and development in the region observed, while top-level bureaucrats in the region often produced "textbook" blueprints for reform, these have often been "dead letters in the absence of implementation capacity, which only a vibrant civil society appears to be able to provide" (Henry and Springborg, 2001: xiv).

An expanding body of development literature has highlighted the conditions under which "state–society synergy" (Evans, 1996) or "co-production" (Ostrom, 1996) of public goods and effective policy implementation takes place. For instance, Peter Evans explained successful industrial policy in East Asia as a form of "embedded autonomy," where autonomous, meritocratic public bureaucracies made use of institutionalized linkages with business groups to promote industrial innovation and production (Evans, 1995). Even under authoritarian rule, or where state–society relations are generally exclusionary and antagonistic, networks of local state officials and local communities have created momentum for policy changes in particular sectors and around specific issues (Mernissi, 1997; Tendler and Freedheim, 1994). O'Rourke, for instance, argues that community campaigns against pollution in Vietnam helped create incentives for local public authorities to take action even under conditions of single-party rule (O'Rourke, 2004).

Policy change, particularly under authoritarian rule, can be traced to the activities of networks that coalesce around distinctive policy domains or issues. For Egypt, scholars have traced the influence of state–business networks in promoting neoliberal economic reform, resulting in a political economy that Waterbury memorably described in terms of a "public–private symbiosis" (Waterbury, 1993). Many of these analyses analyzed networks as the means by which public and private actors jointly influenced policy outcomes (Haddad, 2004; Sfakianakis, 2004; Sowers, 2003; Springborg, 1989).

In seeking to explain why authoritarianism in much of the Arab world was so durable, despite internal and external pressures, Heydemann argued that these regimes were characterized by "dense, decentralized, and broadly inclusionary networks" (Heydemann, 2007: 27). Fueled by hydrocarbon revenues and populist ideologies after World War II, Heydemann argues that the expansion of the state apparatus into managing the economy and political life provided "the institutional skeleton for the construction of network polities across the region," replacing earlier forms of informal governance, such as direct patron–client ties in rural areas (ibid.). In this account, networks tying together state officials, business groups, and experts did not become widespread mechanisms for distributing and controlling access to resources, information, and authority as a result of weakly institutionalized or predatory states or unchanging patterns of patrimonialism. Rather, the rapid expansion of state bureaucracies provided fertile terrain for the construction of a multiplicity of public–private networks. Across the Middle East and North Africa, market reforms, (partial) privatization, and attempts to shrink sprawling state bureaucracies did not destroy these networks spanning state and social institutions, but instead restructured them.

To understand environmental governance in specific policy domains and over time, however, we need more fine-grained analyses of networks, including their participants, their institutional bases, and the opportunities and constraints available to mobilizing distinctive kinds of authority. Several scholars of environmental politics have conducted such analyses for other regions of the world and other kinds of environmental networks. These scholars have identified "epistemic communities" (Haas, 1990), transnational advocacy networks (Keck and Sikkink, 1998), and bilateral activists (Steinberg, 2001) as important mechanisms for environmental policy change. Epistemic communities share a commitment to professional norms that produce scientific consensus around the causes of environmental degradation over time (Haas, 1990). Transnational advocacy networks are generally distinguished by a set of shared normative commitments or principles, such as opposition to slavery or whaling (Keck and Sikkink, 1998). Both epistemic communities and advocacy networks are generally held to be centered in the more wealthy, industrialized countries, from which they draw resources and expertise to shape the framing of environmental problems and solutions in the developing world. In contrast, Steinberg's bilateral activists draw on their intimate knowledge and experience of domestic politics to more successfully use resources and publicity drawn from the international sphere.

Transnational advocacy networks have been considered particularly important agents for promoting change in authoritarian regimes and countries with closed political opportunity structures. For Keck and Sikkink, activists generate a "boomerang" effect as they lobby international organizations and open political structures in other countries to create pressures for change in closed regimes (ibid.). Transnational advocacy networks thus target their environmental campaigns to key international institutions, such as the World Bank, or to developed countries with aid and trade flows to exclusionary authoritarian regimes.

The study of Egyptian environmental networks yields a different cast of characters and a different balance of power between domestic and transnational actors. Network participants are generally more "rooted" in domestic institutional arrangements and interests and, as in the case of economic reform, most networks are public–private hybrids of state officials, environmental experts, and international consultants. Managerial and activist networks work out of state-affiliated and sanctioned organizations as well as advocacy organizations and NGOs.

The salience of domestic actors and state institutions in Egyptian environmental policymaking, and the correspondingly limited role played by transnational advocacy networks, stems in part from the fact that the Egyptian regime is largely insulated from international political pressure and transnational environmental organizations. Egypt's geopolitical significance for the United States and Europe, including its key role in normalizing relations with Israel and its strategic position as a transit route for oil (through the Suez Canal) and natural gas (through the SUMED pipeline), has limited external pressures. Geopolitical factors have also ensured that Egypt receives relatively large aid flows compared to other developing countries. International environmental campaigns have rarely targeted Egypt or other countries of the Middle East, in part because well-known international organizations, such as Greenpeace or Friends of the Earth, operate only in the more open political venues in the region, such as Lebanon or Israel. Until the 2011 revolutions, these organizations found it difficult to gain a foothold elsewhere in the region. Egypt, like much of the Arab world, is also relatively immune to environmental concerns raised by the World Bank or other development banks, as it can muster domestic and regional resources to fund development projects that outside funders might find questionable on economic or environmental grounds (Sowers, 2003).

Transnational connections still matter for Egyptian environmental networks, however. As participants in international and regional "epistemic communities," Egyptian environmental experts have long played a significant role in generating regional and global environmental discourses around issues of desertification, water scarcity, demand management, and nature conservation. Egypt's scientists and technocrats often help define regional environmental agendas and shape possible policy solutions, as Waterbury observed with regard to the World Bank-supported Nile Basin Initiative (Waterbury, 2002).

Until the January 25 revolution in 2011, the most comparable set of cases for understanding emerging environmental networks in Egypt was found in other evolving authoritarian and transitional regimes in which market reform and social activism had intensified in the absence of formal democratization or regime change. China and Vietnam constitute such cases, as do other countries where hegemonic parties and a degree of centralized planning persist, and where market reform spawned dense public–private networks. In China, for instance, incremental yet consistent environmental reform facilitated what one analyst termed "embedded activism," where "the divide between civic organizations, state, and Party is extremely blurred" by the sheer variety of informal networks based on numerous and often overlapping institutional linkages (Ho and Edmonds, 2008: 3).

## Egypt's environmental networks: managerial and activist

Two types of environmental networks can be abstracted from the Egyptian experience: managerial networks and activist networks. During the Mubarak period, these networks often differed in terms of their participants, institutional origins, goals, and strategies. Managerial networks based their interventions on claims to technical expertise and invoked the authoritative role of the state as the basis for public policymaking. Participants in these networks held overlapping or rotating positions as appointed officials, environmental scientists, university researchers, and environmental consultants. These individuals became linked together through the repeated experience of working together on discrete "projects" (*mashari'a*) in a given policy domain and by staffing environmental reform units and parallel institutions established within existing central ministries. This book analyzes the impact of managerial networks on creating and managing protected areas, promoting pollution control, and restructuring many different facets of the irrigation system in Egypt.

Activist networks drew upon different justifications and tactics than managerial networks. Activist networks mounted campaigns to address specific, egregious sources of pollution, industrial siting, and other issues that have tangible impacts on local communities. Participants in activist networks often came together through a collective undertaking, namely the conduct of a campaign (*hamla*) to publicize their case, mobilize local communities, and influence decision-making. Activist networks grounded their environmental discourses in risks to public health, livelihoods, and urban identities. They often derived a sense of coherence from either a shared value orientation, such as a commitment to human rights or labor organization, or a shared sense of place, as in the provincial cities of Alexandria and Damietta (Chapter 4).

The scope and substance of Egyptian environmentalism has been increasingly redefined by the prominent role of activist networks and popular mobilization. Activist campaigns became more effective in influencing decision-makers during the late 1990s and 2000s with the rise of an independent media, the strategic use of existing but weak formal political institutions (such as the Majlis al-Sha'b, the elected parliamentary house, and the judiciary), and the increased willingness of ordinary people to engage in direct action.

Managerial and activist networks have typically arisen in different locations, in the distinctive landscapes and projects that served as catalysts for network creation and activity. Different places thus offered different opportunities and constraints for networks seeking to mobilize legal, discursive, and infrastructural forms of power. As Michael Mann observes, networks have "spatial contours" that shape the kinds of power they seek to exercise (Mann, 1986: 10). The spatial contours of environmental networks have inevitably been intimately linked with broader transformations in Egypt's political economy and its landscapes.

Since the 1980s, the Mubarak regime sought to attract private investment by creating special economic zones free of typical regulatory frameworks governing taxation, labor, and import duties. These zones included free zones, port authorities, industrial zones, tourism zones, new cities, and qualified industrial zones (QIZs). Many of these zones grew only slowly, particularly when not in close proximity to transport, trade, and population center. But some of these new areas produced intensified investment in industry and tourism. The effect was most pronounced in the breakneck development in real estate, tourism, and industry along Egypt's coastlines, from the Mediterranean coast in the north to the Gulf of 'Aqaba and the Red Sea coast in the southeast. Severe environmental impacts attracted the attention of managerial networks working in such policy domains as industrial pollution, marine ecology, and habitat protection.

In "old" urban areas and rapidly expanding peri-urban areas, densification of settlement, inadequate public service provision, and industrial pollution contributed to rising public concern with pollution impacts. The result was the emergence of activist networks that drew upon existing social fabrics in urban areas to contest industrial siting decisions and urban pollution. The major participants, policy domains, and geographic foci for Egyptian environmental networks analyzed in this book are summarized in Table 1.1.

*Table 1.1* Environmental networks in Egypt

|  | *Managerial networks* | *Activist networks* |
| --- | --- | --- |
| Catalyst for network creation | Donor-state projects | Issue campaigns |
| Participants | Experts<br>Consultants (Egyptian and expatriate)<br>Scientists | Community activists<br>Journalists<br>Advocacy and professional organizations<br>Parliamentarians |
| Spatial-policy focus | Industrial pollution hotspots (Chapter 3)<br>Protected areas (Chapter 5)<br>Irrigation/drainage system in Nile Delta and Nile Valley (Chapter 6)<br>Restructuring government ministries (e.g. irrigation, agriculture, environmental affairs) | Industrial siting and pollution (Chapters 4, 7)<br>Rights to resources—land, water, fisheries (Chapters 4, 5, 6, 7) |

## Networks and power

Managerial and activist networks seek to influence outcomes by acquiring and exercising legal, discursive, and infrastructural forms of authority. The next three sections situate these forms of authority within the Egyptian political context.

### *Legal authority: fragmentation and conflict*

Rule-making or legal authority is often associated with the formal regulatory and legislative powers delegated to state agencies, courts, and legislatures. These include rules that create or restructure property rights, allocate resources, and establish regulatory standards. In Egypt as in most of the Arab states, rule-making authority has been largely vested in executive institutions. Authority wielded by the executive—personified by the president, the Cabinet, and executive appointees within the central ministries and provincial governments—trumped that of the other branches of government, local administration, civil society, and the business sector. The 2004 Arab Human Development Report characterized this governance arrangement as "executive hegemony" and argued it was a key element in a broader regional "architecture" of authoritarian rule (United Nations Development Programme, 2005). Even where legislation is formally approved by parliament, substantive portions are issued directly by the executive branch through administrative decrees. Such was the case, for instance, with the environmental regulatory standards contained in Law 4 for 1994 (revised in Law 9 for 2009).

In practice, however, legal authority has not been as centralized or standardized as the idea of "executive hegemony" might suggest. "Executive authority" is delegated to a variety of officials charged with various projects, programs, and activities, and thus multiple entities are entitled to issue various kinds of administrative regulations. In addition, the president and his associates rotate high-ranking personnel in some ministries to avoid the emergence of alternative power centers. The result has been a continual proliferation and fragmentation of administrative law and decrees that, in aggregate, produced confusion and uncertainty in most policy areas. Overlapping, conflicting rules and regulations in turn required ongoing, additional administrative decrees to clarify contradictions and omissions.

The accumulation of fragmented, vague, and conflicting rule-making around any given policy issue was often associated with the ministerial reigns of different individuals and the bureaucratic turf of different ministries. But in some instances, fragmented legal authority also reflected the de facto cultivation of what Ho terms "intentional institutional ambiguity" (Ho, 2005: 3). Institutional ambiguity arises when executive authorities avoid sorting out multiple claims or clarifying ambiguous regulatory decrees in order to avert intensified social conflict, a tactic Ho argues is frequently employed by party officials in China.

Institutional ambiguity, overlapping mandates, and conflicting rule-making authorities open space for contestation and influence by environmental networks. To deal with legal fragmentation and conflict, managerial networks seek executive authority to issue rules for their initiatives, projects, and organizations. In some instances, environmental experts attain sufficient access to high-ranking individuals to write legislation and administrative decrees directly. Activist networks also seek to leverage ambiguities and conflicts in legal authority. They strategically engage the rule-making jurisdictions of the court system, Parliament, local municipalities, and provincial governors.[3] During the late Mubarak period, Egyptian courts, in particular, emerged as a significant venue for activists to constrain the prerogatives of executive power (Moustafa, 2007).

## *Discursive authority and environmental narratives*

The significance of networks and the discourses that they employ are intrinsically linked. I approach networks not as functionalist categories, but as social constructions constituted in large part by the shared understandings of participants. In what Bevir and Richards describe as a "decentered" theory of networks, they note that "the 'facts' about networks are not 'given' but are constructed by individuals in the stories they hand down to one another. The study of networks, therefore, is inextricably bound up with interpreting the narratives on which they are based" (Bevir and Richards, 2009: 8).

Several environmental historians of the Middle East have shown how colonial and postcolonial states created dominant environmental narratives that continue to influence how environmental problems are understood, implicitly circumscribing the range of possible policy solutions (Davis and Burke, 2011). The coupling of postcolonial expansion in state power with top-down visions of development has made these environmental narratives salient for understanding contemporary environmental politics. The "transformative programs" (Keshavarzian, 2007) and "grand missions" (Richards and Waterbury, 2008) pursued by political elites in Middle Eastern states often dramatically restructured property rights and reshaped landscapes through large-scale, state-sponsored projects. Regimes often whole-heartedly appropriated colonial-era arguments about the causes of environmental degradation and possible solutions. For instance, French colonial narratives about the role of pastoral populations in creating desertification through overgrazing have frequently resurfaced in contemporary policy prescriptions in North Africa (Davis, 2006).

Successive Egyptian governments, alongside international donors, have long framed Egypt's environmental problems primarily in terms of a demographic crisis, drawing on British colonial and elite preoccupations with population growth and a paucity of arable land (Ayeb, 2002; Mitchell, 1991). Bush and Sabri argued that this framing permeated environmental discourse; writing in 2000, they noted that "Egyptian environmental policy discussion focuses almost exclusively on the relationship between population pressure, scarce water resources and limited cultivable land, echoing the neo-Malthusian sense of crisis in much development discourse on Egypt" (Bush and Sabri, 2012: 243).

This book shows, however, that managerial and activist networks disseminate but also rework dominant environmental narratives. In doing so, they draw upon long-standing tropes, new scientific understandings, and changing political contexts. Managerial networks seek to translate ecological concerns into discursive framings emphasizing economic returns that resonate with governmental authorities, while activist networks mobilize popular concern through resonant framings that link environmental issues to health, livelihoods, and the vitality of local economies. In the wake of the 2011 uprising, activist and expert networks alike have sought to situate environmental campaigns in terms of broader demands "by the people" for rights, justice, and equity.

### *Infrastructural authority: reaching local constituencies*

For environmental initiatives to be effective, networks must be able to influence decision-makers or mobilize constituencies involved in a specific environmental issue. These constituents may include, for example, firms producing pollution, local communities experiencing environmental harm, or farmers involved in water user associations. Networks must make (often creative) use of evolving forms of infrastructure, organization, and communication to coordinate social action, drawing on the "logistical techniques" at the heart of the idea of infrastructural power (Mann, 1984: 192). The notion of infrastructural power thus draws our attention to how networks use and adapt specific material infrastructures, technologies, and organizational capacities to reach constituencies.[4] Networks organize collective action using opportunities provided by specific social–technical infrastructures, such as social media, communication technologies, electricity stations, roads, and ports (Mitchell, 2009). Mobilizing infrastructural authority requires networks to engage in "capacity building" across different environmental policy domains and in different physical locations. Those involved in the routine operation of infrastructures and institutions have often been overlooked as agents in top-down plans for natural resource management and environmental protection, even as it is widely recognized that local actors may employ a myriad of techniques to avoid, subvert, and transform top-down interventions (Scott, 1985).

Egypt's water-agricultural sector provides a good example of the challenges of building infrastructural authority, explored in Chapter 6. Expert networks have long pursued a series of technological interventions in the irrigation and drainage systems that shape how water is extracted, distributed, and used. In doing so, they encounter a variety of agents at various layers of these social–technical infrastructures that shape whether state and donor initiatives reach their intended constituencies.

In contesting industrial land use decisions, activist networks have made creative use of existing urban infrastructures, filling central squares with protesters, blockading roads and ports, and publicized their campaigns through state-owned and independent media outlets. They have also employed coordination mechanisms familiar to activists elsewhere in the Arab world, by establishing "popular committees" to coordinate various social groups and to establish common sets of demands and grievances.

## Research approach

This book relies heavily on information and insights gathered from participants in activist and managerial networks in Egypt, where I conducted research intermittently between 1997 and 2011. Research trips ranged in duration from an initial dissertation immersion of eighteen months, to a semester, to shorter stays of three weeks or a month. I conducted over 200 interviews with firm managers, environmental experts, activists, government officials, and donor representatives, often returning to insightful interviewees over time. These interviews were conducted primarily in Cairo, Alexandria, southern Sinai, and the new cities of Tenth of Ramadan and Burg al-'Arab. I have also made extensive use of "gray" material, including unpublished reports, surveys, conference papers, and documents, authored by international donors, government ministries, and non-governmental associations, in addition to conventional forms of published material.

Field research helps overcome limitations on publicly available information, since interviews and unofficial documentation serve as checks on officially circulated statistics and narratives.[5] Field research is furthermore uniquely suited to tracing the dynamics of policy change in authoritarian and transitional regimes. Authoritarian regimes are, by design, opaque political spaces, where information about policymaking is closely held, if not hoarded, by decision-makers. The observations of an Egyptian business executive in 1998 still hold, even as activists demand more transparency and accountability:

> There are two competing cultures of secrecy in Egypt. One is the government and the military authorities and the second is the emerging corporate culture of secrecy, where company information is confidential. Both of these have disastrous effects on environmental policies.[6]

Despite these limitations, one of the most significant developments for environmental research on Egypt has been the steadily improving collection of environmental information, often in the form of reports produced by the managerial policy networks analyzed in this book. Much of this information, however, focuses on questions of project evaluation or scientific and technical parameters. Issues of policy implementation, effectiveness, or politics writ large are rarely addressed explicitly. While information about some environmental issues is relatively accessible, others are harder to track down reliably. Of great help has been the development of relatively independent media outlets, particularly newspapers and satellite channels. An expanding number of local environmental experts, community organizers, journalists, and consultants also provided welcome insights and sources of information.

## Environmental case studies

The environmental issues examined in this volume engage complex sets of stakeholders, and catalyze donor funding, media coverage, state initiatives, and political activism. The cases of pollution control, protected area conservation, and water management require coordination across economic sectors and among influential actors, such as military officials, provincial governors, and business enterprises. They also involve a range of actors from local communities in urban and rural areas.

Chapter 2 analyzes how managerial networks of scientists, consultants, donors, and technocrats created national legal frameworks for environmental protection. I trace the origins of early expert networks to debates about the environmental impacts of constructing the Aswan High Dam in the early 1970s and to the participation of Egyptian environmental scientists in several United Nations projects. Managerial networks worked to establish a national environmental agency (1983), a legal regime for protected areas (1983), and a comprehensive environmental law (1994, revised 2009). Managerial networks also mediated the increasing flow of international environmental aid into Egypt. Network participants worked on rotating assignments in international and domestic consulting firms, government agencies, and local universities on a variety of projects sponsored by international donors and governmental institutions. They also participated in regional networks and information sharing, working temporarily in the Persian Gulf and other parts of the Middle East on environmental initiatives.

Chapters 3 and 4 analyze the respective roles of managerial and activist networks in tackling issues of pollution and land use in urban areas. In Chapter 3, I explore how managerial networks promoted strategies of pollution control, such as "clean production" and "pollution prevention," that relied on assumptions about firm behavior in market economies. Yet the discursive framings and organizational capacities embedded in these approaches did not match the institutional contexts and political logics underpinning firm-level decision-making in Egypt's transitional political economy. Instead, state-owned enterprises and partially privatized firms engaged in protracted bargaining with government ministries and international donors, seeking comprehensive external assistance to upgrade their production lines. The consequence, however, was limited progress on addressing pollution in an effective or timely manner.

Moving from the top-down efforts of managerial networks to control industrial pollution to the bottom-up activities of activist networks, Chapter 4 explores urban protest campaigns against pollution and land use decisions. Environmental awareness among the Egyptian public is generally high for activities that have a direct impact on neighborhoods and public health. Activist networks framed their concerns with local officials and broader popular constituencies by emphasizing a shared popular (*sha'bi*) urban identity and shared risks to local health and economy. In terms of mobilizing infrastructural authority, activist networks drew upon an existing state-sanctioned infrastructure of corporatist institutions and syndicates, political parties, and emerging privately owned media. These organizational avenues ensured that activist demands gained traction in national debates and political institutions, such as Parliament.

Chapter 5 analyzes how managerial networks sought to build infrastructural and legal authority for protected areas and, in doing so, increasingly contested rapid tourism development on Egypt's coastlines and lakes. Managerial networks established some forms of legal and infrastructural authority in the 1980s and 1990s, particularly in South Sinai. Effective management of protected areas, however, was increasingly threatened on the country's coasts by explosive growth in tourism investment, facilitated by state incentives and global demand. New activist networks, drawn from the diving industry, have emerged to seek stronger enforcement of environmental regulations to protect fragile coastal habitats. In turn, managerial networks have increasingly adopted activist strategies to contest central land use decisions that affect protected areas, even as they work to build formal institutional capacities for conservation.

The last environmental policy domain, explored in Chapter 6, examines efforts to restructure water management. Egypt's irrigation and drainage networks are some of the most complex in the world, distributing water for industrial, municipal, and agricultural use. In light of market liberalization in agriculture, increased demand for water, and increasing pollution loads, networks of water experts promoted ideas of decentralization, participation, and integration of water resources through a series of donor and state-sponsored interventions. Many of these interventions did not develop adequate forms of infrastructural authority to gain the cooperation of local farmers and lower-level officials. The re-engineering of the irrigation and drainage system and the communities that use the system, through the introduction of new technologies and organizational structures, continues to be a focus of donor funding and governmental intervention.

The concluding chapter examines trends in environmental politics during Egypt's ongoing political upheaval, sparked by the mass street protests in January and February 2011. Simultaneous, sustained protests across Egypt ended the long reign of Hosni Mubarak and prompted leading military figures to temporarily take power. This revolutionary moment has intensified social mobilization around environmental issues, such as land use and land rights, industrial pollution, and access to natural resources. From the Nubians in southern Egypt to the Bedouin in Sinai, the tactics and discourses of activist networks have been adopted by a much greater array of actors. These protests and campaigns have produced *ad hoc* concessions from governmental authorities at both the central and provincial levels, across a number of policy arenas formerly closed to public input.

Experts and activists in environmental networks have begun to adapt to these new political circumstances. Managerial networks of experts have adopted more populist environmental discourses, made use of new infrastructures and techniques of mobilization, and sought to mediate between mobilized communities and governmental authorities. Environmental activist networks have proliferated, and sought to build more sustainable forms of political engagement by supporting new infrastructures of collective action, including small producer unions, the revitalization of local councils and governance structures, and ongoing use of litigation, sit-ins, strikes, and blockades to tackle issues of environmental and social justice. Egypt's revolutionary moment has thus opened opportunities for a more participatory, contested, and dynamic phase in the country's environmental politics.

# 2 Managerial networks

## Domestic institution-building and international engagement

For years, the late Professor of Botany Mohamed 'Abd al-Fattah Kassas faithfully showed up early each morning to his Cairo University office. Former president of the International Union for the Conservation of Nature (IUCN), the professor was an internationally respected expert on arid ecologies, with a particular affinity for the diverse species of plants, insects, and other under-appreciated denizens of desert areas.[1] His office was full of papers, reports, and monographs, stacked precariously on bookshelves lining every wall, but he could find obscure conference documents in a matter of seconds. Down the corridor from his office was a small library housing the most complete archive on conservation and biodiversity in Egypt, composed largely of his personal document collection.

Kassas, like a handful of other environmental scientists, had been involved in promoting environmental protection in Egypt since the 1960s. Environmental scientists, along with well-placed officials and international donors, constituted key participants in managerial networks that established national-level environmental institutions and laws during the 1980s and 1990s. Catalyzed by environmental controversies around the construction of the Aswan High Dam, new international initiatives from the United Nations, and the increased focus of international donors on environmental issues, scientists such as Kassas lobbied Egypt's political leadership to establish national environmental legislation and institutions. By the early 1980s, environmental scientists found fellow travelers among several middle-class associations advocating public health and environmental protection, and among top officials concerned with the impacts of polluted water and air. The result was the issuing of a number of decrees and laws establishing environmental standards, the creation of national-level institutions, expanded graduate training in environmental sciences, and an emerging cadre of environmental professionals to staff state and donor projects.

Egypt's environmental professionals were supported by two developments explored in the second half of this chapter. The first was the influx of international environmental aid that provided opportunities for environmental experts to work on donor projects. The second was the phenomenon of temporary migration to other Middle Eastern countries, particularly the oil exporters of the Gulf, where employment opportunities for scientists and professionals abounded in the 1980s and 1990s.

Managerial networks comprised of relatively small numbers of scientists, donors, and technocrats encountered significant obstacles, however, in creating effective forms of infrastructural authority despite significant donor aid and evolving local environmental expertise. These problems were compounded in the late 1990s and during the 2000s as Mubarak increasingly appointed officials from the military and internal security forces to leadership positions at the environmental agency, displacing environmental professionals with significant expertise. The national-level account in this chapter thus provides the institutional context for the specific environmental cases examined in subsequent chapters.

## Origins of managerial environmental networks

During the 1960s, various regulatory initiatives emerged in Egypt, accompanied by rising donor interest in funding public health and environmental projects. In 1962, the government passed Law 93, which specified standards for industrial and agricultural discharges to urban sewer systems, principally in Cairo, Alexandria, and Egypt's port cities. In 1969, executive decrees established procedures for addressing oil pollution from petroleum exploration operations. According to several of Egypt's scientists involved in passing these laws, these efforts at rule making remained largely paper exercises with no enforcement capacities developed. Similarly, the Ministry of Health commissioned a committee to study air pollution from cement factories in the Cairo suburb of Helwan during the Nasser period but, according to one of the participants, the commission encountered strong opposition from industry and accomplished little.[2]

International aid to Egypt during this period increasingly focused on public health, agricultural modernization, and irrigation and water resources. In so doing, donors helped establish organizations that served as nodes for managerial environmental networks. One such organization was the High Institute of Public Health at the University of Alexandria. Founded in 1955 by Nasser's regime, with aid from the US Foreign Operations Administration and curriculum assistance from the University of California at Berkeley, the institute provided Egyptian students with training in epidemiology, sanitary engineering, statistics, health education, and public health administration (Gallagher, 1990: 173). Professors associated with the High Institute for Public Health served as environmental consultants on many state and donor-sponsored environmental projects in subsequent years.

It was not until the 1970s, however, that protection of the environment *per se* began to emerge as a distinct domain of policymaking, triggered by several significant international and domestic developments. The first of these was the debate that erupted over the environmental side effects of constructing al-Sadd al-'Ali, or the High Dam, at Aswan. As is well known, the High Dam became the centerpiece of the Free Officers' development plans after they overthrew the Egyptian monarchy in 1952. The dam was designed to hold years' worth of the annual flood of the Nile River in a massive manmade reservoir, Lake Nasser. Egypt could therefore rationalize its distribution of Nile water as needed, insulating its farmers and industries from periodic floods and droughts. A predictable water supply ensured the extension of perennial (year-round) irrigation to new agricultural areas, while cheap hydropower was supposed to fuel rapid industrial development (Waterbury, 1983: 64). The High Dam was an extension of earlier Nile River control projects undertaken by the British and Egyptian governments, including a previous dam at Aswan built in 1902 (Waterbury, 1979).

While experts concurred on the need for a system of dams to store multiple years of floodwaters, the choice of one massive dam, rather than a series of smaller dams, reflected the Free Officers' vision of remaking the country through centralized hydroengineering. Like proponents of the Tennessee Valley Authority in the United States, and the Soviet advisers who assisted with the High Dam, the Free Officers embraced large-scale social and environmental engineering as a means to promote development. These grandiose visions were enabled by a commitment to what James Scott terms authoritarian high modernism—using the resources and coercion of the state to enact grand transformations in nature and society without public consent or participation (Scott, 1998).

From its inception, the Aswan High Dam was a sensitive political and security issue. After the United States blocked proposed World Bank funding for dam construction, Nasser nationalized the Suez Canal so that Egypt might use the transit revenues to underwrite the construction itself. Despite Egyptian promises of compensation to Suez Canal Company investors, France, Britain, and Israel attacked Egypt with the purpose of retaking the Canal in 1956. After the United States and USSR helped broker a ceasefire, Nasser turned to Soviet expertise and assistance, and construction on the dam began using an Egyptian firm, the Arab Contractors, in 1960. It was finally completed in 1970.

The 1956 attack and increasingly authoritarian system established by Gamal Abdel Nasser made it very difficult for Egyptian scientists to openly assess the dam's environmental impacts, which were widely expected to be significant. The dam held back not only Nile floodwaters but also the silt and sediment that replenished the soils of the Nile Delta and kept it above sea level. Alongside the High Dam's protective benefits in terms of mitigating floods and droughts, the Delta's fertile agricultural lands became no longer, in the words of two well-known scientists, "a functioning delta but, rather, a subsiding and eroding coastal plain" (Stanley and Warne, 1998: 794). In a 1998 assessment, these experts enumerated the most significant impacts of the High Dam on the Nile Delta:

> Symptoms of the destruction phase of the Nile delta include accelerated coastal erosion and straightening of the shoreline, reduction in wetland size, increased landward incursion of saline groundwater, and buildup of salt and pollutants to toxic levels in wetlands and delta plain. Without seasonal flushing by floods, the former delta plain surface is now incapable of recycling and/or removing agricultural, municipal and industrial wastes generated by Egypt's rapidly expanding population.
>
> (Ibid.)

For many years, however, the Egyptian government did not support systematic examination of deleterious long-term effects by its small scientific community or investigate potential remedial actions. As Professor Kassas recalled:

> In 1968, I attended a conference on Environment and Development at Arlington House, which was the first forum to ask the World Bank to prepare an environmental impact assessment of the High Dam. I presented a paper about how river control systems on the Nile would affect coastal erosion patterns. It ended up causing lots of problems as the Western media picked up on the story, and I was considered against the project, anti-party [Nasser's single party]. We kept telling the government and party leaders that they should not confuse technical and political issues, but keep them separate. Although a few of us established a commission on side effects of the High Dam, it was not until twenty years later that the Ministry of Water Resources established an institute to study these effects.[3]

While some scholars have argued that scientific communities are more likely to be consulted when uncertainty surrounding ecological outcomes is significant (Haas, 1990), it is just as likely that officials cultivate ignorance of negative environmental impacts (Ascher, 1999). For Nasser's regime, ecological issues paled in comparison to the political and economic imperatives that they believed mandated the construction of the dam.

The construction of the Aswan High Dam was not the only catalyst for Egyptian scientists to pay close attention to emerging ecological problems. The increasing involvement of UN agencies in issues of environmental protection provided new forums for Egyptian scientists to interact with a global "epistemic community" of environmental scientists (Haas, 1990), and work with colleagues on domestic environmental initiatives.

The Man and Biosphere Programme, launched by UNESCO in 1970, was an early example of how UN initiatives gave Egyptian environmental scientists new research and advocacy opportunities. This program provided funds to designated "biosphere" reserves in participating countries, many of them in the developing world. The UN use of the term biosphere reflected an emerging global framing of environmentalism, in which the natural world needed to be safeguarded from human-induced degradation. Protecting specific places as biosphere reserves was intended to establish a representative, global network of threatened ecosystems and cultures. Reflecting UNESCO's broader mission of protecting cultural heritage, biosphere reserves were selected to encompass the diversity of human–natural interactions, or ways of life distinctive to different places.[4] Additionally, the reserves were to receive sustained support for systematic research on what, in modern scientific parlance, is termed coupled natural and human systems. These applied research and community-building initiatives are still ongoing; as of 2009, the World Network of Biosphere Reserves contained 564 sites in 109 countries.

In Egypt, the creation of the Egyptian Man and Biosphere Commission brought together academic scientists, officials from the Ministry of Irrigation, and representatives of several voluntary organizations for the first time.[5] The Ministry of Education and 'Ayn Shams University soon asked the commission to develop postgraduate education programs in environmental sciences (ibid.). Using the precedent established by the biosphere commission model, a similar committee was established in the late 1970s to draw up plans for national-level environmental institutions in Egypt.

Chaired by Professor Kassas, the committee proposed creating an environmental agency to coordinate environmental initiatives among central ministries. Agency activities were to be supported by a special fund for the environment, a national network to monitor environmental conditions and generate data, a program for applied natural resource management, and the creation of environmental training programs in universities and government research centers.[6]

The League of Arab States, the regional organization with twenty-two official member states, also played a small role in fostering early managerial networks in Egypt and the Arab countries. The League's educational, scientific, and cultural organization held a regional conference on environmental issues in 1971. As Professor Kassas recalled, the conference was attended by Maurice Strong, one of the key organizers of the UN's 1972 Stockholm Conference on the Human Environment.

For scientists like Kassas, the 1972 Stockholm Conference and subsequent creation of the United Nations Environment Programme (UNEP) marked a watershed in their involvement in global and local environmental issues. The organizational structure of UNEP, and the informal connections cultivated at Stockholm and subsequent international meetings, offered Egyptian scientists the opportunity to promote environmental protection at home by leveraging international interest and resources. As "bilateral activists," they played an important role in bridging the international and domestic spheres (Steinberg, 2001).

Mostafa Kamal Tolba, who served as UNEP's second executive director, became one of the best-known Egyptian scientists straddling domestic and international roles. Tolba's career exemplifies how Egyptian scientists held multiple positions in managerial environmental networks, rotating from positions in the Egyptian government and academia to international institutions and back again. A science professor at Cairo University with a doctorate in microbiology from Imperial College, London, Tolba was appointed Minister of Youth and President of the Egyptian Academy for Scientific Research and Technology in the years before the Stockholm conference (Canan and Reichman, 2001: 51). He then served from 1974 to 1992 as executive director of UNEP, where he played a pivotal role in facilitating the international negotiations on ozone-depleting substances which resulted in the Montreal Protocol in 1987. During this period, he helped draft environmental legislation and participated in a number of environmental initiatives in Egypt. After retiring, he established a voluntary association and environmental consulting firm in Egypt.

## The discursive foundations of environmental initiatives

Given their natural science backgrounds, Kassas, Tolba, and other environmental scientists emphasized the "nature" side of environmental issues—the protection and conservation of ecosystems. As suggested by the involvement of Egyptian scientists in UNESCO's Man and Biosphere Programme, their environmentalism was grounded in emerging concepts of ecology. As early as 1979, Kassas and other scientists from the state-supported Academy of Scientific Research and Technology called for development plans that would exploit natural resources but protect environmental balance (*muhafaza 'ala tawazun al-bi'a*) (Academy of Scientific Research and Technology, 1979: 2).

In reports and memoranda produced during the early and mid-1980s, these scientists sought to translate emerging notions of ecological science into government plans for development. In a draft national action plan for protected areas put forward in 1981, for instance, scientists argued that protected areas and parks should safeguard local varieties of plants and wildlife, rather than simply serve as tourism sites. These and other developmental objectives could be attained only through *ta'min al-wiratha* (safeguarding the [natural] inheritance). *Ta'min al-wiratha* required protecting natural resources through the adoption of multisectoral, mutually reinforcing policies. In addition to establishing protected areas, policy prescriptions included addressing water pollution and soil contamination, creating genetic seed banks, and supporting applied research through experimental farms and plots (National Committee to Preserve Nature and Natural Resources, 1981: 5–8). The diversity and specialization of flora and fauna endemic to Egypt's natural inheritance, these scientists argued, would help create drought- and insect-resistant strains of crops to improve productivity and lessen dependence on food imports (ibid.: 5–8).

While Egypt's small cadre of conservation scientists framed nature conservation as a strategy for ensuring Egypt's future, other experts focused on grounding environmental concerns in Egyptians' well-founded association of polluted water with disease. For decades, media and popular discourse had linked polluted water with outbreaks of infectious disease, various forms of cancer, and liver and kidney diseases. During the turbulent 1940s, epidemics of malaria (1942–4), relapsing fever (1946), and cholera (1947) rocketed public health and polluted water to the top of the Egyptian political agenda (Gallagher, 1990: 3). The rapid spread of schistosomiasis (also termed bilharzia), a waterborne parasitic disease carried by freshwater snails that accompanied the expansion of perennial irrigation in the late nineteenth century, was a long-term public health crisis, prompting a variety of campaigns to control infections. In one of the more infamous consequences, government campaigns to inject the peasantry with tartar emetic in the 1950s and 1960s were later linked to the highest rate of hepatitis C infection in the world, because many government health workers had used unclean needles on villagers. Water contamination remains a critical public health issue, particularly in rural areas, secondary cities, and informal settlements with inadequate potable water and sanitation systems.

The perils of water contamination by agricultural chemicals was also firmly embedded in popular awareness through several well-publicized tragedies. In 1971, 3,000 water buffalo and an unknown number of farmers were paralyzed by or died from exposure to the pesticide leptophos, licensed in the United States for use on the cotton crop (Alpern, 1976; Brown, 1977; Richards, 1977).[7] The discrepancy in accounting for human and animal losses was a result of Egypt's insurance practices: the Ministry of Agriculture paid compensation for loss of registered buffalo, but there was no system in place to claim compensation for human casualties.[8] The problem of pesticide contamination persists: in 1998 alone, 5,300 pesticide poisonings were recorded in Egypt (United Nations Development Programme, 2001: 71).

Doctors, professors, and officials with expertise in public health thus urged the government to strengthen legal standards for pollutants and chemicals. Several formed advocacy and educational associations that undertook awareness campaigns on issues ranging from smoking to pollution. One of the better-known organizations, Jam'iyyat Qanun al-Tib (Association for Medical Law), began holding conferences and lobbying officials on smoking rules, transplants, and poor prison conditions during the 1970s, according to one of its founders.[9] By the early 1980s, the association turned to advocating enforcement of air and water pollution laws.

Environmentalism framed as public health found a receptive audience with Ahmad Fu'ad Muhi al-Din, a professor of industrial health who was appointed prime minister from 1982 to 1984. Muhi al-Din created and chaired a committee to establish a national legal framework for environmental protection. Reflecting public concern with water pollution, one of the first laws issued was Law 48 (1982) to regulate discharges to the Nile River. Law 48 authorized the Ministry of Irrigation to issue and revoke licenses of industrial projects discharging to the Nile. It also designated patrols from the Ministry of Interior to monitor pollution to the Nile and linked canals (Lajna al-Khadamat, 1992: 42). The government further imposed a tax on international travel to fund environmental protection activities. The fund was to be administered under the shared jurisdiction of the Ministry of Tourism, the prime minister, and a newly created environmental agency.

The environmental agency was established by presidential decree in 1982 (Presidential Decree No. 631/1982). The Gihaz Shu'un al-Bi'a (Egyptian Environmental Affairs Agency or EEAA) was mandated to coordinate the environmental initiatives of other ministries, and was not elevated to the status of a Cabinet-level ministry (*wizara*). Parallel to the creation of the agency and its executive director (titled chief executive officer), the government created the post of Minister of State for Environmental Affairs to represent the environmental portfolio at the Cabinet level. Creating the position of Minister distinct from that of the head of the environmental agency created two bureaucratic entities that from the outset had the potential to clash or at least compete (Gomaa, 1997).

This spate of environmental regulatory activity was somewhat exceptional. Muhi al-Din's successor as prime minister, General Kamal Hasan 'Ali, had previously served as the Minister of Defense and Military Production under President

Sadat. He downgraded the environmental committee and removed it from his portfolio. No subsequent prime minister took such a key leadership role in promoting environmental institutions.

## Limited legal authority at the national environmental agency

The environmental agency established in 1982 was reorganized in 1985, 1991, and again in 1994 as part of the passage of a more comprehensive environmental law. Neither the initial authorizing decrees nor the later institutional reorganizations endowed the agency with executive authority vis-à-vis established sectoral ministries governing water, agriculture, investment, and industry (ibid.: 7).

Participants in environmental managerial networks took different positions on this legal outcome. Some, like Mostafa Tolba, argued that unless the agency became a ministry for the environment, it would never successfully carve out jurisdiction over existing sectoral ministries. Others, among them Kassas, feared that a Cabinet-level environmental ministry would not be able to compete with existing, well-entrenched ministries, particularly in the water and agricultural sectors with their extensive reach and large numbers of employees. To set the environmental agency against these ministries would thus make it ineffective from the outset.[10] As another environmental expert observed, these experts also feared that an environmental ministry would simply replicate the flaws of most governmental institutions: underfunded, hierarchically run, and overburdened with redundant employees in order to fulfill the state's promise to offer employment to all college graduates. The alternative of a small, streamlined agency that would coordinate with existing ministries, employing relatively few numbers of people, seemed a possible institutional solution. As an environmental engineer working at the environmental agency observed:

> I thought the *idea* of the EEAA was pioneering—an umbrella agency to coordinate the environmental departments of other ministries, such as the Ministry of Irrigation. The idea was to have many interlocutors on environmental protection, each ministry having a small department of environment. As the experience of the US Environmental Protection Agency shows, one central agency cannot do it all. At the environmental agency, we made a strategic decision to keep the numbers of employees small and their expertise high. But in reality, the planned coordination with other ministries didn't happen.[11]

### *Strong legal authority for protected areas*

Several prominent environmental scientists, including Tolba and Kassas, were appointed to the board of directors for the EEAA in 1982. One of the first proposals of the EEAA's board was a protected areas law, Law 102, issued in 1983. The executive regulations for the law contained several remarkable provisions compared with subsequent environmental laws, reflecting the access that conservation scientists had obtained in drafting these statutes (Sowers, 2007). Law 102 vested executive authority for implementation and oversight with a protected areas division within the EEAA. While the agency itself did not enjoy executive legal authority, the parks division, later called the Nature Conservation Sector (NCS), did. Law 102 provided a long-term funding mechanism, through the creation of an Environmental Fund to collect park entrance fees and levy fines for violations, such as damaging coral reefs or oil spills. Law 102 further gave the NCS authority over coastal setback areas, in practice considerably expanding its spatial jurisdiction.

Managerial networks working on conservation thus played a crucial role in formulating national environmental institutions and endowing the Nature Conservation Sector with executive authority. This success, however, was not easily replicated. Managerial networks attempted to strengthen the legal authority of the EEAA as part of promoting a new environmental law in the early 1990s. According to one participant, the text of the 1994 law was written by a small network of prominent environmental experts, including Tolba, Kassas, Mohamed al-Gindi, and Amin al-Gamal. Al-Gindi, a lawyer, was a former attorney general in Egypt and the vice president of Egypt's Court of Cassation.[12] Amin al-Gamal was then a deputy from the Ministry of Health and the founder of Jam'iyyat Qanun al-Tib.

The 1994 parliamentary debates around the new environmental law revealed how contentious the prospect of a legally strengthened environmental agency was to other ministries. The environmental law was stalled in the Majlis al-Sha'b, the elected lower house of parliament, for four years, reflecting significant opposition from powerful sectoral ministries. Such delay was unusual for government-sponsored legislation, as the Mubarak regime, like those of Sadat and Nasser, ensured that the government's National Democratic Party held a dominating majority in Parliament through systematic electoral manipulation. In addition, as in the case of environmental laws, the substantive parts of legislation were typically issued as executive regulations, drawn up directly by the concerned ministries and the executive office. As one participant later recalled, "The problem was with the ministers themselves. The Ministry of Petroleum was fighting us for three or four years."[13] Private businessmen also viewed provisions in the law requiring environmental impact assessments with concern.

With international environmental aid increasing, bilateral and multilateral donors joined environmental experts in pressuring the government for more adequate national legislation (Gomaa, 1997). A former chief executive officer of the environmental agency in 1999 recalled intervening with Fathi Sorour, then the parliamentary speaker: "I explained to him that a law without strong legal provisions will not please donors, and I will stand up, withdraw the bill, and tell donors and parliament that the law is useless."[14]

Despite intense donor and expert lobbying, the ratified 1994 law added only a few executive functions to the EEAA. The EEAA's legal authority was limited to establishing environmental standards, implementing pilot projects and monitoring networks, setting procedural guidelines in such areas as environmental impact assessments, and generating national reports and action plans (ibid.: 49). While the *person* of the Minister of State for Environmental Affairs retained authority to fine or close firms temporarily, this authority did not extend to the EEAA, which remained designated a *jihaz*, an agency, rather than a *wizara*, a Cabinet-level ministry. The minister was thus a minister without portfolio. While the EEAA could sign protocols with other ministries to carry out activities, it did not enjoy autonomous budgetary or regulatory authority, in stark contrast to its own Nature Conservation Unit. Although Law 4 was revised again in 2009, the EEAA remained a coordinating agency.

Lacking the executive authority granted to other ministries, the EEAA faced significant challenges in building infrastructural authority and the ability to establish routines and infrastructures to reach the parties that it was supposed to regulate. A former head of the agency, who had previously worked in an upper-level management position at the state-owned petroleum company, highlighted the challenges that emerged, contrasting the EEAA's legal standing with that of its Nature Conservation Unit:

> Protected areas are easier to enforce than the provisions of Law 4 because, for protected areas, the Nature Conservation Unit within the agency was the only designated authority—except the military, of course. But for other environmental issues, the problem with the EEAA is that to get something done, you have to deal with other ministries. For instance, to get a list of staffing, you have to go through the Ministry of Finance. Or to deal with hazardous waste, you need the permission of the Ministry of Health. What I did in six years at the EEAA, I could have done in two years with a sector like the petroleum sector. It was a big struggle, and very frustrating.[15]

## International environmental assistance

The environmental agency thus enjoyed weak legal and infrastructural authority, with the initial exception of its parks division. With the 1994 law and the reorganization of the agency, newly appointed environmental experts began to focus on developing the organizational capacities of the agency. Managerial networks felt that if the environmental agency attracted outside assistance, it might be better able to induce other governmental ministries to cooperate. A former CEO at the agency recalled reaching out to donors, as well as the sensitivities this provoked among other ministries and companies:

> When I took over in 1991, we had two demonstration projects worth LE30 million. With some environmental consultants that we hired, we essentially shopped for financing from outside donors. Soon we had increased the budget to LE1.6 billion. This made some people uneasy, especially in the petroleum sector and among the industries. However, I had checked with the prime minister first to make sure this was all right.[16]

In the early 1990s, aid to the environmental agency was largely channeled through one internal unit, the Technical Cooperation Office for the Environment. This office was itself a project funded by the United Nations Development Programme (UNDP) from 1991 to 1995, tasked with attracting and coordinating projects. During this period, it was the most institutionally developed and well-staffed section of the Egyptian Environmental Affairs Agency (El Baradei, 2001). Senior staff in this unit recalled that they prepared extensive lists of potential projects for outside donors. The 1997 draft consultative document for a national environmental action plan, for instance, presented 168 pages of ongoing and potential projects across different environmental sectors, specifying timeframes, needed actions, and potential domestic partners (Egyptian Environmental Affairs Agency, 1997). These were formalized into detailed investment packages and incorporated into the 2001 National Environmental Action Plan (Ministry of State for Environmental Affairs, 2001b).

From 1980 to 1999, Egypt obtained significantly more official development assistance (ODA) for the environment than most other developing countries. Overall, environmental aid to Egypt during the 1990s was at odds with general trends in aid to developing countries, which declined as a share of industrialized countries' GDP. Egypt was the second largest global recipient of international environmental aid during the 1980s, receiving a total of US$2.2 billion (Hicks *et al.*, 2008: 61–2). During the 1990s, it was the seventh largest recipient of worldwide environmental aid with an inflow of US$3.2 billion (ibid.: 62). More strikingly, in per capita terms, Egypt received more environmental aid than any country except Argentina (Figure 2.1). By 2002, at least eleven bilateral donors and eight multilateral organizations were involved in funding environmental projects in Egypt.[17]

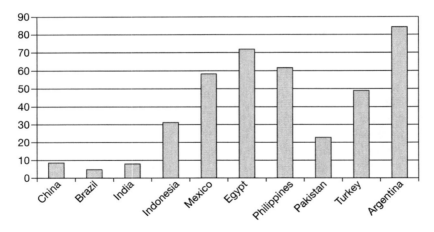

*Figure 2.1* Top ten global country recipients of environmental aid, per capita, 1980–99
(US$ per person)

Source: Calculated from aid figures in PLAID database, Hicks *et al.*, 2008; Population figures from World Development Indicators 2007, compiled by the World Bank, http://ddp-ext.worldbank.org/ext/ddpreports/

Aid flows to Egypt reflected geopolitical calculations in donor countries. Large flows of US aid reflected Egypt's role as the first Arab state to normalize relations with Israel through the 1977 Camp David Accords. The European Union channeled aid to Egypt as part of broader concerns about stability, migration, and development in the southern Mediterranean. The EU steadily increased its commitment as part of the Euro–Mediterranean partnership process, making Egypt the top recipient of European Commission funds from 1986 to 1998, receiving 25.2 percent of all funds committed to the region.[18] Table 2.1 lists the top five donors to Egypt for environmental aid, by volume.

*Table 2.1* Top five environmental donors to Egypt, 1980–99, US$

| United States | 1,760,000,000 |
| World Bank | 134,000,000 |
| European Union | 119,000,000 |
| West Germany | 52,300,000 |
| United Kingdom | 46,800,000 |

Source: Hicks *et al.*, 2008: 61

## Sustaining managerial networks: donor projects and consultancies

The use of environmental aid in iterative projects helped catalyze new managerial networks and provided income and employment for environmental scientists, engineers, and consultants, some of whom eventually founded their own consulting firms. Donor-funded environmental projects also created further demand for environmental studies and professional training programs. As of 2008, educational programs in environmental science and engineering had been established at Cairo University, the University of Alexandria, the University of Helwan, the University of Asyut, the University of Minya, and the American University in Cairo, among others.

Opportunities to work with donor projects helped expand and retain the ranks of environmental professionals, as traditional public-service positions (outside the uppermost echelons) did not offer a decent livelihood. Employment prospects in government for younger professionals had become particularly dire. As part of neoliberal reforms to shrink government employment, the government had decreed that new positions were to go first to civil servants laid off elsewhere in the public sector. Such rules did not apply to hiring on donor-funded projects.

Local environmental experts were hired directly as consultants on donor-funded projects, or under short-term, temporary work contracts through public sector authorities. Either form of work, however, typically paid considerably more than standardized, long-term government employment. These differences in remuneration are shown in Table 2.2, which gives ranges of salary figures for one donor project in 2000.

*Table 2.2* Salary scales for sample donor project, Egyptian Environmental Affairs Agency, 2000 (thousands of US$ per year)

| Employment category | EEAA civil service | EEAA one-year contract employee | Donor project |
|---|---|---|---|
| Engineer | 2,000–4,000 | 3,000–5,000 | > 10,000 |
| Accountant | 1,800–2,500 | 2,460–3,000 | > 10,000 |
| Secretary | 1,800–2,500 | 2,100–3,100 | > 11,000 |
| Driver | 1,440–2,100 | 2,100–3,000 | > 3,500 |

Source: Personal communication, Egyptian Environmental Affairs Agency, December 11, 2000

For young professionals who did find employment in donor projects, several observed in interviews that they gained advanced skills and acquired familiarity with emerging environmental management techniques.[19] They also reported that they found it difficult to adjust back to the low pay and esteem accorded to typical civil servants. They thus preferred further work with donors, consulting, academia, and business opportunities at home and abroad over government employment.

Donor projects thus provided employment but also over time decoupled participants in managerial networks from newly established environmental institutions. Junior positions at the environmental agency turned over rapidly, as young graduates with little experience (though considerable enthusiasm) left the agency when possible to seize opportunities to work with a donor project or an international institution. Senior environmental experts increasingly established their own consulting firms to respond to the upsurge in donor-funded environmental projects. These local firms usually partnered with international contractors from donor countries to implement environmental projects. Sometimes these arrangements were formalized into longer-term affiliations, such as that between Chemonics, a US-based firm working on United States Agency for International Development (USAID) contracts, and Chemonics Egypt, an Egyptian joint venture. In 1999, Chemonics Egypt spun off another local consultancy, Environics.

By 2001, when USAID compiled a directory of environmental consulting firms in Egypt, 251 companies offered environmental consulting, design, and engineering services (Ministry of State for Environmental Affairs, 2001a). Most firms provided environmental audits, impact assessments, and voluntary certifications, while others were primarily suppliers and importers of pollution abatement technologies. Of the 251 firms listed in the directory, the majority (approximately 100) were privately owned domestic companies, while another forty were local agents of multinational firms. The remainder were state-owned, foreign-owned, or joint-venture enterprises between multinational and local consulting environmental firms.

Egyptian experts and their consulting firms thus served as development brokers, linking international donors and local officials in the implementation of projects. Rather than being nested primarily within the environmental agency, however, managerial networks comprised of scientists, donors, and technocrats emerged in the process of working together on a series of projects.

## Sustaining managerial networks: temporary migration

Egypt managed to retain some of its environmental experts given employment opportunities created by donors and governmental authorities for consultancies and short-term contracts with environmental projects. Opportunities to work on environmental initiatives elsewhere in the Middle East, particularly in the oil-exporting countries of the Persian/Arab Gulf, supplemented domestic labor markets. Temporary migration, particularly to the Gulf, is a common avenue for Egyptians looking to provide for their families and improve their economic prospects.[20] As of 2001, an estimated 1.9 million Egyptians were working temporarily abroad (Zohry, 2003: 30).[21] Highly skilled Egyptian workers constituted between 40 and 70 percent of the total Egyptian workforce employed in Saudi Arabia, Libya, Kuwait, UAE, Qatar, Yemen, and Oman (ibid.).

Egyptians leave to work abroad for periods ranging from months to years, and often leave repeatedly. What one scholar termed the "permanence of temporary migration" means "all professions migrate temporarily, ranging from scientists and technicians to production workers" (Farrag, 1999, cited in Zohry, 2003: 30). The single largest category of Egyptian temporary migrants in 2002 was for scientists and technicians, comprising 41 percent of total temporary emigrants.

The temporary migration of technical professionals is facilitated in several ways. Many experts are hired out by public and governmental authorities to their counterparts in the Gulf through official secondment, usually arranged through personal contacts or official requests (Zohry, 2003: 30). Others find employment with Egyptian or Arab Gulf companies that win contracts in the Gulf.[22] As with donor projects, temporary contracts around the Middle East provided additional opportunities for environmental professionals working in a particular policy domain to come together repeatedly.

Almost every mid-career environmental scientist and professional I interviewed over the years had worked abroad, and had foregone additional opportunities to do so. Many interspersed work outside Egypt with their careers at home in order to secure the futures of their families. Because of family ties and obligations, and a commitment to Egypt, several senior scientists recalled deciding not to migrate permanently. One leading consultant for the EEAA, also a public health professor at the High Institute of Public Health, provided a fairly typical illustration of the interlocking government, academic, regional, and donor employment trajectories of environmental professionals:

> I earned my Ph.D. from the University of North Carolina in civil engineering in 1973. I was offered a job at NASA, but chose to return to Egypt as a faculty member at the High Institute for Public Health. Then I taught civil engineering in Sapporo, Hokkaido for one-and-a-half years, and later took a job with the United Nations environmental coordination group for West Asia, stationed in Baghdad. I then returned to the High Institute for several years, worked as a

regional adviser again, and then worked as a consultant on various USAID-funded projects on pollution prevention. And so on: I have worked in about fourteen countries but kept returning to the University of Alexandria. I have now been working for three years with the EEAA as a technical consultant. I left Egypt on temporary jobs to secure my children's future. I didn't emigrate permanently because Egypt is my home. Here I have a mission. But you make sacrifices. At the UN, I made US$9,500 a month, and I came back to my salary here of US$400 per month. But even if that is the salary, you should fulfill your obligations—to your students, your university, and your country.[23]

Regional migration opportunities were also available to expatriate consultants employed on donor projects. This was particularly the case for environmental sectors where the Gulf countries were active. Saudi Arabia and Oman, for instance, placed considerable emphasis on conservation and protected areas beginning in the 1970s. As a result, conservation professionals often circulated between positions in Egypt and the Gulf.[24]

## Environmental aid and weak infrastructural authority

International environmental aid and temporary migration to regional environmental projects thus strengthened the economic fortunes and accumulated expertise of Egypt's environmental experts, both locally born and resident expatriates. As suggested in Chapter 1, however, this expertise has not been used as effectively as it could have been. To understand why, we have to look at the difficulties that managerial networks encountered in building infrastructural authority within the environmental agency. Using environmental aid to build effective forms of infrastructural authority has been limited due to several factors.

A significant proportion of "environmental" aid went to conventional infrastructure projects administered by government ministries in water, agriculture, health, and housing.[25] Water infrastructure projects—in irrigation and drainage, drinking water, and sanitation—accounted for the majority of environmental aid (Hicks *et al.*, 2008). As Hicks *et al.* noted, water and sanitation projects are appealing to donors as they "are highly visible, location-specific, and of immediate benefit to specific communities" (ibid.: 44). For the same reasons, recipient governments also tend to prefer concrete infrastructure investments to capacity-building projects.

Despite this, aid channeled to the environmental agency was still significant. From 1991 to 2001, the EEAA was involved, in some capacity, with donor projects worth about LE2.4 billion, 91 percent of which was disbursed as grants and 9 percent as loans (El Baradei, 2001: 39). However, given the agency's limited executive authority, the majority of these projects consisted of the agency coordinating environmental initiatives with other government ministries. As shown in Table 2.3, 89 percent of total aid flows between 1991 and 2001 were designated for the environmental agency to coordinate projects with other ministries, while only 7.5 percent of aid went directly for capacity building within the agency itself. Between 2002 and 2008, this figure increased modestly to 11.1 percent.

*Table 2.3* Role of Egyptian Environmental Affairs Agency in international environmental
assistance projects to Egypt, 1991–2008

| Role of environmental agency | 1991–2001 (51 projects) (%) | 2002–8 (36 projects) (%) |
|---|---|---|
| Main beneficiary: institutional and capacity-building projects (excluding protected areas) | 7.5 | 11.1 |
| Sole authority administering natural protectorates | 3.1 | 30.6 |
| Coordinating agency with other governmental authorities | 89.5 | 41.7 |
| Lead implementing authority (e.g. compliance with international treaties) | 0.0 | 16.6 |

Source: For 1991–2001, El Baradei (2001: 43); for 2002–9, data compiled from the EEAA 2007
Annual Report (Cairo: January 2008) and *Egypt State of the Environment Report* (2008), Chap. 14,
http://www.eeaa.gov.eg/English/info/report_soe2008.asp (accessed January 10, 2010)

Just under half (42.9 percent) of all environmental aid to the agency was in the
form of policy support programs (ibid.: 41–2). Used particularly by the USAID,
policy support programs meant that donors released tranches of discretionary
funding directly to government agencies once specified policy benchmarks were
achieved. USAID credited policy support programs with prodding the Mubarak
regime to liberalize the agricultural sector through the Ministry of Agriculture in
the late 1980s, and to undertake macroeconomic reforms in the 1990s. However,
leading officials could simply overlook and ignore such benchmarks, even when
enshrined in administrative decrees.

Other bilateral donors, working with far smaller budgets than USAID, preferred to keep direct control over their smaller environmental aid budgets.
Although projects targeting institutional capacity building within the EEAA
accounted for only 6.3 percent of total environmental assistance flowing
through the agency, small-scale capacity-building initiatives were the most
common type of donor project (ibid.: 41). However, such initiatives were
fragmented and often provided little long-term continuity in building administrative capacities.

### Military and security appointees to the environmental agency

Compounding these difficulties, the Mubarak regime increasingly appointed ex-
military and security officials to leadership positions across the environmental
agency during the 2000s. During the 1980s and 1990s, these positions had generally been filled with environmental experts, with experience working in specific
environmental policy areas. In the last decade of Mubarak's rule, however, many
environmental experts argued that senior leadership positions went largely to
ex-military and police officials with little technical knowledge of environmental
issues.[26] This practice was rare at such key ministries as Finance, Planning, Trade,

and Irrigation, where top appointees typically combined demonstrated loyalty to the regime with recognized technical expertise.

The last Mubarak-era Minister of State for Environmental Affairs, Maged George, appointed in 2004, was a case in point. He was the chief of the Engineering Authority for the Armed Forces from 2002 to 2004, and had previously worked as the military works management director, chief of general staff for military works and project management, and the Egyptian defense attaché in Rome, Italy. As minister, George pressed donors for projects that produced tangible infrastructure investments, rather than agency capacity building, occasionally suspending projects not primarily focused on infrastructure.[27]

A similar pattern held for the management of the EEAA's Environmental Protection Fund. Top officials at the Environmental Protection Fund were increasingly appointed from the military and security forces. The director of the fund in 2008, for instance, had been a military attaché for financial affairs in the United Kingdom until 2006, and previously worked in the military academy's financial affairs division. In contrast, the more long-standing mid-level professionals serving directly below the director had extensive background in the financial administration of environmental donor projects.

Fragmented capacity-building efforts and inadequate leadership produced what environmental professionals in Egypt described as a process of "deinstitutionalization," "demobilization," and "demotivation" at environmental agency in the late Mubarak period.[28] As one long-time senior consultant observed, "There is a critical mass of technicians and know-how, but at the upper levels there is no leadership, and a lack of responsiveness."[29] Another professional, the principal of an environmental consulting firm, argued that:

> Danida and USAID spent lots of dollars, but there are still no systems or guidelines in place. The sustainability of the agency has not been achieved. The agency is still working on a project basis, not being proactive. This became clear to the donors, who downgraded their projects and moved a number of projects to other ministries.[30]

As shown in Table 2.3, between 2002 and 2009, donors decreased the total number of projects at the environmental agency from fifty-one to thirty-six, focusing the remaining projects on protected areas and institutional capacity building.

## Conclusion

Over the past three decades, managerial networks of environmental experts, donors, and technocrats helped construct new national institutions and regulatory frameworks for environmental protection in Egypt. By the early 1970s, leading scientists in Egypt began to consider the environmental implications of the Aswan High Dam and to participate in environmental initiatives sponsored by UN agencies and the Arab League. They staffed local research institutes and some played key leadership roles in new international environmental institutions, such as the

International Union for the Conservation of Nature and UNEP. These "bilateral activists," together with middle-class professionals heading voluntary associations and reformist technocrats, helped create national-level environmental institutions during the 1980s and 1990s. These initiatives included the establishment of national environmental standards, an environmental agency, a fund for environmental protection, and a system of protected areas.

With the increase in donor assistance targeting the "environment," the spread of educational training programs in environmental sciences, and opportunities for temporary regional migration on environmental contracts, managerial networks in Egypt proliferated and specialized during the 1990s. Egyptian environmental experts increasingly served as development brokers in networks that brought experts together with international donors, foreign consulting firms, and government technocrats. These networks were not nested primarily within national environmental institutions; instead, participants developed long-standing ties through repeated consultancies for governmental and donor-funded projects.

The evolution of these managerial networks was part of a broader restructuring of state power and policymaking in Egypt. Their rotation through multiple professional roles—as consultants in the private and public sectors, as temporary contract employees at home and abroad—reflected broader trends toward the privatization and hybridization of "public policy" making and implementation in the region.

What these expert environmental networks lacked, as has often been the case in Egyptian efforts to "reform" state practices and policies, were linkages to broader constituencies. Managerial networks remained firmly grounded in a technical approach to environmental problems that decoupled environmental problems from political and economic decision-making. Although they effectively framed environmental problems in terms of public health impacts and ensuring Egypt's natural inheritance for the political leadership, these discursive framings did not catalyze broader environmental social movements. In this respect, developments in Egypt during this period diverged from the experience of other large developing countries, such as India, Brazil, and China, where environmental experts and scientists played some role in fostering broader social movements (Guha, 2000; Hochstetler and Keck, 2007; Lemos, 1995; Ru and Ortolano, 2009).

While developing infrastructural authority in the absence of trusted institutional linkages between social constituencies and state entities is difficult, managerial networks faced additional difficulties given the limited legal authority vested in the environmental agency. To compound the problem, the Mubarak government increasingly used leadership posts at national environmental institutions as sinecures for officials retired from the military, security, and police sectors. Most of these individuals had little environmental expertise and even less experience in building linkages to firms or communities. The erosion in capacities at the national environmental agency led managerial networks to focus their efforts even more on working with external donors through consultancies and short-term contractual arrangements.

# 3   Persistent hotspots of industrial pollution

## Managerial networks, state-ownership, and poor environmental performance

"*Al-hukuma akbar mulawith fi Misr.*"
(The government is the biggest polluter in Egypt.)
> Interview with construction contractor, Alexandria, May 17, 1998

"What is wrong about this government is that while it declares that it is moving the country towards a market economy, it still behaves like a government at the helm of a command economy."

> (Al-Said, 2006)

In a slim volume entitled *Buhayrat al-Mawt* (Lake of Death), published in 1990, the Egyptian lawyer Ahmad Qazamil chronicled the destruction of Egypt's Lake Manzala through increased flows of wastewater from industry, cities, and agriculture (Qazamil, 1990). While numerous government reports had documented the degradation of the lake, the authorities had done little to slow these processes. Qazamil's account of Lake Manzala's deterioration and the lack of effective remediation applies equally well to the other northern lakes of the Nile Delta. Up until the 1980s, the "four sisters"—the coastal lagoons of Lakes Maryut, Edku, Burullus, and Manzala—were highly productive fisheries, sustaining thousands of families. For the past two decades, however, they have served largely as waste basins, receiving the discharge of major irrigation canals, agricultural drainage networks, and sewage systems from Cairo and the Nile Delta (Lajna al-Khadamat, 1992: 25). In Lake Maryut, fish catches have declined dramatically and large portions of the lake are eutrophic, with 60 percent of its dwindling water area covered in aquatic vegetation (Alvarez and Beevers, 2009).

For Lake Maryut, on the western side of Egypt's second largest city, Alexandria, Egyptian scientists and international aid agencies have long documented the sources and consequences of the lake's pollution loads. In 1978, the United States Agency for International Development (USAID) released one such study. USAID was concerned about the discharge of concentrated industrial effluent into a new treatment plant and sanitation network funded largely by American aid. Since concentrated industrial wastewater shortened the life and effectiveness of the new sanitation infrastructure, USAID's consultants recommended immediately stopping the direct discharge of industrial wastes from tanneries, petroleum companies, power stations, and engineering firms into waterways, the lake, and the Mediterranean (Camp Dresser & McKee, 1978a: 10–32). As of 2009, however, many of these firms were still discharging directly into Lake Maryut and the nearby coastal bays of al-Mex and Abu Qir. These areas remained designated critical "hotspots" of pollution, not only in Egypt but the Mediterranean as a whole (El-Kholy and Beltagy, 2002).

Adequate legal standards for industrial pollutants have been in place in Egypt since 1994, when Parliament passed a comprehensive environmental law. Yet few firms have taken compliance with these standards seriously. A 2006 survey of the fifty-five largest industrial firms in Alexandria remarked on the "'soft' enforcement of the environmental regulations," that encouraged firms to adopt an "adaptive strategy of 'soft' implementation" (El-Zayat *et al.*, 2006: 213).

In the 2006 survey, all fifty-five companies reported receiving inspections from the Ministries of Health, Labor, and Environment during the previous year. All reported that they had been cited for exceeding regulatory standards, while 36 percent reported receiving fines, though often for paltry amounts (ibid.: 209). Based on interviews with firm managers responsible for environmental compliance, the survey authors concluded that "most respondents were fairly acquainted with the environmental regulation...and seemed convinced that the regulations were reasonable and should be followed" (El-Zayat *et al.*, 2006: 210). Awareness of environmental laws, citations, and fines, however, did not translate into firms taking substantive measures to reduce pollution. Over half of the firms surveyed (58.2 percent) had no wastewater treatment system in place, while 60 percent had no air pollution control equipment (ibid.: 212). The majority (63.6 percent) did not keep a complete environmental register as required by Egyptian law, and 18.2 percent kept no register at all (ibid.: 210).

While firm awareness of environmental issues and regulations has increased since the passage of Law 4 in the mid-1990s, as have routine environmental inspections, these measures have not resulted in firms making consistent efforts to control pollution. In this chapter, I analyze why "soft enforcement" and half-hearted compliance persists among some of the most polluting firms in Egypt. Most gravely polluting firms in Egypt are state-owned enterprises (SOEs) or quasi-privatized entities under a variety of hybrid state–private ownership arrangements. Regulatory initiatives and international environmental aid have prioritized these firms as the worst environmental performers, funding "pollution prevention" and "clean production" initiatives. These approaches to pollution control identify a variety of measures to reduce consumption of inputs, improve production efficiencies, and generate less pollutants per unit of production, some of which cost little to implement.

I argue, however, that these approaches to pollution control rely on assumptions about firm behavior in market economies, which did not match decision-making by public sector firm managers in Egypt's transitional political economy. Rather than embracing pollution prevention, state-owned and newly privatized firms engaged in protracted bargaining with government ministries and international donors for packages of external assistance, under the rubric of comprehensively modernizing production and upgrading their facilities. In such negotiations, pollution loads were a kind of asset, rather than a liability, as the greater the pollution loads, the more likely firms would receive outside assistance for "industrial modernization." Because such packages were costly and time-consuming to put together, and were successfully implemented at relatively few firms during the 1990s and 2000s, gravely high pollution loads continued at many state-owned and partially privatized firms in the interim.

This argument is laid out as follows. The next section highlights the principal challenges of pollution control in state-owned and privatized firms in transitional political economies. I then turn to the political economy of industrial production in Egypt, focusing on trends in state ownership and the spatial distribution of industry. The subsequent sections analyze early, ineffective attempts to regulate pollution through law, the rise of managerial networks specifically focused on pollution control, and the discourses and initiatives put forward by managerial networks to tackle pollution loads. The limited success of these initiatives is examined in terms of the limited legal and infrastructural forms of authority wielded by managerial networks and by Egypt's environmental agency.

## Challenges of pollution control in transitional economies

Controlling pollution in political economies moving from state-led planning and investment in industry to greater private-sector ownership has long proved challenging, whether in Eastern Europe, the former Soviet Union, Vietnam, or China. In many cases, government initiatives at central and local levels have often been characterized as ineffectual. Some of the most commonly cited problems include competing priorities among central government ministries (Ohshita and Ortolano, 2006), concern about the costs of pollution control for struggling domestic firms, lack of effective civil society mobilization to press for more adequate enforcement, and inadequate capacity at the local level to enforce environmental laws (Morton, 2005). An additional challenge, identified particularly by scholars working on transitions from communism and state-led capitalism, is the proliferation of fragmented, hybrid ownership structures for firms that mix state and private ownership without clear lines of environmental accountability (Hellman, 1998; Ho, 2005). Such hybrid property forms are often explicitly promoted by government investment laws that create industrial free zones, investment zones, and other enclaves where existing regulatory frameworks are suspended to attract private capital (Tan, 2002: 336).

SOEs have historically lacked effective management mechanisms, with firms subject to conflicting demands from the political leadership, government ministries, and workers (Luong and Weinthal, 2010; Waterbury, 1993). In particular, governing elites and enterprise managers are tempted to use the revenues of SOEs for a variety of political, populist purposes, creating weak systems of accountability and limiting mechanisms for internal and external scrutiny (Luong and

Weinthal, 2010). At the same time, many SOEs are starved of reinvestment funds necessary for adequate pollution control. SOEs are often required to sell their goods and services at below-market prices for domestic consumption (an indirect subsidy), overstaff their factories to provide employment, and undertake grandiose "prestige projects" that provide patronage opportunities for political leaders (Ascher, 1999; Waterbury, 1993). These political functions are rarely matched by predictable reinvestment and SOEs are typically starved of the resources necessary to invest in new production lines, upgrade technologies, and produce competitive products. The result is pollution loads that often far exceed those predicted in the original specifications for a given technology.

Kornai's classic work on the behavior of state-owned firms under command economies helps explain the ensuing incentives for firm managers vis-à-vis the state. Many state-owned enterprises enjoy a monopoly or an oligopoly on the production or distribution of goods and services, or supply a politically important sector (such as fertilizers, oil, or chemicals). Hence they are well positioned to bargain within the state bureaucracies for outside budgetary assistance since they are too large to fail (Kornai, 1992: 124). In Kornai's terms, SOEs in a command economy encountered a soft budget constraint, where they could consistently expect outside assistance irrespective of profitability (ibid.). As Luong and Weinthal note, governing elites and enterprise managers therefore typically engage in "implicit bargaining, which not only increases opportunities for corruption but also reinforces personalism as the basis for allocating resources" (Luong and Weinthal, 2010: 49).

Tightening the soft budget constraint, however, can also produce disincentives for firms to undertake costly investments in pollution control. Programs of privatization, liquidation, and economic restructuring of the public sector often make managers at state-owned enterprises and sectoral holding companies risk-averse, focused primarily on firm survival (Tan, 2002: 337). In China, state-owned enterprises were restructured into entities jointly owned by local governments and townships. These municipally owned firms often emphasized extraction of short-term profits over costly environmental investments. That is, local townships searching for revenue tightened budget constraints on their enterprises, but in doing so they constrained the ability of firms to invest in significant upgrades of technologies and production lines. Such was the case in the coal sector, where firms chose not to invest in costly, cleaner coal technologies in the face of local government pressures for short-term financial returns (Ohshita and Ortolano, 2006: 84–6).

Despite these obstacles, several countries have successfully promoted pollution control in particular economic sectors during transitions from command economies to market-oriented ones. The Czech Republic successfully imposed "hard environmental constraints" on the steel sector in the decade following the end of state socialism in 1989 (Novy, 1999). This achievement came about through a combination of credible regulation, tightened budget constraints on enterprises, significant privatization, and a progressive system of fines (ibid.). The Czech government eliminated subsidies and government loan guarantees to the steel sector, moved rapidly on privatization, and lifted wage and price controls. Strengthening budgetary constraints on enterprises was accompanied, however, by the government's reinvestment of pollution control fines into an environmental investment fund that provided loans to firms for pollution control (ibid.). The government assessed charges on every unit of pollutant emitted, regardless of whether these were above legal standards; for every unit in excess of statutory standards, fines were increased. Firms paid these fines into the environmental fund that awarded low-interest loans and grants, but (crucially) not necessarily to the same firms that had paid punitive damages (ibid.).

As importantly, the government also established positive incentives for environmental performance and clearly specified environmental liability for privatized firms. The government offered managers of state-owned firms the option to buy up to 15 percent of the shares in newly privatized companies if the companies met environmental standards and adopted newer technologies. For private investors, privatization agreements specified targets for remediation and limits on liability, while in some cases the government allocated privatization funds to compensate investors for cleanup costs (ibid.: 275). There were two additional conditions in the Czech Republic's steel sector that enabled these environmental achievements. First, significant pollution reductions could be achieved right away through relatively modest investments. Second, market demand remained strong for the products in question, generating revenue to pay environmental fines and restructuring costs. These conditions hold for some Egyptian industrial sectors but by no means all.

In contrast to the Czech Republic, the Egyptian government never pursued a consistent or sustained transition to a market economy. In the decades since Sadat announced the policy of *infitah*, the (re)opening of the economy to private domestic and foreign investment in 1974, the regime enacted market reforms fitfully. The government lacked a clear public mandate, particularly as the benefits accrued largely to a relatively small number of elite business conglomerates in the public and private sectors. Privatization of SOEs was conducted independently of pollution control efforts. Indeed, as one bank president noted, potential investors faced significant uncertainty regarding future environmental liabilities arising from old state-owned enterprises, as the government had established no clear guidelines for environmental responsibility.[1]

Similarly, managers at state-owned enterprises were not provided with clear incentives to enact pollution control through systems of progressively strict fines or shares in newly privatized companies. Instead, Egypt's SOEs encountered layers of governmental authorities with nominal oversight of firms, including central ministries and the sectoral holding companies (such as the Holding Company for Chemical Industries). These agencies held often conflicting agendas regarding firm restructuring and lacked a commitment to prioritizing pollution issues. In order to appreciate what was at stake in efforts to oversee pollution control at SOEs, the next section provides an overview of the political economy of industrial production in Egypt, focusing on the spatial distribution of industry and resultant health hazards.

# The political topography of industrial pollution in Egypt

## *Co-location of industries, urban population, and fresh waterways*

In 2007, the Ministry of Industry reported that there were 28,184 registered industrial facilities in Egypt (Ministry of State for Environmental Affairs, 2009: 231). Many large polluting enterprises are within or adjacent to densely populated cities and limited freshwater sources, making industrial pollution a significant health threat to many Egyptians. Most old industrial enterprises are concentrated in a handful of densely populated urban suburbs. New cities and designated industrial zones originally located outside of urban areas are now on the outskirts of burgeoning conurbations, fueled by population growth and rural-to-urban migration. As expanding urban areas engulf industrial areas, and population density increases in old residential–industrial areas, a significant number of Egyptians live in close proximity to industrial pollution. This problem persists despite ongoing efforts to create new industrial cities in the desert and attempts to relocate particularly hazardous small and medium enterprises, such as lead smelting operations, to new desert locations. In recent years, new facilities producing petrochemicals, fertilizers, and related industries have been sited near established cities, particularly ports with good sea and land transport linkages (Figure 3.1).

Industrial enterprises of all sizes remain particularly concentrated in and around Egypt's two traditional metropolitan areas of Cairo and Alexandria. Egyptian environmental officials often claim that Greater Cairo and Alexandria contain approximately 80 percent of the industrial activities in Egypt, though this accounting reflects only formally registered firms, excluding vast numbers of small and informal enterprises (Hamed and El Mahgary, 2004). In recent years, the Greater Cairo metropolitan area has continued to receive the largest share of private industrial investments, with additional new investment gravitating to industrial zones in the northern Delta and along the Suez Canal.[2]

Within Cairo, heavy industry has long clustered in the northern suburb of Shubra al-Khayma and the southern suburb of Helwan. In 2008, the environmental agency reported 1,300 to 1,900 registered industries in these areas, including smelters, iron and steel foundries, chemical and metals plants, kilns, potteries, brick, textile, and car factories, and oil refineries (Ministry of State for Environmental Affairs, 2009: 39). The neighboring urbanized governorates of Qalyubiyya and Giza are also highly industrialized, as are adjacent, rapidly urbanizing areas, such as Kafr al-Zayyat. State policy of relocating industry to "new" industrial sites, such as Kafr al-Zayyat, often merely displaces pollution to new areas if undertaken without substantial investment in pollution control and ongoing enforcement efforts.

The confluence of urban populations and industrial areas emerged in the late nineteenth century. Private industrial investment focused on Cairo and Alexandria since these cities were close to waterways, trading houses, banks, and key transport routes (Mabro and Radwan, 1976: 93). The northern Cairo district of Shubra al-Khayma, for instance, became a center of textile manufacturing and power generation, while the southern suburb of Helwan, once famous for its hot springs,

*Figure 3.1* Fishermen in front of state-owned Misr Fertilizers Production Company
(MOPCO), Damietta, November 22, 2008
Jeannie Sowers, 2008

became the emblem of the industrial era and its attendant pollution with the establishment of two cement plants, Tura Cement in 1927 and Helwan Cement in 1929. Several towns near Alexandria, particularly Kafr al-Dawwar, expanded with the spinning and weaving of cotton textiles during the interwar period along freshwater canals such as the Mahmudiyya, which supplies Alexandria with Nile water.

As with textile firms, most industries rely on access to a reasonably clean water supply. Clusters of heavy and intermediate industries are often thus located near freshwater intakes from irrigation canals, the Nile River, and the northern coastal lakes, discharging effluent directly into drainage canals, lakes, shallow manmade ponds, or wells. Water is used and reused as it flows through the Delta, distributed through an elaborate network of irrigation and drainage canals, with some seeping into the shallow aquifer underlying the river system. Eventually, in much reduced volume, flows of water terminate in the northern lakes or in discharge to the Mediterranean in the form of agricultural drainage and urban–industrial wastewater.

### *Nationalization of industry under Nasser, 1957–67*

The expansion of state ownership in industry under the Nasser regime intensified industrial pollution loads in urban areas. Following the overthrow of the monarchy and the advent of military government under Nasser, the new regime eliminated the private "haute bourgeoisie" between 1957 and 1967 by nationalizing, either wholly or through majority shares, the banking, mining, manufacturing, public transport, and insurance sectors, as well as leading retail stores (Abdel-Malek, 1968; Issawi, 1963; Waterbury, 1983). By 1966–7, 95 percent of industrial enterprises employing 500 or more employees were state-owned, while 65 percent of firms employing 100–499 workers were also under state ownership (Mabro and Radwan, 1976: 97).

The Egyptian government, like other developing countries during this period, looked to state investment in heavy and intermediate industry to transform their economies, at the expense of investment in social services and agriculture (Kornai, 1992: 171–80). Influenced by the Soviet model, the regime created a Ministry of Industry in 1956 and presented its first Five-Year Plan that year. Through injections of foreign financing from the USSR, the United States, and other countries, and its extension of control over agricultural revenues, the state mobilized US$1.4 billion for the industrial sector between 1960 and 1965 (Waterbury, 1983: 85). Public-sector investments in intermediate goods, such as chemicals, metals, paper, refining, and basic engineering, accounted for 46 percent of all public investment between 1957 and 1965, although many of these projects were not completed until the 1970s (ibid.: 193). The government nationalized and expanded existing industrial establishments in Helwan, Mahalla al-Kubra, al-Mex, and Shubra al-Khayma. New projects were started in Suez, the middle Delta, Abu Qir outside of Alexandria, Aswan, and Nag 'Hammadi (Lajna al-Khadamat, 1992: 23). Hydropower made available by the completion of the Aswan High Dam also prompted new industrial investments, such as the Kima fertilizer plant and aluminum smelters near Aswan in Upper Egypt.

The devastating consequences of the 1967 war with Israel, including the loss of the Sinai Peninsula, restricted government investment in industry. By 1974, the dominant role given to state-owned enterprises and public bureaucracies in controlling investment, prices, and output in the economy had produced economic stagnation, shortages, and a scarcity of private sector investment. The result was *infitah*, or opening the Egyptian economy to foreign and domestic investment. *Infitah* also reflected the strategy of Nasser's successor, Anwar al-Sadat, to revive Egypt's economy through rapprochement with the United States.

### Return of the private sector, 1974–present

Sadat's policy of *infitah* liberalized investment laws and trade regulations, and established incentives for foreign and domestic private investment. These incentives included long-term tax exemptions, cheap land, state-subsidized infrastructure, and exemptions from import and currency exchange restrictions (Law 1943 of 1974, modified 1977 and 1989). New company laws were introduced (Law 159 of 1981), which allowed Egyptians to once again establish companies without government participation. The government established the General Authority for Industrial Development (more recently the Industrial Development Authority), which designated several industrial free zones, including some of the new industrial cities on the outskirts of Greater Cairo. While interest among investors was initially limited, by 2005 approximately 2,700 factories had located to the industrial zones in the new towns. Concentrated particularly in the cities of Tenth of Ramadan and Sixth of October, these enterprises employed approximately 250,000 people, the vast majority of whom commuted from Greater Cairo and other established urban areas (Madbouli, 2005: 60).

The government also began to privatize state-owned firms. Throughout the privatization program, the regime was concerned with labor protest, fears of increased unemployment, and political criticism from opposition parties, syndicates, and other corporatist interest groups. As a result, periods of intensified privatization alternated with delays, though calls for re-nationalization of privatized firms were generally resisted. By 2010, 282 out of 314 state-owned enterprises slated for sale were partially or wholly privatized. Of these privatized firms, eighty-five were sold to anchor investors (private owners with majority shares), while another thirty-eight listed majority shares on the Egyptian stock exchange but significant shares were retained under state control, as shown in Table 3.1.

With the exception of anchor investments, many privatization transactions did not produce clear changes in ownership. Instead, firms were in essence quasi-privatized, and oversight authority was fragmented among public-sector banks, holding companies, and state officials. In terms of environmental accountability, quasi-privatization posed problems similar to those of state ownership.

*Table 3.1* Egyptian companies privatized or liquidated (through May 31, 2010)

| Method of privatization | Number of companies | Sale proceeds (LE million) |
|---|---|---|
| Majority through public offering (stock exchange) | 38 | 6,064 |
| Minority through public offering | 23 | 11,003 |
| Liquidation | 34 | – |
| Asset sale | 44 | 3,437 |
| Anchor investor | 85 | 32,208 |
| Employee Share Association (ESA) | 33 | 932 |
| Leasing | 25 | – |
| Total | 282 | 53,644 |

Source: EGID Egypt, Monthly Bulletin, May 2010, Egypt for Information Dissemination, Produced by the Egyptian Exchange, http://www.egidegypt.com (accessed June 18, 2010)

## Persistence of state ownership in industry

In addition to hybrid state–private ownership for many former SOEs, outright state ownership in pollution-intensive industrial sectors remains significant. The share of the private sector in GDP during the 2000s leveled out at slightly over 60 percent, as shown in Table 3.2.

*Table 3.2* Industrial activity and ownership in Egypt, 1991–2008

| | 1991/2 | 1996/7 | 2001/2 | 2007/8 |
|---|---|---|---|---|
| Share of private sector in total GDP (percent) | 61.2 | 66.4 | 65.4 | 61.9 |
| Industry, value added (percent of GDP) | 33 | 31 | 35 | 36 |
| Manufacturing, value added (percent of GDP) | 17 | 18 | 20 | 17 |
| Manufacturers' exports (percent of merchandise exports) | 35 | 38 | 35 | 19 (2007) |
| Foreign direct investment (millions of US$) | 1,140 | 770 | 1,235 | 11,578 |

Source: Compiled from American Chamber of Commerce in Egypt, Business Studies and Analysis Center, http://www.amcham.org.eg/BSAC/EconomicIndicators/EcIndicators.asp (accessed June 17, 2010); World Development Indicators Database, September 2009

Several factors account for the continued presence of state ownership in Egypt's industrial sector. First, privatization opportunities were limited for some firms because investors proved unwilling to buy them, viewing them as unprofitable ventures. Second, Egypt's natural endowment in fossil fuels provides a strong incentive for state ownership, as these resources supply hard currency to the government. In 2007–8, energy and energy products (the petroleum-related sector) still accounted for 50.3 percent of all export products.[3] The oil and natural gas sector remains state-owned under the Egyptian General Petroleum Company (EGPC) and three affiliated holding companies, although multinational oil firms are involved via production-sharing contracts (United States Energy Information Administration, 2010).

The 2006 survey of large firms near and around Alexandria discussed at the outset of this chapter illustrates the continued importance of state ownership in industry. The survey classified ownership of large industrial enterprises in terms of five categories: the public (i.e. state) sector, the private sector, the EGPC, the investment sector, and the military sector (El-Zayat *et al.*, 2006: 208). Of these, three are fully state-owned (the public, EGPC, and military sectors) while investment enterprises, formed under specific investment laws, are typically hybrid joint ventures between government authorities and private investors, either foreign or domestic (Waterbury, 1983). The majority of large industrial firms in Alexandria remained state-owned (61.8 percent), while nine were undergoing privatization at the time of the survey. The authors provided no indication of the numbers of firms affiliated with the military sector or the EGPC, nor state ownership in hybrid "investment firms," reflecting the ongoing sensitivity of questions about state ownership in industry.

## *Industry and pollution*

The intermediate and heavy industrial sectors favored in both state plans for investment and private capitalists are inherently large consumers of energy and materials, making them pollution-intensive. To compound these challenges, much of Egypt's heavy industry established during the heyday of Egyptian–Soviet cooperation under Nasser is now outdated. Egypt paid for technology imports from the Soviet bloc via barter arrangements, using cotton and other exports as payment. Cooperation in industrial investment with the Soviet bloc later left many state-owned enterprises unable to acquire spare parts or adapt their Soviet-era production lines with the reorientation of Egypt's political economy towards the West. In visits by the author to some of the most polluting state-owned industries during the 1990s and 2000s, it was common to see production lines dating from the 1960s and early 1970s, imported from Romania, East Germany, and Poland.

Industrial emissions are thus a significant contributing factor to severe air pollution in Egypt's cities. For Greater Cairo, a 2001 source attribution study found that industrial emissions accounted for 32 percent of the total annual load for fine particulates, while open burning of solid municipal waste accounted for 36 percent. Vehicle exhaust made up 26 percent of air pollution loads, and open burning of agricultural waste another 6 percent (Ministry of State for Environmental Affairs, 2006). Egypt's arid climate, which features little precipitation, seasonal temperature inversions, and seasonal sandstorms and winds (especially the *khamsin* winds in the spring), also contributes to acute episodes of air pollution. To compound matters, industrialized areas north of the capital, such as Abu Za'bal and Musturud, are situated such that prevailing winds carry industrial pollutants and smoke from agricultural burning over the capital.

All of these factors combine to create the notorious "black cloud" (*al-sahaba al-sawda'*), prolonged episodes of intense air pollution that first appeared in the late 1990s and return each season to blanket the capital, often in the fall (ibid.: 39). When the "black cloud" first appeared, the columnist Salah Montasser reminded readers of the state-owned *Al-Ahram Weekly* that the "post-1952 'revolutionary' governments" were partially to blame, as they built factories very close to the capital "for propaganda purposes" (Montasser, 1999).

Industrial loads to waterways also remain significant. At the beginning of the privatization process in 1992, the environmental agency estimated that 330 large state-owned industries consumed approximately 638 million $m^3$ of water annually, 65 percent of which was drawn directly from the Nile. The report estimated that 80 percent of the 549 million $m^3$ discharged by these facilities was untreated, with 57 percent discharged directly to the Nile and other irrigation channels, 21.5 percent to drainage canals, 12.9 percent to sewage lines, and 8.9 percent to lakes and estuaries (Egyptian Environmental Affairs Agency and Ministry of Industry, 1995: 22).[4]

Through the late 1990s and early 2000s, as confirmed by the author in visits to a number of large state-owned industrial facilities, only a few firms had invested in water treatment systems. Most used straight dilution techniques to lower concentrations of contaminants. Metal finishing plants, for instance, discharged wastewater contaminated with chromium, copper, and nickel directly to canals, ocean outfalls, or municipal sewage networks if they were connected to the system. Industrial plants without access to sewage networks often discharged wastewater to shallow drainage wells and unlined septic tanks. Since the Delta water table is only a few meters below the surface, it was likely that effluent was leaching into groundwater reserves.

As USAID had warned in Alexandria, industrial effluent discharged to municipal sanitation systems raises operation costs, shortens the longevity of these infrastructures as acidic effluent corrodes the pipes, and poses grave problems for sludge disposal. Industrial discharges to waterways not only adversely affect human and marine health, but also threaten government plans to treat and reuse wastewater for agricultural crops.

### The military sector

Military enterprises, while a small number of Egypt's total industrial firms, comprise a significant number of the most polluting firms. In the period of expansive state ownership under Nasser, new military-industrial districts, such as Abu

Za'bal and Abu Rawwash, were established in Cairo, while the regime also established military firms in established residential areas, such as the upscale suburb of Ma'adi. Three governmental authorities—the Ministry of Military Production, the Arab Organization for Industrialization, and the National Service Products Organization—have long overseen (at least) twenty-nine large industrial enterprises associated with the military. These large-scale operations with large numbers of workers employ outdated production lines with heavy pollution loads.

Helwan Factory 9, for instance, operated the "biggest integrated complex of ferrous foundries for cast iron and steel casting in Egypt" in 1997, according to the company's promotional literature. The company produces metal parts for spinning and weaving machines, cement factories, railway wagons, and water pumps, as well as for cannons, missiles, and launchers. Since goods produced are generally of poor quality and non-competitive in private markets, most military-owned firms primarily supply other state-owned enterprises.

Pollution loads at military plants are particularly acute. One environmental engineer recalled that while studying at Helwan University in the mid-1990s, training in sampling wastewater was conducted at several military production plants. He reported routinely measuring concentrations 500 times the legal standards.[5] In 1999, only two companies under the Ministry of War Production reported having end-of-pipe facilities to treat chemical discharges, including chromium and other heavy metals (Hussein, 1999).

US–Egyptian co-production of the M1 tank offers a further glimpse into the lack of environmental controls at state-owned facilities. In 1984 General Dynamics signed a contract with the government of Egypt for the construction and start-up of a tank facility. The facility enabled Egyptian policymakers to push successfully for a program of tank co-production during the 1990s, rather than importing complete tanks as preferred by US manufacturers (United States General Accounting Office, 1993). The United States provided tank technology in phased "packages," enabling the United States to withhold critical technical elements. While these packages included quality control measures, neither the Egyptians nor the Americans created requirements for environmental controls, although several production processes used toxic materials that would have been subject to hazardous waste laws in the United States. A military attaché at the American Embassy in Cairo kindly provided a concrete example: the inside of tank cannons were plated with chromium, but there were no provisions to monitor either the volume applied or disposal.[6]

Military firms have also contracted with other public sector industrial establishments to supply environmental goods and services. The Engine Factory, one of the nine factories under the Arab Organization for Industrialization, expanded its services from the manufacture and repair of aircraft engines to include the design, installation, and maintenance of wastewater treatment plants. The Engine Factory secured contracts with eight publicly owned oil and soap companies for the installation and maintenance of such wastewater treatment plants, and bid for projects at five other firms (El Maadawy, 1999: 2). The Helwan, Abu Qir, and Abu Za'bal Engineering Companies signed contracts with local governments to produce composting plants. The Ma'sara Company for Military and Civil

Industries produced not only machine guns and rifles, but also water meters under license from Andrae GmbH of Germany and three types of incinerators (ibid.).

Environmental services and technologies provided by these firms were often inefficient and outdated. In contrast to efforts by managerial networks to promote pollution prevention and clean production, as explored in subsequent sections, military-owned firms typically supplied end-of-pipe treatment technologies that simply diluted or displaced pollutants into other media.

## Early attempts to regulate industrial pollution

Attempts to regulate pollution began in the early 1960s and were fragmented among government authorities responsible for different land uses and discharges into different media. Law 93 in 1962, under the authority of the Ministry of Housing and New Communities, specified standards for industrial and agricultural discharges to urban sewer systems, principally in Cairo, Alexandria, and the port cities. In 1969, executive decrees issued by the Ministry of Petroleum established procedures for oil pollution from petroleum exploration operations. The following decades saw additional Cabinet decrees, executive orders, ministerial edicts, and governorate proclamations aimed specifically at controlling various types of industrial pollution. A 1975 Ministry of Housing resolution set out guidelines for siting industrial enterprises near residential areas. In 1979, local administrative agencies were given authority to supervise industrial establishments in order to protect public health (Local Administration Code No. 43).

The government also passed a series of laws designed to address water pollution. The principal regulatory mechanisms employed in these laws were permit procedures for new industrial projects and the authority to suspend existing industrial licenses (Shawky, 1993). The Ministry of Industry, for instance, issued a 1982 decree that required new or modernizing factories, including foreign companies and joint ventures, to obtain a license specifying pollution control devices (Lajna al-Khadamat, 1992: 42). Law 38 (1982) authorized the Ministry of Irrigation to issue and revoke licenses of industrial projects discharging into the Nile (ibid.). The Ministry of Housing was tasked with sampling and analysis of wastewater discharged at specific facilities. Law 38 also appointed the river patrols of the Ministry of Interior to monitor pollution of the Nile River and canals. The river police, however, were hardly equipped to carry out sophisticated monitoring of water quality.

Parliamentary reports from the early 1980s reveal that the government was aware that these measures had been entirely ineffective, particularly with respect to state-owned enterprises. In 1985, an agreement was signed by the Ministries of Health, Industry, and Irrigation to implement twenty-five projects targeted at ameliorating industrial pollution from nineteen state-owned companies, at an estimated cost of LE75.3 million. But the money was not allocated and the projects were not implemented at that time (Qasim, 1993: 112). Similarly, the Ministry of Industry produced a study of environmental investments needed for state-owned enterprises between 1983 and 1987; recommendations for a series of significant investments at selected firms were disregarded in state budget allocations (ibid.: 110–11).

## Managerial networks in pollution control

By the mid-1990s, international donors and environmental experts began calling for more substantive pollution control efforts at large industrial facilities. These efforts moved along two tracks: the creation of donor funds to support pollution control efforts at specific enterprises on the one hand, and attempts by environmental networks to establish rudimentary organizational capacities for pollution control at the environmental agency on the other.

For environmental experts, the most immediate challenge was the lack of basic, verifiable information about industrial pollution loads and firm responses. As the director of the Industrial Compliance Unit wrote in 1999, "Major sources of compliance information—industrial self-monitoring and reporting, inspections, citizen complaints, and ambient monitoring—are all inadequately functioning, if not non-existent" (Sharif, 1999: 3).

Monitoring of water pollution began in the 1980s by the Ministries of Irrigation and Health, with little coordination or information sharing between them. These efforts expanded during the 1990s and 2000s with donor assistance. By 2000, the Ministry of Irrigation monitored water quality along the Nile River, irrigation canals, and drains in 232 stations, and operated another 203 stations to monitor groundwater pollution (Ministry of Water Resources and Irrigation, 2005b). The Ministry of Health, responsible for potable water quality, ran 154 monitoring sites along the Nile and large canals, near intakes for drinking water plants and large polluting plants. The Ministry of State for Environmental Affairs (MSEA) operated its own smaller network along the Nile.

For air quality, ambient air monitoring of basic indicators only began in the early 1990s. The USAID-funded Cairo Air Improvement Project expanded the existing air pollution monitoring network in 1999. But monitoring stations quickly fell into disrepair and, in a few years, the agency reported that only a few were working. As with many donor-funded projects, the technologies and protocols for environmental monitoring reflected those employed in donor countries, regardless of their suitability to local conditions. With supplemental USAID funding, monitoring stations were renovated in 2004 and 2005 with additional stations brought online (Ministry of State for Environmental Affairs, 2006). By 2006, however, the coverage across all of Egypt was a mere fifty-four monitoring stations. Only thirteen of these were in industrial areas with high air pollution loads (ibid.).

Although the World Bank and other international institutions had developed simple protocols for sharing ambient pollution information with the public, based on color-coded alert levels disseminated by the local media, these practices were not adopted in Egypt. Thus, while donor-funded initiatives expanded air monitoring networks, there was almost no attempt to share this information with the public. Ambient monitoring also did not provide environmental experts with usable data on firm-specific pollution loads. As a senior consultant in the industrial compliance office noted in the late 1990s, "We simply had no information on pollution loads from the private sector, and only limited information on the public sector."[7]

## Framing pollution: hotspots, clean production, and pollution prevention

Egyptian environmental experts, beginning in the 1970s, had long argued that Egypt faced serious pollution loads in critical "hotspots." These "hotspots" typically consisted of clusters of large, primarily state-owned industrial complexes. Some environmental experts hoped that by framing pollution in terms of hotspots, they could avoid politically sensitive questions about pollution loads from state- and military-owned firms. As one environmental scientist working as a consultant in the Industrial Compliance Office noted, "We have merely been trying to point out that there are pockets of high density pollution in Egypt—and totally unacceptable practices of polluting in these pockets."[8]

Managerial networks of pollution control experts and consultants for donors and government ministries produced numerous maps and listings of pollution hotspots during the 1990s and 2000s. Experts used a variety of qualitative rankings based on risks to public health, drinking water, and economic productivity to identify such areas (El-Kholy and Beltagy, 2002: 50). Mapping pollution hotspots emerged as a regular feature of action plans, government investment plans, and donor documents regarding industrial pollution (Egyptian Environmental Affairs Agency and Ministry of Industry, 1995; World Bank, 2005b). These documents highlighted the same clusters of state-owned firms that had been well-known sources of pollution for decades. For instance, many of the same coastal Alexandrian firms listed in the 1978 USAID study as requiring immediate pollution abatement or closure appeared as major polluters in Egypt's *State of the Environment Report* for 2008.

Alongside framing pollution in terms of hotspots, international donors and local experts promoted two approaches to pollution control that had gained widespread acceptance in industrialized countries during the 1990s, namely pollution prevention and clean production (Hamed and El Mahgary, 2004). Rather than focusing on end-of-pipe treatments, which often simply transferred pollutants from one medium to another, managerial networks argued that industry should focus on reducing pollution at the source. Key elements of these approaches, as outlined in a 1991 report on coastal Alexandria, included process modifications to reduce consumption of inputs and minimize waste, recycling and reclaiming of waste products, and incorporating environmental considerations in new technology decisions (Hamza, 1991: 2–7).

Of the ten plants identified for pilot studies of pollution prevention in this 1991 study, eight were state-owned enterprises, most of which were partially privatized in the ensuing decade (ibid.: 122–4). USAID's Environmental Pollution Prevention Project (EP3), which ran from 1993 to 1998, hired Egyptian environmental consultants to conduct free pollution prevention assessments at these firms as well as others (Gallup and Marcotte, 2004: 219). These assessments identified no-cost and low-cost measures for firms, on the assumption that such measures were affordable. For instance, these firms could adopt simple housekeeping measures to reduce the volume of inputs used and thus the volumes of pollution generated.[9]

Pollution prevention was premised, however, on the assumption that firms operate in a market context, where reduced consumption of inputs, quality of production, and reduction of pollutants matter for firm profitability. But for state-owned enterprises, such small financial savings were unimportant in the face of large debts, soft budget constraints, and the uncertainty of privatization. Firms had little reason to change routine practices or invest in incremental managerial and technological innovations to lower consumption or produce more efficiently with fewer resources.

These problems with applying pollution prevention approaches to state-owned and quasi-privatized enterprises were in many ways predictable. During the 1980s, a team of Egyptian and American consultants conducted six environmental audits of highly polluting SOEs for USAID. These audits found that firms did not track pollution discharges nor did they monitor volumes of inputs, as these costs were not reflected in the state's assessments of enterprise performance or in allocations of budgetary resources to enterprises. By 2004, a cumulative review of USAID's experience promoting pollution prevention across several developing countries included a critique of focusing aid efforts on the most polluting firms without attention to firm ownership or management. As the report noted:

> There is a tendency for pollution prevention programs to focus on the firms with the worst pollution problems. That may not be the best approach to achieve a sustained impact. Pollution prevention efforts stand a better chance of success if they identify and work with the more progressive and better-managed firms.
>
> (Ibid.: 224)

### State-owned enterprises and the costs of pollution abatement

While many SOE managers I interviewed in Alexandria expressed concern about pollution impacts, they also felt that the government and donors should finance any improvements. As one manager at a state-owned chemical firm declared, "The state should help us or all this stuff about environment is *kalam fadi* [empty words]."[10] An official at the Metallurgical Holding Company agreed, observing, "The private sector can help themselves. We must help the public sector in order to make it possible for them to comply with pollution laws."[11]

These assertions were widely accepted by managerial networks of experts and international donors. Donor funds established for pollution abatement in "hotspots" primarily targeted SOEs. From 1996 to 2008, the German technical assistance agency KfW provided grants and technical assistance under its "Environmental Facility for Public-Sector Industries" program. The World Bank and Finnish government funded the Egyptian Pollution Abatement Project from 1998 to 2005, which financed twenty-five pollution abatement projects at twenty-one facilities (Ministry of State for Environmental Affairs, 2007; World Bank, 2005b). Between 1999 and 2004, a total of eleven funds financed by international donors and managed by domestic commercial banks offered soft loans and grants for pollution control and abatement.

Concessionary lending expanded dramatically under the World Bank's second Egyptian Pollution Abatement Project (EPAP II), approved in 2006, which established a US$20 million loan fund (World Bank, 2005b). EPAP II leveraged an additional US$145 million from the Japan Bank for International Cooperation, the European Investment Bank, Agence Française de Developement, and the Government of Finland. These funds were deposited with the state-owned National Bank of Egypt, to be distributed to selected firms on the terms of 20 percent grant and 80 percent loan (ibid.).

This financing was further paired with an additional US$7 million from the Global Environmental Facility for pollution abatement at "hotspots" in Alexandria, Lake Maryut, and Cairo (ibid.). As shown in Table 3.3 at the end of this chapter, of the fifteen companies listed as candidates for receiving funds under EPAP II, four were state-owned enterprises, seven were partially privatized state-owned enterprises, and the remaining four were private firms. In 2007, under the EU's European Neighbourhood Policy, the EU committed to a US$558 million aid package, which included an energy and environment component, and Egypt was declared eligible to borrow additional funds from the European Investment Bank. This influx of assistance continued to prioritize state-owned and quasi-privatized enterprises in hotspots.

The assumption that state-owned firms could not afford pollution abatement encouraged managerial networks of donors and experts to privilege large, polluting state-owned enterprises for pollution abatement funds. Yet surveys of firms in Egypt did not bear out key elements of this assumption. In the previously cited survey of fifty-five large firms in Alexandria, a large proportion of which were state or military-owned, only fifteen managers interviewed (27.3 percent of the sample) thought that achieving compliance with environmental standards was too costly for their firm (El-Zayat *et al.*, 2006). Of these fifteen, six reported that their firm had already received outside financial assistance, though none of the six managers considered this assistance "sufficient" (ibid.: 212). The other forty-three firms surveyed had not received financial assistance, yet most did not rank cost as a primary obstacle to environmental compliance.

For large state-owned firms that successfully installed basic water treatment plants and rerouted their discharges away from the Nile River, these costs were typically covered by central government allocations combined with self-financing (Egyptian Environmental Affairs Agency, 2002). How did such companies manage to "self-finance" pollution abatement costs, when most firms were chronically indebted, saddled with excess labor and inefficient and outdated production lines, and producing poor quality products?

## Inside the soft budget constraint

The answer lies in a host of opaque, intra-public sector financial transactions between enterprises, public-sector banks, and government agencies. Two major sources of investment for SOEs were Egypt's National Investment Bank (NIB) and the Public Savings Fund (PSF), which allocated money to central ministries which, in turn, divided it among holding companies, and then among affiliated state-owned enterprises. Neither the NIB nor the PSF publicized their balance sheets, and nor were these institutions subject to parliamentary scrutiny. State-owned enterprises could draw on off-budget sources of "deficit" financing, provided by other state-owned entities, as well as the NIB and the PSF, in order to fund pollution abatement.

The Extracted Oils and Derivatives Company, for instance, with LE400 million in annual turnover, claimed to have unpaid debts amounting to LE900 million from the Ministry of Supply in 1997 and to be operating at a loss. The company, however, self-financed LE7.5 million in pollution controls by drawing on overdraft credits from the NIB (Soil and Water Ltd, 1998: 11). These loans were, in turn, credited to a state-owned military factory that supplied industrial wastewater treatment projects for two of the firm's plants in Alexandria. Thus, when SOEs invested in pollution control, the equipment was supplied largely by other state-owned agencies and financed by intra-public sector transactions. In this context, firms had little incentive to pursue pollution control strategies based on clean production or pollution prevention.

Most managers at large SOEs were far more concerned with what they termed industrial modernization. Managers sought aid from donors, holding companies, and the central ministries for comprehensive upgrading of production lines through donor and governmental transfers. In surveys, managers ranked improved product quality, increased production, and cost reduction as their primary concerns, not pollution control (El-Zayat *et al.*, 2006). They argued that international donors should focus on industrial modernization, to replace and update production processes entirely, and thereby improve product quality and competitiveness in contexts where privatization and competition were increasing.

Managerial concern with the need for comprehensive industrial modernization became more acute as Egypt liberalized access to its domestic market. Beginning in the late 1990s, Egypt signed a number of multilateral and bilateral trade agreements that opened domestic industry to global pressure. These included Egypt's accession to the World Trade Organization (WTO), bilateral trade agreements giving preferential access to the US market (such as the establishment of Qualified Industrial Zones, which include minimum content requirements from Israel), and the EU–Egypt Association Agreement, which came into effect in 2004. All of these agreements provided for lower tariff barriers in key industrial and service sectors, opening up protected markets to competition with multinational and domestic private firms. State-owned and quasi-privatized enterprises thus bargained to "soften" environmental legal constraints, in a similar manner to softened budget constraints.

### *Rakta Pulp and Paper*

The case of the Rakta Pulp and Paper Company in Alexandria illustrates the mismatch between expert framings of pollution control as critical "hotspots" in need of immediate, low-cost interventions to reduce pollution, and the incentives for managers at a quasi-privatized enterprise to bargain with the government and with donors for more comprehensive and costly packages of external assistance.

Founded in 1958, Rakta Pulp and Paper was nationalized in 1961 and partially privatized in the late 1990s. The firm owns eight plants producing paper products out of rice straw, with some sugarcane bagasse and scrap paper inputs as well. Rakta's paper is largely sold to other state-owned enterprises and government-owned presses.[12] Rakta has long been identified as an Alexandrian pollution hotspot, since its production process consumes a great deal of water and wastewater discharges contain high concentrations of total dissolved solids. Pulp and paper production at Rakta consumes between 81,500 and 137,200 cubic meters of water per day (El-Bestawy *et al.*, 2008: 1521). Pulp and paper plants accounted for the largest water pollution loads in the Alexandrian metropolitan area, estimated at 35 percent of total waste loads (Hamza, 1991: 103).

Rakta's water pollution has been a focus for managerial networks for decades. When I visited the plant in the late 1990s, the production manager showed me dozens of donor-funded studies, conducted over years, on how to address the company's pollution problems. Privatization and a rise in international paper prices had brought a flood of cash into the company. Yet, as the manager explained, upper management in the firm and the affiliated holding company had not acted on these reams of recommendations. The firm was instead waiting to hear about an industrial modernization package from the World Bank's Pollution Abatement Fund.[13]

In part, difficulties in addressing pollution stemmed from adapting technology to local inputs. In an interview, the production manager observed that:

> We wanted industrialization at any cost and now we are paying the price, both in terms of profitability and pollution. We looked at paper, a strategic industry, and determined that we could make paper with rice straw, since it was locally available. So we imported German machinery, and adapted it to conditions here. But now we have a big problem, as international firms don't use rice straw as an input.[14]

Rakta's production processes using rice straw discharge large quantities of "black liquor" effluent that have proven difficult to treat before discharge. Egyptian researchers, however, have increasingly identified several cost-effective techniques for doing so (El-Ashtoukhy *et al.*, 2009; El-Bestawy *et al.*, 2008). Yet untreated "black liquor" discharge largely persists (ibid.).

Rakta's decision to wait for external assistance characterized the approach of many partially privatized enterprises toward pollution control and environmental management. As much as pollution was a liability for the general public, it thus served as a peculiar kind of asset in terms of intra-bureaucratic bargaining and qualifying for external assistance.

## Constraints on legal and infrastructural authority for pollution control

Large industrial firms could take a leisurely approach to pollution control in large part because of "soft enforcement," the lack of infrastructural and legal authority to compel firms to prioritize pollution control. The difficulties of inducing state-owned and quasi-privatized firms to embark on pollution prevention and clean production measures reflected the absence of credible enforcement mechanisms and limited legal authority. As discussed in Chapter 2, the 1994 environmental law (Law 4/1994, revised as Law 9/2009) conferred limited authority for pollution control upon the Egyptian Environmental Affairs Agency (EEAA). Instead, legal authority for pollution control remained vested in the "administrative authority" with oversight over a given enterprise or responsible for allocating land to the firm.[15] Administrative entities vested with enforcement authority thus included municipalities, urban districts, the provincial governments (governorates), special investment authorities, the Ministry of Industry, or various agencies affiliated with the military.[16] Law 4/1994 did provide the Minister of State for Environmental Affairs with some authority to intercede directly with these administrative agencies. Specifically, the minister was empowered to request provincial governors to close polluting factories temporarily or to shut off water and electricity supply to a violating plant.

Such extreme actions, however, were obviously reserved only for exceptional cases. More typically, pollution control networks sought to coordinate with other administrative authorities by creating inter-ministerial protocols and joint committees. A 1998 draft protocol between the EEAA and the Federation of Egyptian Industries specified that a joint committee would serve "as a means for exchanging viewpoints and consultations on the problems of factories…and for reaching compromises between factories, EEAA, and the [state-organized] Federation of Egyptian Industries" (Egyptian Environmental Affairs Agency, 1998: 3). Another protocol signed with the Ministry of Labor stipulated that the EEAA would provide additional training for 150 occupational health and safety inspectors in order to combine environmental inspections with existing occupational health and safety inspections (Egyptian Environmental Affairs Agency, 1998).

The executive regulations for Law 4, issued in 1995, provided industrial establishments with an automatic three-year grace period to comply. A survey of 1,000 facilities undertaken in 1997 by Egyptian pollution control experts found that only a small percentage of new facilities complied with the standards of the law (Sharif, 1999: 3). Over half reported that they had taken no action, 25 percent reported they had taken some measures, and only 5 percent reported that they complied. Yet—as in surveys conducted a decade later—only 10 percent reported that lack of technical assistance and financing were insurmountable obstacles to achieving compliance with environmental standards (ibid.). Of fifty-three public and private firms that submitted data to the USAID-funded Environmental Pollution Prevention Project (EP3) between 1994 and 1997, only 17 percent of firms surveyed said they knew about the requirements of Law 4, none had taken additional measures to comply with the law, and only 11.3 percent had pursued water treatment options other than simple dilution.[17]

A senior consultant to the environment minister observed that, at the end of the grace period, the agency still lacked any credible infrastructural authority through which to reach polluting firms:

> We are saying that Law 4 is coming into force. We are bluffing on that, for the regulatory instruments are lacking. With at least 25,000 industrial establishments, one thousand have a level of pollution we can feasibly measure, but we can't even adequately monitor even six or seven factories. How are we supposed to monitor all of them?[18]

Faced with these organizational deficiencies, the then-environmental minister, Nadya Makram Ebeid, launched a campaign in 1998 targeting thirty-four large, state-owned "hotspots" that discharged effluent directly into the Nile, all concentrated around Greater Cairo. The campaign was conducted by the newly established Industrial Compliance Office within the environmental agency, staffed by a handful of pollution experts. Most were hired directly as consultants by the Minister of State for Environmental Affairs or by the CEO of the environmental agency.

Without reliable means for the agency to gather ongoing information on pollution loads, the minister authorized surprise inspections (Ebeid and Hamza, 2001). The Minister of State for Environmental Affairs also publicly announced that she would request the relevant administrative authority to shut down egregiously polluting plants, shutting off electricity and water to the plants if they did not comply. These threats and surprise inspections received extensive coverage in the state-owned media, heightening pressure on otherwise largely unaccountable enterprises. Faced with intensified media coverage, spot inspections, and fines, environmental experts reported that ten state-owned enterprises spent slightly over LE320 million during 1998 on water treatment and recovery systems (ibid.). The environmental agency reported that another twenty-one companies stopped dumping effluent down drains that emptied directly into freshwater resources by 2002, at a cost of LE120 million.

Many of these firms, however, simply redirected their wastewater discharges from the Nile River into urban sanitation networks. The Cairo and Alexandria sanitation utilities, established under donor auspices as quasi-autonomous cost recovery organizations, became increasingly concerned about the effects of industrial effluent on the longevity and effectiveness of their infrastructure and treatment capacities. Under pressure from donors, the Cairo and Alexandria sanitation agencies were granted executive authority to autonomously raise fees and impose fines. They used this authority to increasingly impose fines on industries discharging untreated effluent into their networks.

The Cairo Sanitary Drainage Organization, for instance, levied a LE1.1 million surcharge on the Egyptian Starch and Glucose Firm (ESG) in Cairo, prompting plant managers to quickly install an on-site treatment facility in order to get the surcharge waived (ibid.). The contrast between Rakta's delays in addressing its discharges of "black liquor" and ESG's attempt to quickly treat wastewater discharges in-house highlight why environmental networks emphasized the importance of creating institutions with adequate legal authority. The Cairo and Alexandria drainage authorities, endowed with the legal authority and infrastructural capacity to impose fines, had some success in forcing companies to install basic wastewater treatment plants.

### Compliance action plans

Given the limits of the environmental agency's legal authority, managerial networks attempted to provide positive inducements for more firms to begin to collect basic information about pollution loads and to begin to address their pollution problems. The challenge for managerial networks was how to create linkages with polluting firms, that is, to build infrastructural authority. Expert consultants at the Industrial Compliance Office decided to offer all firms, not just those in "hotspots," an additional two-year grace period to comply with Law 4 if they would submit "compliance action plans." These plans were to set out how firms would monitor their pollution loads and a timeframe for pollution abatement.

Managerial networks publicized this initiative through their public roles as staff at the environmental agency and their private roles in private consulting firms. According to the project manager for the World Bank's Egyptian Pollution Abatement Project (EPAP), the most effective means of reaching enterprises was that private environmental consulting firms began soliciting enterprises directly, by offering to prepare the compliance action plan for a fee.[19] For companies, preparing such a plan was attractive even in the absence of credible enforcement mechanisms, since managers saw the plan as signaling their intent to comply with formal regulations and gain the environmental agency's stamp of approval to delay compliance for several more years. The Industrial Compliance Office reported that, within several months, they had received 190 submissions from enterprises by late 1997 (ibid.). Private environmental consulting firms had prepared most of the action plans.

The limits of the EEAA's legal authority to undertake even these kinds of initiatives soon became clear, however. The prime minister announced that extending the grace period would reflect poorly on the government's commitment to environmental enforcement and refused to authorize the promised extension of time. This stance was ironic, as the same Cabinet had taken no real steps to pressure governmental ministries to comply. Environmental experts in pollution control networks faced a dilemma: they could not legally accept (or reject) the already-submitted compliance action plans, but publicly admitting this fact would stop firms from submitting such plans. They opted to continue accepting firm submissions, and notified companies that their submissions had been received without extending a formal grace period.

Despite this legal limbo, some firms continued to hire consulting firms to prepare compliance action plans, since environmental consultants working with donor projects used the plans in putting together projects for external assistance. In addition, some donors, such as USAID, sought to create more demand for private environmental consulting firms. Preparing a compliance action plan thus became a prerequisite for gaining access to environmental aid. In contrast to the original purpose envisioned by managerial networks, the compliance action plan was thus increasingly decoupled from regulatory enforcement.

## Conclusion

Environmentalism in Egypt includes widespread public concern about the effects of industrial pollution on health and local environments. Increasing attention to pollution from international donors helped spur the growth of managerial networks focused on pollution control. The expansion of external concessionary financing spurred demands for environmental goods and services supplied by private environmental consulting firms. Through iterative projects undertaken by donors and state agencies, network participants rotated through multiple roles in private consulting firms, government ministries, academia, and donor projects.

Despite efforts to build authority, however, these networks were unable to implement credible sanctions or supply sufficient inducements to promote rapid, substantive change in firm environmental performance. Managerial networks promoted pollution prevention and clean production as cost-effective approaches to pollution control, and advocated focusing on critical pollution "hotspots." In emphasizing critical hotspots, managerial networks helped focus regulatory efforts and financial assistance on a limited number of large-scale, state-owned, and quasi-privatized firms. Since these large clusters of polluting firms were numerically limited, such an approach would seem to facilitate building linkages to regulated industries.

These discourses about pollution control, however, presupposed that managers considered cost savings on inputs and faced constraints on discharging pollutants. For state-owned and quasi-privatized enterprises operating under a soft budget constraint, these conditions only partially applied. Indeed, in the context of Egypt's transitional economy, highly polluting firms used their pollution loads as an "asset" in implicit bargaining within the state apparatus and with donors for more comprehensive aid packages, folding pollution control into larger negotiations about comprehensive industrial modernization of production lines. In this context, pollution became an asset for large enterprises rather than a liability. The greater a firm's contribution to pollution levels in critical "hotspots," the more privileged its claim to external funds and the better its prospects for delaying action on pollution control. Managerial networks, whose main participants were often based in private consultancies, could not muster sufficient legal, discursive, or infrastructural authority to induce firms to engage in significant, timely pollution control efforts.

In addition, Egypt's implementation of market reforms and privatization through executive decrees offered few opportunities for environmental experts to shape policy. Unlike in some of the Eastern European cases, privatization transactions were not conditioned on environmental improvements, and no systematic approach to enforcement (such as progressive fines based on pollutant loads) was adopted. Instead, executive authority for pollution control remained fragmented among a variety of ministries, provincial governments, and holding companies, often tied to the specific agency granting permission for industrial land use.

Existing regulatory efforts remain insufficient to address pollution issues, whether in "hotspots" such as Alexandria's Lake Maryut or outside them. The result has been mounting protest in urban and rural areas already affected or potentially impacted by industrial pollution. The next chapter thus analyzes the emergence of popular campaigns led by activist networks around pollution issues in several provincial Egyptian cities.

*Table 3.3* Firm ownership and shareholders, proposed projects for Egyptian Pollution Abatement Project II, the World Bank, 2006–13

| Company | Ownership* | Major shareholders** | Proposed environmental project | Cost (millions of US$) |
|---|---|---|---|---|
| National Cement Company (Qawmiyya) | State-owned enterprise (SOE), listed on stock exchange | Subsidiary of Chemical Industries Holding Company | New technologies to control dust emissions | 15.5 |
| Torah Cement Company | Privatized SOE, listed on stock exchange | Italcementi (Italy) | New technologies to control dust emissions | 20 |
| Helwan Cement Company | Private firm, delisted on stock exchange | Suez Cement Company (Egyptian), 98.7%; free float 1.2% | Fuel switching: mazut to natural gas | 3 |
| Egyptian Starch and Glucose | SOE, listed on stock exchange | | 1. Fuel switching: mazut to natural gas | 0.38 |
| | | | 2. Replacement of production line | 8 |
| Arab Abu Saad and El-Saaf Brick Factories | Small and medium firms: 206 brick factories | | Fuel switching: mazut to natural gas | 25 |
| Abu Zaabel Fertilizer | Privatized SOE (2004), listed on stock exchange | Polyserve for Fertilizers and Chemicals | New technologies for dust emissions | 15 |

| Company | Ownership* | Major shareholders** | Proposed environmental project | Cost (millions of US$) |
|---|---|---|---|---|
| Middle East for Paper Manufactoring (SIMO) | Publicly listed, mixed state–private ownership | Free float 35.4%; Holding Company for Chemical Industries 10%; National Financial for Investments 8.9%; individuals 38.3%; Employees Association 6.7% | Fuel switching: mazut to natural gas | 0.4 |
| El Nasr Company for Rubber Products (Narubin) | SOE, up for privatization | Holding Company for Chemical Industries | Installation of new pollution control technologies | 0.495 |
| Swailem for Pottery | Private SME | | Installation of new filters to control dust emissions | 0.2 |
| Amreyah Cement | Private firm, established 1989, acquired by Cimpor Egypt 2006, listed on stock exchange | Cimpor Egypt Cement, subsidiary of Cimpor (Cimentos De Portugal) 96%; free float 1.8%; Misr Insurance 1.7% | Installation of new filters for dust emissions | 9 |
| Misr Chemicals Industry | Partially privatized SOE (1994), listed on stock exchange | Holding Company for Chemical Industries 53.1%; free float 30.6%; Banque Misr 15.6% | Fuel switching: mazut to natural gas | 0.44 |
| General Company for Paper Industry (Rakta) | Partially privatized SOE, listed on stock exchange | Holding Company for Chemical Industries 77.9%; free float 10.6%; Social Insurance Funds for government sector employees 6.9%; physical shares 2.5%; Misr Insurance 1.5% | Fuel switching: mazut to natural gas | 4.5 |

*Continued*

| Company | Ownership* | Major shareholders** | Proposed environmental project | Cost (millions of US$) |
|---|---|---|---|---|
| Amreya Petroleum Refining Company | SOE | | Rehabilitation of production units to reduce pollutants in wastewater | 10 |
| National Paper Company | Privatized SOE (2005), listed on stock exchange | Emak for Paper Manufacturing 99.1%; free float 0.9% | Installation of waste treatment plant | 8 |
| Wood Equipment Company | Private company, Merghem Industrial Zone | | Rehabilitation of production lines to reduce pollutants in wastewater | 0.4 |

Sources: Data compiled from the EEAA, *Egypt State of the Environment Report* (2008: 283–5) for EPAP projects and costs; shareholder information from Emerging Markets Information Service, A Product of ISI Emerging Markets, downloaded June 18, 2010

*Firm listed as state-owned enterprise (SOE) if 50 percent or greater of shares held by government entities. Shares comprising less than 1 percent of total are not listed.

**Ownership totals do not equal 100 percent due to rounding and exclusion of shareholders with less than 1 percent of total shares.

# 4 Activist networks and anti-pollution campaigns in the provinces

People mobilize not only because they can, but also and probably even more readily when they are compelled to do so: when they feel their sense of justice or morals, their basic rights, or the possibility of offering decent living conditions to their children are being attacked.

(Beinin and Vairel, 2011: 22)

The uprising that erupted in early 2011 in Egypt brought large numbers of people together in street demonstrations, strikes, and other direct actions loosely coordinated by networks of activists. The cascading mass protests in Cairo, Suez, Alexandria, Mansoura, and other Egyptian cities revealed that, while the government had circumscribed the activities of civic associations and political parties, large-scale popular mobilization simply could not be contained. In the decade prior to 2011, however, all kinds of more limited protest campaigns had emerged, led by loose networks of activists that coalesced around issues of wages, labor and human rights, political reform, and environmental issues.

This chapter analyzes the emergence of environmental protest in two provincial cities, exploring how activist networks coalesced in the conduct of "campaigns" (*hamlat*) against official decisions perceived as threatening the urban environment and public health. In Alexandria, a mid-1990s *hamla* partially resolved a long-running dispute that had emerged in the 1970s over whether the city's partially treated sewage should be dumped in the Mediterranean or used to irrigate desert land. In another port city on the Mediterranean, Damietta, a 2008 coordinated campaign blocked plans by the Canadian firm Agrium to build a large fertilizer plant in the area. In an era when the Mubarak regime was more avidly pursuing market reforms, this campaign succeeded in compelling the central government to revoke investment approvals for a multinational firm, a first for Egypt's environmental activists.

These campaigns, however, did not simply pit "civil society" against a monolithic "state." Instead, activist networks made full use of state-legitimated infrastructures, such as the media, courts, universities, and professional associations. Egypt's fragmented system of legal authority allowed campaigners to press their claims in multiple state institutions, filing court cases and conducting work stoppages at the same time that they petitioned for parliamentary inquiries. In both the Alexandria and Damietta cases, activists framed their campaigns in discourses that emphasized the preservation of distinctive urban identities and local livelihoods, in the face of centralized decision-making that favored foreign donors and investors over locals.

The impact of such popular campaigns on policymaking in the Arab world has been remarkably understudied. As the Moroccan scholar Saloua Zerhouni observed, "Even if the impact of various actors on policymaking processes remains relatively limited, there are diverse spaces for participatory activity by a wide range of actors with varying degrees of influence" (Zerhouni, 2008: 260). While the uprisings across the region in 2011 began to make these spaces more contested than in previous years, the patterns of activist agitation analyzed in this chapter remain, in large part since the organizing routines and structures of the state apparatus in Egypt remain intact. At both the central and provincial level, appointed officials reliant on the executive continue to make decisions and allocations regarding public works, infrastructure, and investment. Exploring how activist networks made use of political opportunities under sustained authoritarian rule not only helps us to understand Egypt's past patterns of protest, but also reveals what will continue to be common strategies by activists to influence policy choices.

## Civic activism under Mubarak

From the post-uprising vantage point, it is tempting to recast the history of contentious politics under Mubarak as one of a valiant civil society battling the various minions of a repressive state. Much of the scholarly literature on the emergence of civil associations in the Arab world during the 1990s invokes this sort of imagery. And, to some extent, this simple depiction captured important elements of the coercion and confinement of civil and political society. Under Mubarak, the state sought to limit the organizational and financial autonomy of formal associations through a combination of outright repression, legal restrictions, and informal, extra-legal measures.

Civic activism was limited by explicit regulations governing the formation and activities of private voluntary organizations and general Emergency Laws that withheld basic civil and political rights. In addition, the government maintained a system of "state corporatism" that enshrined government ownership and control over professional associations (syndicates), universities, trade unions, and media houses (Bianchi, 1989; Waterbury, 1983).[1] Lastly, the regime used the state security agencies for the surveillance, harassment, arbitrary detention, and torture of activists and their families, as was well documented by Human Rights Watch, Amnesty International, the Egyptian Organization for Human Rights, and other local human rights organizations.

Yet these restrictions did not fully stifle associational life, and nor were civil society and the state locked into an exclusively adversarial relationship. Despite the highly restrictive legal environment and the state's targeted repression, varied social movements and activist campaigns diffused strategies through which activists could express grievances and, sometimes, influence policy choices. It may well be that, in Mubarak's last years, these informal feedback loops eroded as the aging leader and his confidants closed ranks and relied ever more heavily on the ubiquitous internal security forces (Springborg, 2009). For much of the Mubarak period, however, the elaborate institutional structure of the authoritarian state was "restrictive but conducive" to associational life, as one scholar has termed activism in contemporary China (Ho and Edmonds, 2008).

The 1980s and 1990s saw the proliferation of voluntary associations in Egypt as throughout the Middle East (Abdelrahman, 2004: 5–8; Ben-Nafissa and Kandil, 1994; Kandil, 1998; Norton, 1995; Schwedler, 1995; Sullivan, 1994). The expansion of the private voluntary sector occurred in a number of domains, increasing the number of professionalized non-governmental associations, welfare and charity associations, business associations, and religious organizations. The Egyptian press reported official statistics claiming that 14,738 NGOs were registered in 1996–7, 75 percent of them involved in social welfare and 25 percent in development (Tadros, 2000).

In part, the government tolerated this proliferation of voluntary organizations because their charitable and welfare functions provided public services that the state was retracting. As the 2004 *Egyptian Human Development Report* argued, "To date, civil society—through private activities—has created parallel systems or informal practices to compensate for poor or failing state services" (United Nations Development Programme and Institute of National Planning, 2004: 13). A survey of voluntary associations in Egypt in the late 1990s found that the most common form of private association was social service and welfare organizations run by religious institutions, such as non-state mosques and churches. These "faith-based" groups, in fact, accounted for half of all registered welfare associations in the late 1990s (Bayat, 2009: 79).

Despite this seeming toleration, the Mubarak regime continued and deepened existing legal restrictions on the operations, funding, and governance of voluntary organizations. It continued to rely on the Emergency Law (Law 162) which restricted rights to assembly, speech, printing, and organizing, and allowed the government to deem any meeting, organization, or publication subversive of national security. First enacted in the midst of the 1967 Arab–Israeli war, the Emergency Law had been continuously extended with the exception of an eighteenth-month period in 1980–1 during Sadat's last year in power. After the 9/11 attacks by Al Qaeda in the United States, the Mubarak government passed a new Anti-Terrorism Law that further expanded the government's authority to circumscribe basic civil rights in the name of national security (United Nations Development Programme and Institute of National Planning, 2008: 10). Not surprisingly, the lifting of the Emergency Laws was a central demand of the 2011 mass protests, but as of this writing the Supreme Council of the Armed Forces (SCAF) had not yet repealed them, and was in the midst of drafting various new restrictive laws restricting the right to protest or strike.

The Mubarak regime also maintained additional laws specifically controlling the formation and activities of voluntary associations despite repeated promises to relax such restrictions. In 1964, the Nasser regime enacted the Civic Association Code (Law 32/1964), which gave the government the right to approve, dissolve, or merge associations as it saw fit (Agati, 2007). Successive laws elaborated on these state powers. From the short-lived Law 153 (1998), declared unconstitutional in 2000 by Egypt's Supreme Constitutional Court on procedural grounds, to its successor regulation, Law 84 (2002), key restrictions on civil society have remained in place. These measures included mandatory registration of associations with the Ministry of Social Affairs (later renamed the Ministry of Social Solidarity), where state security officers within the ministry wielded the power to approve or deny registration (ibid.). Law 84 also granted the ministry the right to send representatives to any meeting of the registered associations, review all of their minutes and agendas, remove their board members, and block or cancel projects that they sought to undertake with international partners (South Asia Human Rights Documentation Network, 2002). An association's membership as a whole could be held criminally liable for the actions of any one member. All foreign funding for NGOs had to be reviewed and approved by the ministry. Post-revolutionary Cabinets have reiterated their opposition to outside funding of civil society groups without governmental supervision (Strasser, 2011; Yassin, 2011).

In practice, this sweeping legal authority was selectively applied. The government was least tolerant of advocacy groups focused on human rights, torture, and land and tenancy issues. Even those groups, however, found ways to continue their activities. During the 1990s, environmental and advocacy organizations denied registration by the government registered as civil companies. Well-known groups such as the Egyptian Organization for Human Rights and the Land Center for Human Rights were repeatedly denied state recognition as associations, yet operated for years despite their uncertain legal status.

This informal toleration, however, did not signal acceptance of any legal basis for independent associations. Indeed, the obstacles to complying with various formal regulations were so great that most civil associations operated in *de facto* violation of one decree or another. Thus, the regime could target specific associations with legal violations at a whim. For instance, the government repeatedly tried to discredit groups monitoring elections and human rights by charging them with receiving foreign funds and spreading "rumors" harmful to the state. One of the most well-known cases in the early 2000s was that of Egyptian–American sociologist Saad Eddin Ibrahim and twenty-seven employees of the Ibn Khaldoun Center for Development Studies, a research center that sought to monitor elections. Ibrahim served fourteen months in prison while appeals of his case wended their way through Egypt's legal system. He was ultimately acquitted by Egypt's highest court, the Court of Cassation, which overturned two guilty verdicts rendered by a state security court (Sachs, 2003). In the post-uprising period, the center proudly changed its name to the Center for Democratic Studies.

Formal restrictions, especially on foreign funding, cut many voluntary associations off from the resources and organizational capacities of international organizations and networks. The 2008 *Egypt Human Development Report* found that only 5 percent of the 4,300 civil associations devoted to the field of development participated in global or Arab networks (United Nations Development Programme and Institute of National Planning, 2008: 10). In the environmental field, Egypt was one of the few large developing countries with no presence from such well-known international advocacy groups as the World Wildlife Fund, Nature Conservancy, and Greenpeace.

Given these limitations, critical assessments of the effectiveness of nongovernmental organizations burgeoned in the late 1990s and early 2000s. Writing under titles such as *Civil Society Exposed* and "Too Much Civil Society, Too Little Politics," scholars sought to debunk the notion that an expanding civil society, understood as the proliferation of NGOs, made a democratic transition more likely (Abdelrahman, 2004; Langohr, 2005). These authors rightly argued that the regime's legal and extra-legal restrictions circumscribed the financial, legal, and organizational autonomy of civic organizations. Some also showed how even more stringent controls over overtly political activity, such as party mobilization, pushed activists into non-governmental organizations that tended to focus on single issues with limited cross-class appeal (Langohr, 2005: 216–17).

These characterizations generally applied to environmental associations as well. Gomaa (1994) identified sixty-two associations in 1992–4 that were linked to some aspect of the environment: twenty-two dealt with general environmental issues, twenty-one focused on a specific environmental issue, such as industrial waste or wildlife, and the remainder were scientific associations with almost exclusively professional memberships.

Most of the groups were run by a few influential individuals and had small memberships (Gomaa, 1997). Like other non-governmental organizations, environmental organizations were often criticized for lacking mass constituencies, relying on foreign funding and/or experts, and employing a technocratic, elitist approach to tackling their chosen problems.

By focusing almost exclusively on formal associations, however, critiques of Egyptian civil society overlooked the multiple informal networks and infrastructural opportunities within and without the state apparatus that periodically allowed protest campaigns to emerge without relying on formal NGOs. Focusing on a particular organizational form (such as the NGO), or a particular institutional venue (such as Parliament or elections), obscured these other forms of activism, and underestimated how activist networks could occasionally challenge state decisions and influence public debate.

During the late Mubarak period, the landscape of civic activism was changing rapidly, fostered by structural economic change that expanded private economic activity and, therefore, economic resources. As importantly, new technologies of coordination and communication and new cohorts of Egyptians eager for greater political engagement facilitated larger popular protests. Comparing environmental campaigns in Alexandria and Damietta, separated not only in place but also in time, illustrates many of these changing conditions.

## Wasting wastewater? Controversies over sanitation in Alexandria, 1979–97

Controversy over Alexandria's wastewater surfaced in 1977, when the United States Agency for International Development (USAID) proposed a sixteen-year project, the Alexandria Wastewater Systems Expansion Project. By all accounts, Alexandria's wastewater situation was dire, as it was in many cities in the developing world at the time. Only some of the city's 2.25 million inhabitants had sewage collection networks, which discharged untreated wastewater to the Mediterranean via short pipes scattered along the shoreline (Camp Dresser & McKee, 1978a: Sect. 3–93). Sewage discharges contaminated local beaches and caused a variety of bacterial ailments and waterborne diseases, particularly during the summer months, when Alexandria's population swelled with tourists. In the winter, rains overloaded sewage collection pipes, flooding neighborhoods and ponding in vacant areas. Industries discharged effluent directly into the shallow coastal lagoon of Lake Maryut or the sea, and agricultural drainage canals discharged into the lake and coastal waters.

As a result of the Camp David Accords and the ensuing significant increases in US economic assistance to Egypt, USAID began investing in the sanitation and potable water infrastructure of Cairo and Alexandria in the late 1970s. US assistance was initially set at US$405 million, with Egypt providing US$85 million (El-Kilany, 1997). USAID later appropriated an additional US$35 million to fund design of a second phase of sewage expansion (1995–2000) to cope with urban growth and population increase (Joynce, 1994).

USAID found investing in large-scale wastewater treatment systems attractive because these projects could quickly absorb large amounts of money that might otherwise go undisbursed (Dorman, 2007: 220). Investment in the wastewater sector also brought tangible benefits to local urban populations and brought aid dollars back home, in the form of fees collected by American contractors to do feasibility studies, design work, construction of the system, and training in operation and maintenance. Indeed, US contractors have been continuously involved in Alexandria's wastewater system for over three decades. As we shall see, the outsize role of USAID funds and American contractors served as a focal point of contention in Alexandria.

In 1979, the US firm Camp Dresser & McKee (CDM) devised a master plan for Alexandria's wastewater system under contract for USAID. The master plan sought to limit sewage flooding in the city by expanding collection systems, rehabilitating and expanding an existing treatment plant in eastern Alexandria, and building a new treatment plant on the western side of the city. Alexandria's existing central collection network had been constructed in 1890. Ongoing urban expansion had led to the construction of several unconnected collection networks that drained to the sea, while poorer areas had been left unsewered.

USAID and American contractors portrayed their investments in Alexandria's sanitation system primarily in terms of addressing public health issues. Using epidemiological studies conducted by the High Institute of Public Health from

1970 to 1974, the master plan and its accompanying environmental impact assessment (EIA) highlighted that infant mortality rates and incidences of typhoid, hepatitis, and dysentery were higher in Alexandria than in Cairo or Egypt as a whole (Camp Dresser & McKee, 1978b: Sect. 3–93).[2] The report also stressed that cholera outbreaks were also more likely in Alexandria than in other Egyptian cities. "Nowhere is the public health justification for a wastewater treatment project clearer than in Alexandria, for the current environment is an ideal setting for extensive outbreaks of disease similar to the cholera epidemic that infected the city in 1970" (ibid.: Sect. 3–90). The American consultants also observed that "clearly diagnosed outbreaks of cholera have never been officially recognized by the Egyptian government which, instead, prefers the term 'acute enteric summer disease.' There is, however, no question about the identity of the disease" (ibid.: Sect. 3–94). According to statistics gathered by Egypt's Ministry of Health and reported to the World Health Organization, the 1970 cholera outbreak registered incidence rates (per 100,000 people) in Alexandria four times higher than those reported in Cairo, Giza, and Qalyubiyya, the governorates that together comprised Greater Cairo at the time (ibid.: Sect. 3–95). Within Alexandria, the incidence of cholera was strongly correlated to neighborhoods that suffered from inadequate or backed-up sewers or lacked sewage connections entirely (ibid.).

The CDM reports include vivid descriptions of the city's poor sanitary conditions by appalled American consultants. Sewage regularly flooded streets and blocked traffic, they wrote, flowing into irrigation canals and through informal areas where "squatters" regularly bathed, cooked, and washed clothing. "The conditions have to be seen to be believed," the Americans concluded (Camp Dresser & McKee, 1978b: Sect. 3–97).

The CDM master plan laid out phases for the construction of Alexandria's wastewater system. The first phase would rehabilitate an existing treatment plan and build a new plant on the other side of the city, using the coastal lagoon of Lake Maryut as a low-cost "natural" treatment system for effluent after primary treatment. Effluent would then be pumped to a sea outfall via an existing pumping station at al-Mex, a village to the west of the city (Lager *et al.*, undated: 2). In looking ahead to the second phase, CDM considered various secondary treatment options, but argued these remained prohibitively expensive. Instead, the report recommended continued sea disposal of primary-treated effluent through a new, long submarine pipe that would empty far offshore. As the US contractor summarized in a 1978 letter to the Ministry of Housing:

> Discharge to the sea through long submarine outfalls is clearly the most feasible and economical alternative for the disposal of wastewaters from the presently developed areas of Alexandria. Significant savings in both capital and operating costs will be possible using marine disposal as compared to all other alternatives.
>
> (Grantham and Cullivan, 1978)

American experts thus portrayed future options for sewage disposal primarily in terms of keeping costs low.

In light of Egypt's scarce water resources, however, several university professors in the faculties of engineering and agriculture at the University of Alexandria disagreed with this option. They argued that treated wastewater was a valuable resource that should not be wasted, and proposed reusing municipal wastewater to irrigate desert lands on the outskirts of Alexandria. Such water could be used for cultivation of non-food crops and to provide green spaces for new settlements. These individuals also opposed continued sea disposal of effluent, as they believed that marine circulation patterns would return sewage to Alexandria's beaches and continue to threaten public health.

In accordance with the focus on cost savings, the CDM master plan provided cost-benefit analyses comparing disposal of treated wastewater at sea with the proposed reuse of municipal wastewater in irrigation. The report argued that irrigation was more costly than sea disposal because of the need for expensive secondary treatment and the costs of transport to the desert. Secondary treatment of wastewater was also technically difficult, if not impossible, they noted, unless Alexandrian industries stopped discharging directly into the municipal collection systems and pre-treated their industrial wastewater (Camp Dresser & McKee, 1978a). In addition, they noted, the costs of reusing wastewater in agriculture were between three and five times as high as using freshwater, and that there was not enough land adjacent to the city to absorb the volume of treated wastewater, estimated to reach 1.5 million liters per day by the year 2000 (Kassas, undated mimeograph: 1, 4). Similar conclusions in favor of continuing sea disposal were reached in another review of sanitation options undertaken by the USAID-funded Wastewater Consultants Group a few years later (Montgomery, 1990: 51).

The Alexandria professors were not convinced. Led by a sanitary engineer, Muhammad Sadiq al-'Adawi, they argued the pipeline was costly and risky, because breaks in submerged pipes would be difficult to locate, much less to fix (Wahba, "The Golden Anniversary of Alexandria's Wastewater," 1996). They also argued that the CDM report overstated the costs of reusing wastewater in land reclamation and understated the costs of sea disposal (ibid.). The professors found an initial platform to share their views in a Comprehensive Urban Planning Committee established by the Alexandrian governorate's Department of Local Administration. The committee was appointed by the Alexandria governor at the time, Lt. Gen. Muhammad Sa'id al-Mahi. As one critic of the committee noted, of the appointees only al-'Adawi was a sanitary engineer, while the other six members were from the faculties of agriculture, fine arts, and architecture (Farag, undated).

In a series of decisions, the Alexandria local council and the centrally appointed governor affirmed the findings of this urban planning committee. In 1981, the governor informed Prime Minister Fu'ad Muhi al-Din that he and the city council supported using effluent for land reclamation in 1981 (Wahba, "The Golden Anniversary of Alexandria's Wastewater," 1996). USAID reportedly responded by reminding the Egyptian government that the

United States had invested in Alexandria's sanitation system on the basis of sea disposal. Egypt, USAID went on, would have to bear any technical costs in excess of allocated funds (ibid.).

To adjudicate the dispute, Egypt's national research institutions were brought in. In 1982, the Academy for Scientific Research and Technology established specialized working groups to consider the options for disposal of Alexandria's wastewater.[3] These included Mohamed Kassas and a number of other well-known professors and engineers.[4] The Ministries of Agriculture and Housing provided preliminary studies about the feasibility of conducting land reclamation with treated wastewater around Alexandria (Wali, 1979).

These experts concluded that reusing treated effluent in desert areas should at least be considered by USAID and the Egyptian government. Kassas, in his written comments on the CDM master plan, highlighted some of the complexities of the issue. He noted that the CDM report overlooked data gathered from six years of continuous monitoring of currents, wave patterns, and sedimentation patterns along Egypt's coast by the Academy for Scientific Research, the Institute for Oceanography at the University of Alexandria, and the UNDP. These studies suggested that prevailing currents, wave action, and coastal erosion patterns would most likely disperse sewage plumes from offshore sea outfalls horizontally along the coastline rather than dispersing them out to sea as CDM assumed (Kassas, undated mimeograph: 6). In addition, while sea discharge could provide much-needed nutrients for marine life, the impact on human health of bioaccumulation of heavy metals and toxins in shellfish and fish stocks was not adequately understood (ibid.: 6–7). Just as the CDM consultants had raised the issue of industrial waste treatment, so did Kassas, noting that half of all wastewater was estimated to be industrial in origin by the year 2000. Industrial effluent required pre-treatment by industry whether disposed of in Lake Maryut, piped out to sea, or reused for agriculture.

Kassas also viewed sewage disposal options in terms of maximizing Egypt's scarce water resources in the longer run. This framing resonated with Egyptian officials and activists, but had not figured as prominently in the assessments done by USAID, CDM, and other American contractors. Kassas noted that

> the volume of wastewater estimated to flow in the Alexandria sewers is about 440 million cubic meters per year. This volume of water is equivalent (at the present extravagant and wasteful rate of present agriculture in Egypt, which averages 8,000 cubic meters per feddan per year) to volumes of water used to irrigate 55,000 feddans, a feddan equaling about 1 acre.
>
> (Ibid.: 4)

In contrast to CDM's argument that land suitable for irrigation with wastewater was limited, Kassas pointed out that the Americans had only considered land directly adjacent to the city; irrigation development plans extended well beyond these boundaries, with planned canals reaching 100 kilometers farther from the city than envisioned by CDM (ibid.: 5–6).

Egyptian environmental scientists enlisted the cooperation of UN agencies in exploring Alexandria's sewage disposal options. In 1986, Mostafa Tolba forwarded to the Egyptian government the findings of an international mission of five experts convened by UNEP. As of 1986, one million cubic meters per day of wastewater were being discharged into Lake Maryut and the Mediterranean without any treatment. After USAID's planned improvements up through 1989, the situation would be only partially rectified, with more flows receiving primary treatment before continued disposal in the lake and sea (Ahmad *et al.*, 1986: 30). The UNEP committee report, like both the CDM and Kassas reports, highlighted the problem of industrial wastewater remaining untreated at its source, noting that the state had announced plans to control industrial wastewater only by 2006 (ibid.).

In sharp contrast to the CDM assessments, however, the UNEP mission found that some options for reusing wastewater in irrigation were cheaper than sea disposal options. Their report suggested that primary treatment through a series of oxidation ponds and conveyance systems to desert sites would prove more cost-effective than building treatment plants, pumping stations, conveyance works, and long submarine outfalls (Tolba, 1986). This option was strenuously opposed by several of Alexandria's sanitary engineers, who argued that ponds large enough to cope with the city's wastewater would take up valuable land on the outskirts of the city, could not adequately treat highly concentrated municipal and industrial wastewaters, and that the costs of acquiring large swathes of land for treatment would be prohibitive given competing land uses (Farag, undated).

Several Egyptian engineers most closely involved with Alexandria's sanitary drainage network supported the CDM master plan contention that discharge to the sea after primary treatment was a typical alternative for coastal cities. Indeed, these individuals stressed that the Alexandria General Organization for Sanitary Drainage (AGOSD) could not yet cover operation and maintenance costs for the existing network, let alone cover the costs of ongoing expansions and secondary treatment (ibid.). They also cited the work of oceanographers that suggested that sufficiently deep-sea outfalls would effectively disperse sewage plumes away from Alexandria's beaches.[5]

The controversy over Alexandria's wastewater eventually reached the highest levels of the Egyptian state. In 1985, the People's Assembly (Majlis al-Sha'b) established a fact-finding committee that recommended the reuse of wastewater effluent for desert land reclamation. In 1986, the High Committee for Policies, responsible to the prime minister, took up the issue. Drawing upon the studies done by the Academy for Scientific Research and UNEP, this committee then brought the issue before the Cabinet. The Cabinet directed the Alexandrian wastewater authority and the Ministry of Housing to undertake technical studies on desert disposal, ruling out sea disposal. USAID again apparently informed the Egyptian government that any additional costs incurred for land disposal would be Egypt's responsibility (Zakaria, 1997). In 1989, the Agricultural Bureau at the Egyptian Embassy in the United States requested help from the World Bank, asking their experts to weigh in on the possibility of using wastewater in agriculture "in view of the strong opposition on the part of USAID" to reusing wastewater on land (Al-Gazar, 1989).

In the meantime, phase one of the Alexandrian wastewater system was largely completed as planned. The eastern and western treatment plants came online in 1993, as well as tunnels, collection systems, and seven pumping stations for conveying effluent to Lake Maryut and then to the Mediterranean. These upgrades prevented sewage flooding in the established districts of the city, eliminated direct outfalls along the beaches except in the central district, and began providing primary treatment for two-thirds of the city's wastewater flows before discharge.

The use of basins in Lake Maryut as open-air treatment ponds improved the quality of effluent before disposal to the Mediterranean but at the cost of the coastal lagoon's ecological integrity and support of local livelihoods. Fishing communities, estimated to employ 7,000 fishermen and another 10,000 in fishery-related jobs, saw their catches decimated and family health affected in the years after this "interim" solution for Alexandria's wastewater was adopted (Mesahil, 2008). Rapidly expanding informal urban areas, particularly toward the west of the city, remained unsewered, relying on shallow tanks, ponds, and pits for temporary storage, pumped into trucks and tankers when sewage overflowed (El-Kilany, 1997).

In 1995–6, USAID awarded the firm Metcalf and Eddy a US$22.4 million contract to evaluate options for the second phase of expanding Alexandria's wastewater system up through 2020. Alongside the basic goal of expanding coverage of primary treatment, the firm was to evaluate a range of disposal options, including continued use of Lake Maryut as a large oxidation pond to improve primary treatment before discharge into the sea; establishing secondary treatment at the treatment plants and bypassing Lake Maryut through long sea outfalls; or devising a cost-effective means for secondary treatment and transport for reuse on desert lands (Lager *et al.*, undated).

### Polluted water and dirty politics: the "Diary" of Sa'ad al-Din Wahba

When news broke that USAID had contracted studies for the second phase of wastewater expansion, renewed controversy erupted over Alexandria's wastewater. Authors, journalists, environmental experts, and Alexandrians writing in newspapers and journals sustained a more visible and effective opposition to sea disposal than in earlier decades. The discursive claims and tactics of this loose network of activists were captured in a series of columns penned by the prominent playwright and screenwriter, Sa'ad al-Din Wahba, in the few years before his death in 1997. His column, portrayed as excerpts from his diary, ran intermittently on Saturdays between 1995 and 1997 in the state-owned daily *Al-Ahram*. In the columns, Wahba attacked USAID's continued insistence on sea disposal despite decisions taken at the highest levels of the Egyptian government in the late 1980s to pursue reuse of municipal wastewater.

Discursively, Wahba's pieces framed problems of sewage in Alexandria as part of a broader political and social commentary on corruption, injustice, and incompetence in Egyptian urban governance. In doing so, they sparked significant numbers of readers to write to *Al-Ahram* in an effort to document the degradation of the city of Alexandria through pollution and government neglect. Wahba reprinted many of these letters verbatim in his columns, and he later compiled them in a book, *The "People's Enemy" in Alexandria.*

Wahba was a widely recognizable public intellectual, heralded during the late 1960s as part of Egypt's "new wave" of politically committed playwrights who had emerged after the 1952 revolution (Meisami and Starkey, 1998: 771). These authors wrote in colloquial Egyptian Arabic to make their work accessible to local audiences and also drew on emerging styles and techniques in European drama employed by Brecht, Chekhov, Ibsen, and Sartre (Rubin, 1994: 76). Wahba's early satirical plays focused on exposing the injustice and oppression endured by ordinary villagers at the hands of police, landlords, and the state (Badawi, 1987: 15–152). In addition to plays, Wahba worked as a screenwriter on a number of popular films in the 1960s. He served as president of Cairo's International Film Festival for a number of years and chairman of the Cairo International Book Fair in 1979.

Wahba's opening article, "'Enemy of the People': A Story of Assassinating a City," draws on his background in plays and films. The title, as Wahba explains in the opening paragraph, is that of Ibsen's 1882 play in which a doctor, Thomas Stockmann, finds out that well water supplying the public baths is contaminated. Although he is warned off by the authorities, and ridiculed by the populace, who classify him as an "enemy of the people," Stockmann "decides to fight alone for the good of his country until the last minute of his life" (Wahba, "'Enemy of the People': A Story of Assassinating a City," 1995). The play was on his mind, he wrote, having seen a film adaptation set in rural India by the renowned director Satyajit Ray, in which a doctor finds that contaminated water in a temple is causing an epidemic (*Ganashatru*, 1989, directed by Satyajit Ray). Again, the doctor is ignored, sabotaged, and castigated as an "enemy of the people" for his efforts.

Wahba writes that he has found another such whistleblower, Muhammad al-'Adawi, the engineer and member of Alexandria's master planning committee who had fought against any form of sea disposal since the early 1980s. He reprinted al-'Adawi's pamphlet, "The Case of Drainage of Alexandria—The Crime of This Century," in its entirety, which chronicled how USAID had overlooked numerous decisions taken by various Egyptian authorities to dispose of Alexandria's effluent on land.

This article set out Wahba's staunch opposition to what he saw as USAID's persistent effort to block reuse of treated wastewater. In subsequent pieces, he decried the waste of resources in paying American contracting firms exorbitant sums to conduct research for twenty-one years, even as the Egyptian government had indicated its preference for reusing effluent by 1986 (Wahba, "'Public Enemy' and USAID," 1995). USAID's opposition to reusing wastewater in agriculture, he argued, must originate in US interests in seeing Egypt remain dependent on imports of American wheat. Sea disposal, he wrote, would be the "assassination" of Alexandria by pollution, the real "people's enemy."

Wahba's pieces thus combined simplistic political analysis with a keen eye for critiquing Egyptian decision-makers and their American counterparts, written in a satirical, lively style that attracted readers. Like many of the readers who submitted letters and comments reprinted in *Al-Ahram*, Wahba's columns drew on his own experience living in Alexandria and witnessing its steady degradation and intensifying pollution. Wahba reminded his readers that the debate over pollution from wastewater in Alexandria had gone on for more than half a century and should long ago have been resolved. He remembered studying at Alexandria's University and Police Academy in 1947, where he learned from an army engineer that the fine substance that covered their bodies when they swam off Alexandria's beaches was sewage. "We remained silent out of surprise and disgust," he recalled (Wahba, "'Public Enemy' in Court," 1995).

The articles not only criticized USAID but, also, and even more clearly, lambasted the Mubarak regime. After the publication of his first article, he wrote, members of the public and representatives of USAID had quickly contacted him to provide their viewpoints. In contrast, he recounted, no one from the Egyptian government or Alexandrian governorate had reacted, "because any blame for negligence or any suggestion of an echo of public welfare does not inconvenience those responsible any more" (ibid.). He reprinted in its entirety a petition filed by a lawyer with the High Court of Appeals, who identified himself as "a citizen of Alexandria, the ex-bride of the Mediterranean, horrified by the deteriorating state of the city." The petition requested that the court enforce the decision issued by the Cabinet on October 29, 1986 to drain waste effluent in the desert rather than the sea, and cease all contractual arrangements for sea disposal.

Documents such as this legal petition, along with letters from readers, comprised the bulk of many Wahba columns over the next two years. Written by Alexandrian citizens, academics, businessmen, and government officials, the letters and documents became a forum for the politics of Alexandria writ much larger than sewage. Smog, mounds of refuse, traffic, the destruction of old architecture, absence of street cleaning, unpaved streets, limited public garbage bins, pollution of the Mahmudiyya canal and other irrigation and drainage channels—all these issues were raised by the missives that inundated Wahba.

Many of the letter writers, like Wahba himself, attempted to burnish their discursive authority by emphasizing their long identification with the city. Some writers contrasted the Alexandria of their youth, when in their recollections streets were swept and paved, garbage collected, and the city sprayed for mosquitoes and flies, with the filth, piles of trash, and ubiquitous pests of today. Others noted that the Egyptian Arabic nickname for the city of Alexandria as the "bride of the sea" conjured now nothing more than a memory. Citizen letters also characterized Alexandria's pollution and degradation as a direct failure of the centrally appointed governor, who served at the behest of President Mubarak. The governor and executive council should be held accountable for the ongoing problems of garbage and pollution, as the late 'Adil Abu Zahra, founder of the Alexandrian environmental NGO Friends of the Environment, wrote in Wahba's column (Wahba, "'People's Enemy' in the People's Assembly," 1996).

In a column entitled "'Emperor Jones' in Alexandria," alluding to the 1920 play by Eugene O'Neill, Wahba used wastewater problems in Alexandria as a microcosm of the problems with centralized, corrupt, and unaccountable rule under Mubarak (Wahba, "'Emperor Jones' in Alexandria," 1995). O'Neill's play tracks the fate of an escaped convict from the North American mainland who imposes tyrannical rule over a native population on an unspecified West Indian island. The islanders disappear one night into the forest to stage a revolt, ultimately killing the criminal-ruler, Brutus Jones. In Wahba's retelling, the parallels between the despotic rule of Jones and that of Mubarak and his deputies are clearly laid out:

> The play is about a harsh-hearted emperor who rules an island and tortures his people. In order to rid themselves of his rule, the islanders met and decided to leave. The emperor woke to find himself alone and was maddened. How can he be an emperor with no one left to govern? The emperor and the Governor, all rulers need a nation on whom they can exercise their hobby—injustice— and all sorts of misery... You cannot make an emperor abdicate, a rule that applies to some governors as well. What can the people do? There is only one option: to escape and leave them alone to enjoy the pollution of the sea and of the land.
>
> (Wahba, "'Emperor Jones' in Alexandria," 1995)

These criticisms did not go unanswered. The governor of Alexandria, Isma'il al-Gawsaqi, wrote a long letter to Wahba listing his accomplishments "during the reign of Mubarak, whose soldiers we are." Wahba reprinted this letter in his column, paired with another from Fathi Ragab, an Alexandrian businessman and appointed member to the Shura Council, Egypt's upper parliamentary house. Ragab's letter sought to deflect blame for the sad state of the city from Alexandria's governor to the central government. "Cairo succeeded in snatching from Alexandria the big allocations for hanging bridges, tunnels, new cities—all this the government constructed and funded in Cairo" (Wahba, "The Other Aspect of Alexandria," 1995).

Such quasi-official responses were openly ridiculed in the flood of mail to Wahba's columns that ensued. A letter from a "group of cultured people from Alexandria" observed:

> the most important fact is that during the very long period (ten years) during which the present governor of Alexandria has ruled the city, he absolutely failed in applying the law, despite the fact that he is a man of law... During his rule, corruption spread into the executive departments dealing with the public... During his rule, Alexandria became a candidate for the title of Dirtiest City in the World.
>
> (Wahba, "Enemies of Success," 1995)

In response to the government's oft-repeated claim that a neglectful public was the culprit for the accumulation of trash in urban areas, several letter writers argued, "The people of Alexandria are innocent of this. They are a clean and civilized people, and they are pained to see this filth disfigure their city while the responsible ones remain passive" (ibid.).

Other residents noted that USAID and the governor had failed to bring sanitation and sewage services to the many informal areas, especially the rapidly urbanizing peripheries of the city. A lawyer and resident of the al-'Agami neighborhood wrote that "despite the promises made by the Americans to the head of the AGOSD and the governor of Alexandria," the residents

> live surrounded by sewage water, which overflows the tanks underneath the buildings. The roads are filled with sewage water, causing traffic to stop, while mosquitoes, flies, and epidemics render the inhabitants sick to the bone. The inhabitants are ready to cooperate financially with the government.
> (Ibid.)

USAID and its contracting firms were bewildered by what they saw as public hostility to the Alexandrian wastewater project, hostility which, as they noted, had been absent when USAID invested in Cairo's sanitation network. The American contractor Metcalf and Eddy initially approached the problem as a public relations issue that could be resolved if only the right people could be supplied with the right technical information. They belatedly planned a "media outreach strategy," including a meeting with Wahba and other journalists, and organized a handful of public "scoping sessions" for interested parties in Alexandria (Metcalf and Eddy International, 1995). They provided Wahba with summaries of basic information, which he reprinted verbatim in his column (ibid.). American and Egyptian consultants for the project gave presentations at the American Center in Alexandria (later closed by the US government to save money), the Alexandria Rotary club, the environmental committee of the National Democratic Party in Alexandria (an otherwise dormant entity, by all accounts), and the University of Alexandria, among other venues (Eiteiba and Ali, 1996; "Meeting of the National Democratic Party to Survey the Present and Future Sanitary Drainage Projects," 1996). USAID also enlisted the help of the US Information Service in Cairo and Alexandria to survey the Egyptian press and meet with additional journalists. After reading the news coverage, a US information officer concluded, "The local political situation (more general criticism of certain appointed regional leaders) and academic rivalries (i.e. conflicting opinions on the best method of disposal) are fueling the numerous negative stories which are appearing in the press" (United States Information Service, 1996).

The discursive opening provided by the Alexandrian wastewater situation was not, however, simply about "local" politics, because Alexandria was for all intents and purposes governed directly by the central government in Cairo. Wahba noted that he would keep on writing about Alexandria's sewage overflows, because the issue captured "the representation of governing in Egypt—it is an issue of national power, and an issue of foreign interference" (Wahba, "'People's Enemy' and 'Ashmawi [the Hangman]," 1995).

In 1996, the People's Assembly, the lower house of the Egyptian parliament, took up the US–Egypt grant agreement for phase two of Alexandria's wastewater project. The agreement had already been signed via presidential decree in 1995; Parliament was allowed only to discuss it and pose questions (interpellations) to the government. These procedures did not prevent deputies from raising a number of questions and observations, which Wahba summarized for readers in his column a few days later (Wahba, "'People's Enemy' in the People's Assembly," 1996). Several deputies thanked USAID for its investment in quality sanitation networks, while others noted that disposal to the sea after treatment was an internationally acceptable method. Another observed that adequate treatment of municipal–industrial wastewater for use on crops, particularly cereals, was extremely difficult. Many more parliamentarians, however, questioned why the Americans opposed the reuse of Alexandria's wastewater in agriculture (El-Din, 1996; Wahba, "'People's Enemy' in the People's Assembly," 1996). Parliamentarians also focused on a clause obligating Egypt to spend LE22.5 million annually on Alexandria's wastewater, arguing that low-income consumers should not bear this cost in the form of service rate hikes (Wahba, "'People's Enemy' in the People's Assembly," 1996). Most criticism was reserved, however, for the large expenditures allocated to American contractors to conduct research, studies, and reports. MPs argued that these allocations were a consistent problem with American assistance. "Why should we set aside a large portion of US assistance for things which we do not need?" asked one opposition MP (El-Din, 1996).

## Wastewater reuse and national priorities

By the mid-1990s, therefore, Wahba's "diary" entries had morphed into an activist campaign that took the question of disposing municipal wastewater in the sea or reusing it on land as an opening for a much larger critique of centralized, corrupt, and inept governance. The project manager for the second phase of the Alexandrian wastewater project told me in frustration in 1998 that "The wastewater discharge issue became the opposition's platform. It brought together intellectuals, ideologues, the socialist-Nasserite left, political enemies of the governor, and the media."[6]

To understand the debates over Alexandria's wastewater as the project of a united opposition, however, misreads the character of contentious politics in Egypt in this period. There was no united opposition, nor even a fragmented social movement, but rather a loose network of activists. These engaged citizens employed resonant discursive claims about inadequate services, poor urban governance, and unaccountable leadership, and sought to air their grievances in state-sanctioned venues, such as the media, parliamentary interpellations, and universities, to publicize their cause.

This loose network, however, had a very powerful ally in the preference of the regime itself for reusing municipal wastewater in agriculture. The Egyptian government had long posited that bringing new land under irrigation was the preferred developmental solution to demographic pressures in the Nile Delta and

Valley. In light of Egypt's scarce water resources, the government preferred to be publicly committed to the reuse of wastewater, even if such water largely consisted of mixed industrial–municipal flows as in the case of Alexandria.

This public stance on reclaiming wastewater helped to bolster the government's claims to be using and reusing its Nile water allocations to the hilt, allocations that were increasingly disputed by upper riparian states left out of the 1959 treaty that shared the waters of the Nile between Sudan and Egypt. As the chairman of the Alexandrian wastewater authority was quoted in an Alexandrian paper,

> The issue of draining on land or in the sea is in the first place a purely technical matter…but then we have the political issue, in order to meet the great shortage in the Nile water resources. While the annual population increase continues, state policy at present aims at the reuse of effluent for agricultural purposes.
>
> (Hassan, 1996)

As criticism of USAID's wastewater plans mounted, regime officials publicly embraced reusing effluent for irrigation, making inflated claims about what could be achieved. The governor of Alexandria, al-Gawsaqi, for instance, announced: "Not a drop of effluent shall be disposed of in the sea; instead, all of it shall be used for planting green belts in the desert. In addition, life shall be restored in Lake Maryut after its cleansing of pollutants" ("Disposal of the Sanitary Drainage of Alexandria on Land," 1997; Maksoud, 1996). Irrigation officials announced that Alexandria's wastewater would allow the cultivation of 100,000 feddans (Fiad, 1997).

Thus, while USAID and American contractors saw the issue of Alexandria's sanitation as a local technical decision based on costs, Egyptian activists and officials alike saw it as part of a national question regarding water resources and land use. From available documentation, there is little evidence that the American side ever really grasped the importance that most Egyptian decision-makers gave to reusing wastewater and greening arid areas.

Faced with the unlikely coalition of the regime and vocal activists, one alternative for USAID was simply to stop funding wastewater projects in Alexandria. USAID, however, was unwilling to take this step; not only had the agency sunk millions of dollars in building Alexandria's existing wastewater infrastructure, but the agency had proudly touted institutional reform of the Alexandrian wastewater authority as a prelude to a larger-scale restructuring of the wastewater sector in Egypt. Since 1978, American contractors had sought to endow the AGOSD with the legal and financial authority to operate semi-autonomously, able to impose fees independently to cover its operation and maintenance costs. As with the Cairo sanitation organization, this fiscal semi-autonomy contrasted sharply with Egypt's prevailing practice of centralized financing and budgeting of government agencies.[7]

For USAID and the Egyptian engineers that operated the AGOSD, the primary problem with Alexandria's sewage was not where to dispose of treated effluent, but how to fund ongoing operation and maintenance costs of the existing systems, and how to pay for their planned expansion. Annual operation and maintenance costs for 1992 were estimated at US$14 million. These costs were expected to increase to US$35 million in 1996 as upgrades and expansions of the system continued. Meanwhile, projected tariffs on users in 1992 provided US$5.13 million in revenues, and other fees brought in US$500,000, leaving the Egyptian central budget to fill a US$8 million shortfall (Sewelam, 1992: 10). Central budget allocations for maintaining sewage systems, however, were chronically underfunded, leaving utilities to borrow from other public-sector entities and put off needed maintenance. The wastewater authority, like other public-sector organizations in Egypt, was also significantly overstaffed even as low salaries made it impossible for the agency to retain its most qualified employees.

The general problem of sustaining adequate investment in public infrastructure and public employees is a common one across developing and developed countries alike. Since the global turn toward deregulation and market-oriented economic reforms, three common institutional approaches have been employed. These approaches include increasing tariffs on users ("cost recovery"), creating financially autonomous agencies that can borrow funds and issue bonds, and privatizing service provision. At one time or another, USAID and the Egyptian heads of the Alexandrian wastewater authority would nudge the governorate and the central government toward all three of these solutions, seeking not just to fix Alexandria's problems but also to create an example for the sanitation sector as a whole. By 2004, USAID funded several projects examining the feasibility of privatizing the Alexandrian wastewater utilities on a concessionary basis (Segura Consulting LLC and the Institute for Public–Private Partnerships, 2004).

Ambitious institutional reform agendas, however, quickly encountered a maze of regulatory restrictions and conflicting legal jurisdictions. A 1992 institutional "action plan" for the wastewater authority listed multiple decrees and laws that would have to be enacted by the central government if the utilities were to become financially autonomous utilities (Sewelam, 1992). The list touched upon such politically sensitive areas as public-sector labor laws and the centralized system of revenue collection, planning, and expenditure, all of which were key to the regime's dominant position in Egypt's political economy and its (eroding) role as a provider of low-cost services and employment.

Within these constraints, Alexandria's executive local council and governor had nevertheless raised tariffs for users of the sewage networks by the mid-1990s, charging roughly 18 piasters per cubic meter (Metcalf and Eddy International, 1996). This hike did not come close to covering the cost of primary treatment, which was 35 piasters per cubic meter, but it was considered a better effort than that made by Cairo's wastewater authority. Cairo's sanitary authority was declared ineligible for US assistance, as it had not made commensurate progress in raising tariffs. As a Metcalf and Eddy manager observed, USAID was committed to funding Alexandria's wastewater authority since "Alexandria is the crown jewel in the USAID portfolio in wastewater utilities, and USAID desperately needs success stories."[8]

Given the US commitment to Alexandria's wastewater, Metcalf and Eddy's phase two contract included comprehensive evaluation of several wastewater disposal options, including reuse in desert land reclamation. The assessment process made use of an extensive twelve-month sampling and monitoring program of Lake Maryut, waterways, and the Mediterranean. As we have seen, Wahba and other activists criticized the exorbitant resources diverted to American consulting firms for research, particularly because these studies did not involve transfer of technologies or skills to local universities and research institutes. To partially address this critique, Metcalf and Eddy convened an advisory committee of experts drawn from the major Egyptian universities, though the actual participation of these local experts seems to have been minimal.

Critics such as Wahba, however, often overstated the extent and accuracy of prior environmental studies. Since there was no accurate environmental register of industrial pollutants from Alexandrian industries even by the mid-1990s (see Chapter 3), the actual mix of contaminants in treated wastewater was unknown, and information on the dispersion, flow patterns, and residence times of these pollutants in Lake Maryut was incomplete. The Mediterranean coastline, where Egyptian institutes had more extensive sampling and monitoring programs, was better studied. Moreover, technologies for secondary treatment of wastewater had changed significantly since the round of studies done in the 1980s. A priority for the phase two project was thus to evaluate, through pilot demonstrations, the feasibility of several new approaches to secondary treatment in addition to conventional chemical treatment. These included using natural oxidation ponds and "engineered wetlands" with native plants to take up contaminants (as originally proposed by UNEP) and biological treatment using biotowers. A relatively new technology, biotowers use a plastic or rock medium to grow bacteria and other organisms that feed on organic pollutants.

Metcalf and Eddy's 1997 reports for USAID confirmed several of the earlier contentions made by Egyptian activists and critics of deep-sea disposal. The study found that the risks, costs, and reliability of a long submarine outfall were significant, since the project "would require construction expertise at the forefront of the industry because of the outfall size and depth for the geotechnical conditions to be encountered" (Lager *et al.*, undated: 5). These conditions included the horizontal currents and dispersion patterns along the coastline noted by Kassas and Egyptian oceanographers in the mid-1980s. In terms of costs, the initial capital costs of deep-sea disposal for primary treatment (US$488 million) were estimated to exceed the costs of conducting secondary treatment using Lake Maryut (US$353 million) or bypassing the coastal lagoon with the use of engineered wetlands or biotowers for secondary treatment (US$369 million) (ibid.: 8).

While the deep-sea disposal was still put forward as one option, the 1997 final report by Metcalf and Eddy suggested using biotowers for secondary treatment at the treatment plants, bypassing Lake Maryut, and reusing wastewater in land reclamation as sought by critics. While using engineered wetlands was successful in terms of treating effluent, the report found that limited land availability and the cost of land acquisition made this option unattractive, as several Egyptian and

American engineers had argued in prior years. Using biotowers to treat wastewater effluent offered advantages due to "simplicity, reliability, resistance to shock loads, reduced land requirements, and cost" (ibid.). Reiterating earlier findings, the consultants cautioned that even this treatment method would not meet Egypt's legal standards for chemical oxygen demand (COD) for effluent used in irrigation unless industrial facilities pre-treated their wastewater before discharge to sewers (Lager *et al.*, undated).

Thus, one of the principal problems identified by Egyptian and American environmental experts and analyzed in Chapter 3 remained: the need to compel industry to treat industrial effluent. As two Egyptian oceanographers, Mahmud Ahmad 'Abd al-Mun'im and Hana' al-Din Isma'il 'Asim, wrote in Wahba's column in 1996, "The most dangerous environmental pollutant is the industrial waste, especially if it is disposed in the wastewater...without being treated" (Wahba, 1997). The Alexandrian wastewater authority began an outreach campaign to Alexandrian industry, in tandem with imposing surcharges for industrial waste. As argued in the previous chapter, the semi-autonomous sanitation agencies in Cairo and Alexandria emerged as one of the few governmental authorities with the legal and infrastructural authority to "reach" polluting enterprises and take credible enforcement actions against industrial pollution.

## Protesting foreign industry in Damietta

Concern about water pollution and industry triggered a much more widespread, popularly supported environmental campaign against a proposed fertilizer factory in the port city of Damietta in 2008.[9] Damietta, on the eastern side of the Nile Delta, shares several ecological and economic features with Alexandria on the western side. Like Alexandria, the city borders not only the sea but also a large coastal lagoon, Lake Manzala, which receives agricultural drainage water and semi-treated wastewater from Cairo and other Delta cities. The two cities are considered *masayif*, that is, important summer vacation destinations for the Egyptian middle and lower middle classes, making tourism and second homes a key component of local economies.

Existing uneasily with the tourist economy are large ports and significant concentrations of heavy and intermediate industry. While Alexandria experienced significant expansion of heavy industry some time ago, particularly after nationalization in the 1960s, Damietta's industrial expansion is more recent, coming as the government deepened incentives for investors in the 1990s and 2000s. The government promoted industrial investment in Damietta by investing in a new deep-water port, establishing a free trade zone that included the "Mubarak Complex for Natural Gas and Petrochemicals," and underpricing natural gas as a raw material. The free zone was located directly next to the upscale residential-tourism community of Ras al-Barr and also adjacent to agricultural lands.

One of the first plants to take advantage of the industrial free zone was a large state-owned fertilizer firm, the Misr Fertilizers Production Company (MOPCO). Construction began in 2006, and residents in the vicinity reported that they had no prior knowledge of the complex until it came online in the summer of 2008.[10] They complained of a variety of health and environmental problems, including smoke, dust, dead fish in the canal, odors, skin rashes, respiratory difficulties, and such loud noise that they could not sleep at night (El-Kashef, "Complaint to the Public Prosecutor from the People of Dumyat…," 2008; El-Shazly and El-Kashef, "Signs of a New Crisis in Dumyat…," 2008). Another large-scale plant producing methanol from natural gas, with a 60 percent stake from the multinational Methanex Canada, was also under construction by 2008 (Fikry and Ati, 2008).

When construction began on yet another fertilizer plant, planned to be twice the size of MOPCO and directly next to it, various groups in Damietta organized in opposition. The proposed plant was to be majority-owned by the Canadian multinational, Agrium, in a joint venture with Egyptian state-owned gas and petrochemical companies. The new venture, EAgrium, planned on building one of the largest fertilizer complexes in Egypt, consisting of two ammonia and urea trains producing 1.3 million tons per year (t/y) of urea and 100,000 t/y of ammonia, with associated handling and storage facilities ("Uhde to Build Damietta Fertiliser Plant," 2007). The approvals from the Egyptian government seemed routine. The German firm Uhde, contracted to build the facility on a turnkey basis for EAgrium, had already built six similar fertilizer plants in Egypt, including three in the vicinity of Alexandria, without encountering significant public opposition (ibid.).

In Damietta, however, an effective and large-scale popular movement against the plant quickly emerged. No single party, individual, or interest group monopolized the campaign; instead, activists and concerned community residents formed several popular committees in April 2008 to facilitate coordination. These groups included the Popular Committee Against the Fertilizer Factory (*al-Lagna al-Sha'biyya li-Munahadat Masna' al-Asmida*) and the Popular Committee for the Defense of the Environment. The committees organized protests, held press conferences and workshops, and issued *bayanat* (communiqués), laying out their objections to the factory and calling for presidential intervention. While the Alexandrian wastewater activist network remained limited to a relatively small number of professors, journalists, lawyers, and literate citizens, in Damietta the campaign reached a broader social constituency. Participants in the campaign represented voluntary associations, political parties, Parliament, businesses, universities, popular associations (*jam'iyyat ahliyya*), unions, and professional syndicates, as well as landowners and villagers living nearby the petrochemical plants.

The campaign's broader social base meant that activists could coordinate direct action and protest through a more robust infrastructure than in Alexandria. The campaign against EAgrium unfolded in public squares, residential streets, mosques, courtrooms, government offices, and professional associational headquarters. These various places saw organizers employ a diverse repertoire of protest tactics and mobilizing strategies, including statements, petitions, marches, vigils, litigation, and strikes. As in Alexandria, activists made use of state-owned and opposition media outlets but, in Damietta, media coverage was more extensive, as new, privately owned newspapers and TV stations, as well as regional satellite channels such as Al Jazeera, followed the campaign closely.[11] In particular, the independent daily *Al-Masry Al-Youm* assigned several journalists to cover the campaign on a daily basis through much of 2008. During this period, the paper's circulation numbers increased significantly, from 2,000 to 6,000 copies in Damietta during the protests.[12]

### Framing protest: by the people, for the people

> "Agrium…the destruction of Damietta's economy."
>
> Slogan on a protest banner (Hussein, 2008)

Activist networks in Damietta used several highly effective discursive framings to make their case to officials, the public, and the media. The first was to make their demands in the name of "the people of Damietta"—*sha'b Dumyat* or *ahali Dumyat*, the Egyptian colloquial terms for everyday, ordinary people. These words have class and nationalist connotations, invoking the culture and practices of the middle and lower classes. The first communiqué or *bayan* began, "We, the people of Damietta, announce our total refusal to have the chemical factory on our land, as it endangers our environment" (Zeinobia, 2008). It asked the Prime Minister, the President, and the concerned ministries to reconsider their decision to allow a petrochemical factory in the area, noting that Ras al-Barr was a tourist destination and should be declared a protected area instead (El-Kashef, "Delegation from the People of Damietta…," 2008). Subsequent communiqués consistently invoked the "people of Dumyat" in charging that the plant threatened the area's natural resources, its economic underpinnings, and the health and future of future generations. Similarly, in presenting the campaign to outsiders in Cairo and elsewhere, activists and sympathetic journalists employed such phrases as *ibna' al-muhafaza* (literally "the sons of the province") to convey a collective purpose and sense of communal identity, particularly in contrast to the outsiders, i.e. the foreign company proposing to build the plant.

Members of the popular committees also evoked a sense of distinctive urban identity, much as Alexandrians criticized local governance by depicting their city as an increasingly despoiled "bride of the sea." Located at the confluence of the western branch of the Nile and the Mediterranean, Damietta has a long history as a mercantile port and a contested strategic gateway to the Delta. These historical resonances were sometimes invoked in commentaries and slogans. Writer Samir Farrag, for instance, was quoted at a popular conference arguing that the people of Dumyat had triumphed over the Crusaders in the past and would defeat Canadians today (El-Kashef *et al.*, 2008).[13]

Much of Damietta's economy was tied up with its reputation as a summer tourist destination, particularly the area of Ras al-Barr near the proposed fertilizer complex. The *Ras*, or "head" of land, formed a triangular peninsula that became a prime summertime spot for members of Egypt's elite by the late nineteenth century. Families constructed temporary huts, or *'ishash*, made of reed walls over wooden frames, for the season. These huts could be rolled up and stored for the following year; most were eventually converted to villas and then low-rise blocks of apartments (Muhafaza Dumyat, undated).

Defending the city's historical legacy and present-day tourism economy thus became a central theme of the campaign against the proposed fertilizer factory. In April 2008, the popular committee sent an open message to the Egyptian leadership attending the Davos Economic Forum in Switzerland, arguing that Egyptians welcomed foreign investment as long as it was appropriate to the local geography. Galal al-Ulfi, a parliamentarian from Damietta, noted that LE150–200 million in tourism income would be lost if the project went ahead (El-Kashef *et al.*, "Popular Conference in Dumyat…," 2008). Local businessmen and investors also voiced their opposition, collecting and donating funds to finance the protest campaign (El-Kashef and El-Shazly, "The Government Suggests…," 2008).

The head of the Chamber of Tourist Facilities went further in his opposition. He argued that the project was "a poisoned dagger" aimed at the heart of Damietta, threatening that his chamber and affiliated companies would go on strike if construction of the EAgrium facility continued (El-Ghatrifi *et al.*, "Al-Masry Al-Youm Discovers 'Agrium' Did Not Obtain Agreement…," 2008). When the popular committee held one of several outreach workshops for the citizenry, it rejected compromise with the multinational, titling the workshop, "No to Agrium, No to Dialogue, Yes to Investment in Tourism" (Yassin *et al.*, 2008).

In emphasizing tourism, activists could point to several years of investment in Ras al-Barr by the centrally appointed governor, Muhammad Fathi al-Barad'i, aimed at beautifying the middle-class resort and upgrading its amenities. Drawing on local and national revenues, the governor had mobilized financing to redevelop *al-lisan* (literally "the tongue"), the tip of land at the end of the head of the peninsula where the Nile waters meet the Mediterranean. The governorate had rebuilt the jetty at the end of the tip, marking it with a restored lighthouse and a lighted map inscribed on a monument that traced the Nile's journey from equatorial Africa to Ras al-Barr, and renovated a pedestrian promenade (the "corniche") with shoreline shops and cafés below. The city also repaved and landscaped the main roads in Ras al-Barr, lining them with date palms, and authorized the construction of a new hotel by the ubiquitous firm, the Arab Contractors.

As a promotional brochure from the governorate noted, the governor "took a special interest in developing Ras al-Barr as the real engine for economic development in the governorate," in order to "regain its place as a distinguished Egyptian *masyaf* and to reclaim its position on the Egyptian tourism map" (Muhafaza Dumyat, undated). The brochure, titled "Ras al-Barr: Return to a Beautiful Time," reproduced historical photographs of famous summer visitors, including Gamal Abdel Nasser, the singer Umm Kulthum, and members of the royal dynasty of Mehmat Ali (deposed by the Free Officers in 1952). The accompanying commentary elaborated upon the pastoral qualities and historical resilience of Ras al-Barr:

Ras al-Barr was a suburb of Dumyat where fishermen worked and quail laid nests, where the people of Dumyat took boats for picnics and fishing and sports. Ras al-Barr—the modern name of the place that the Arabs, in the

Middle Ages, called Giza Dumyat, the land that al-Maqrizi visited in the fifteenth century when he wrote his beautiful poem "The Meadow of Two Seas" (*Marj al-Bahrayn*). In the era of the Crusader campaigns, Ras al-Barr witnessed difficult times, for in the year 1169…a Crusader fleet of a thousand ships sat off the coast of Dumyat and besieged the city for 53 days.

(Ibid.)

Tellingly, the governor's introduction noted that he had issued an administrative decree limiting all permitted activities in the area to "tourism activities commensurate with preserving the excellent environment of this unique place" (ibid.). The citizen campaigners were quick to capitalize on this discourse, arguing that Ras al-Barr should be formally designated as a protected area under the jurisdiction of the Environmental Affairs Agency.

Another powerful theme in the campaign was that the Egyptian government and multinational firms were exploiting Egypt's natural resources for the benefit of foreigners. The Egyptian government indeed kept energy prices below prevailing world market levels as part of an overall strategy to attract private investment secondary industries, such as petrochemicals, fertilizers, refineries, and plastics. The cost of natural gas accounts for 50–70 percent of the cost of producing nitrogen fertilizers, such as ammonia and urea; cheap energy is the main reason for multinational fertilizer companies to build plants in the Middle East ("OCI Expands Fertiliser Business," 2009). Egypt thus set the price for natural gas below those that emerged in liberalized futures markets or in prevailing long-term contracts. The Egyptian government reportedly promised to supply natural gas to EAgrium at a price of US$1 per MBtu for five years, at a time when global natural gas prices had risen steeply. Henry Hub prices on the New York mercantile exchange, for instance, climbed above US$11 per MBtu in May 2008.[14]

By keeping prices on energy inputs low, the Egyptian government created a rent, or supranormal profit, that state-owned companies and private consortiums alike were quick to exploit. Strong demand for nitrogen fertilizers for agricultural production in China, India, and Brazil had sent fertilizer prices soaring in 2007–8, and companies scrambled to expand production (ibid.). Unprecedented price increases were also fueled by increased demand for biofuels, such as ethanol. Egypt thus doubled its exports of fertilizers between 2005 and 2007, from LE6 billion (US$1.1 billion) to LE13.4 billion (US$2.5 billion), according to the Ministry of Trade and Industry.

After Mubarak's overthrow in early 2011, public backlash against these policies escalated. Criticism focused particularly on the sale of Egypt's natural gas at below-market prices to Israel, but similar arrangements applied to natural gas contracts with Jordan and with domestic investors in Egypt. In 2008, it was the campaign against EAgrium that popularized this line of attack on state policy. Activists and local opposition party members assailed the "underpricing" of the country's natural wealth for the enrichment of foreigners. Opposition parties joined in: Mahmoud Abaza, the head of the Wafd Party, used a meeting of the party's health committee to criticize the government's energy subsidy to EAgrium, arguing that the agreement allocated the company US$700,000 worth of natural gas per day. The local Wafd deputy similarly argued that outsiders were exploiting the resources of Damietta (El-Kashef, 2012). An independent parliamentarian from Damietta asked the Majlis al-Sha'b to investigate the terms of the natural gas deal with Israel, and called on parliamentarians to join a campaign opposing such policies.

Activists argued that the government was not simply underpricing energy, but also selling valuable coastal land far below market value. When Gamal Mubarak visited Damietta, the popular committees informed him that residents were willing to buy the land allocated to EAgrium themselves (El-Kashef, "Delegation from the People of Damietta...," 2008). The head of the local housing cooperative formally applied to the Ministry of Housing to buy the land for a new tourism development, observing that while the land had been sold to EAgrium for LE39 per cubic meter, the cooperative could resell it to developers for LE100 per cubic meter (El-Shazly, 2008).

The discourse of the Damietta campaign also focused extensively on the unacceptable health and environmental hazards posed by a large fertilizer plant to Damietta's population. At one conference, the local Dumyati deputy of the Ministry of Health told the over 300 participants that the Health Committee of the Majlis al-Sha'b would consider the dangers of the factory for human health (El-Kashef *et al.*, 2008). One scientist said that fertilizer plants were the sixth most polluting industries worldwide, while a botanist at Mansour University noted that the risks associated with such a plant near cities were unacceptable: "The factory will also store 30,000 tonnes of ammonia adjacent to a residential area. Whatever state-of-the-art technology the plant installs it will take a single human error for the entire Delta to be threatened" (El-Sayed, 2008).

Other local researchers highlighted how a large petrochemical plant would "drain the natural resources of Damietta" through water consumption and by threatening Damietta's fishing industry (El-Shazly and El-Kashef, "Experts: Agrium Threatens Fishing Fleet...," 2008). The fishing industry in Damietta was an important economic sector, as the local fleet constituted 65 percent of the entire Egyptian fishing fleet (El-Shazly and El-Kashef, "Dumyat: We Will Prevent Agrium...," 2008). While farmers saw their summer crops suffer from shortages in irrigation water, these commentators noted a factory would consume large amounts of clean water from Damietta's water networks, would discharge polluted water into the sanitation networks, and thus burden the city's public utilities, polluting nearby beaches and imposing large costs on local infrastructure.

The claim that the central government catered to foreign capital at the expense of local health and rights quickly made Damietta into a local protest with national overtones, exactly as in Alexandria. The freedoms committee of the Journalism Syndicate invited Damietta campaigners to join them at their national headquarters in Cairo, where protesters chanted, "Stay away from us you thieves; all we have left is air and water. The government says 'amen' to thieves and the corrupt" (Hussein, 2008). The head of the committee made the linkages to national politics explicit, saying, "the regime that wants to build the factory in Ras al-Barr is the same one that is cracking down on Kifaya [the pro-democracy movement] and arresting the April 6 youth" (ibid.).

Even members of the government's National Democratic Party (NDP) in Damietta joined in the escalating criticism of the government. One local NDP parliamentarian appealed to Mubarak to intervene personally, while another NDP representative wondered how the government could build three fertilizer complexes in the area without consulting the people of the city, arguing that "we are facing a corruption issue. It must be investigated and those responsible held accountable" (El-Shazly and El-Kashef, "National Holiday Festivities Suspended...," 2008).

### Legalizing environmental claims

Participants in the Damietta campaign made extensive use of the openings provided by Egypt's fragmented legal system, filing official complaints (*balaghat*), petitions, appeals, and court cases through various state bodies and organizations. Increasing numbers of government entities weighed in with conflicting verdicts that embarrassed the Nazif government as reports thereof accumulated in the media. In addition, the use of fact-finding committees sanctioned by the government and the People's Assembly turned out to be a further milestone in the "legalization" of activists' central claims.

Local officials in Damietta became some of the most vociferous participants in trying to construct and deploy legal authority. Members of the Damietta Local Council filed complaints with the police, accusing EAgrium of forging their signatures on agreements to build the factory. The consortium denied the charges, but local members persisted, filing additional complaints with the Attorney General. The council head also filed a lawsuit claiming that the company had illegally cut down palm and citrus trees on the construction site in violation of an agreement with the environmental agency. The local councils threatened to go on strike and stop the business of the city if their complaints were not addressed. Indeed, in June, they formally suspended operations (El-Kashef and El-Shazly, "Massive Protests in Damietta...," 2008). Damietta's lawyers went on strike in mid-May, forcing many court cases to be postponed. The local head of the Building and Housing Cooperative for the "Fourth Damietta Neighborhood" appealed to the Ministry of Justice, lodging a complaint with the Committee of Reconciliation of Civil and Commercial Disputes, which met to discuss the issue (El-Ghatrifi *et al.*, "Al-Masry Al-Youm Discovers 'Agrium' Did Not Obtain Agreement...," 2008). Not to be left out, the secretary-general of the youth wing of the NDP filed a court case against the Ministry of Housing, the environmental agency, and the governor for issuing permits to EAgrium. Activist lawyers in Damietta filed cases against then-Minister of State for the Environment, Maged George, charging that the agency could not have done a credible environmental impact assessment, and that the EIA should be released to the public.

A series of subnational decisions halted construction at the Agrium site while these legal claims were pending. In April, the New Communities Development Authority under the Ministry of Housing announced that some of Agrium's structures lacked the proper licenses and would be removed (El-Kashef, "'Housing' Accuses Agrium of Perpetrating Violations...," 2008). A day later, the popular committees filed formal complaints with the Damietta public prosecutor against the governor and other officials for allowing the project to continue, while Egyptian security forces intervened to halt construction at the site. The Damietta Port Authority also decided to halt construction of the company's port platform until the dispute was resolved (El-Ghatrifi *et al.*, "Al-Masry Al-Youm Discovers 'Agrium' Did Not Obtain Agreement...," 2008).

The company's response to this rapidly escalating campaign was that its permits and procedures were valid under Egyptian law and that a significant number of its shareholders were Egyptian companies. The Ministries of Transport, Environment, Agriculture, Industry, Irrigation, and Investment had rubber-stamped approvals for the project to go ahead. The Investment Authority had reportedly licensed EAgrium on the condition that it export 75 percent of its annual production and meet environmental and safety standards. The company also pointed out in press releases and press conferences that while the Canadian firm Agrium, one of the largest global suppliers of fertilizers, owned a 60 percent stake, the other 40 percent was held by Egyptian and Arab state-owned firms involved in petrochemicals, natural gas, and investment.[15] As one company consultant told *Al-Masry Al-Youm*:

> Agrium is an Egyptian company, because the government owns 33 percent of it. We don't need to move our factory from Dumyat, we assure the people of Dumyat that we did not come to damage the city, because we are Egyptians, essentially.
>
> (El-Ghatrifi and El-Kashef, 2008)

The firm thus deployed local managers to emphasize the safety of its advanced technologies and the jobs that the company would provide, but these attempts were largely ineffective in ameliorating public concern.

When the police and port authority stopped construction at the site, Agrium announced it would seek to recoup its sunk costs, equity stake, and lost profits through international arbitration ("New Plant Halted," 2008). Herein lay the central government's dilemma. According to a fact-finding committee appointed by the Majlis al-Sha'b, the firm had indeed obtained the necessary approvals from the central ministries. There was no evidence of corruption, bribes, or other wrongdoing. If the government canceled a lawful contract, it would call into question the integrity of Egypt's system for facilitating foreign investment, the linchpin of the development strategy embraced by Prime Minister Nazif. It did not help EAgrium's case that the prime minister held dual Egyptian–Canadian citizenship, a fact that prompted various charges of vested interest and informal kickbacks.

In an attempt to defuse mounting criticism and buy time for negotiations with the company, the Nazif government announced it would create two more fact-finding committees, in addition to one already convened by the Majlis al-Sha'b. The first would consist of independent environmental experts and the second of government officials. By giving these committees government approval, the Cabinet would also find itself constrained by their findings.

The environmental committee included two national environmental figures, Mostafa Kamal Tolba and Mohamed Kassas, whose careers and roles in Egyptian environmental networks were explored in Chapter 2. The committee's report, released June 8, confirmed the central contentions of opponents to the Damietta project. As summarized by *Al-Masry Al-Youm*, the committee's findings were that the site was chosen with consideration only for the economic interest of EAgrium, and inadequate consideration for the proximity to population centers (El-Ghatrifi *et al.*, "The Expert Report Presented to the Investigative Committee...," 2008). Damietta already hosted a large number of polluting factories, and while the direct outputs of the new complex were not particularly hazardous, the catalysts had to be handled with extreme caution and according to well-defined procedures. The report concluded that tourism was a better development strategy for Ras al-Barr, but admitted that breaking the contract with EAgrium could inhibit foreign investment and invite costly compensation claims (ibid.).

### Creating infrastructural authority

Given the stakes in terms of investor confidence and foreign investment, resonant discourses and legal claims may well not have forced the government to reconsider its contract with EAgrium. Instead, it was the ability of the Damietta activists to mobilize significant numbers of people in direct action and street protests in the spring and summer of 2008 that ratcheted up significant pressure on the governor, the Cabinet, and the Majlis al-Sha'b. Whereas in Alexandria activist networks of academics and journalists generated controversy largely through the media, in Damietta the popular committees made use of a far more extensive infrastructure, including mosques, public squares, workplaces, and associational offices, to engage citizens. They coordinated a series of creative protests on holidays and held special events, boosted by cooperation with environmental advocacy organizations from out of town. The result was mounting popular pressure on the regime and the governor to take action.

The popular committees canvassed heavily at Damietta's mosques, distributing communiqués and flyers after Friday prayers and using the squares and thoroughfares outside of central mosques as staging grounds for large-scale protests (Goma'a *et al.*, 2008). These often became large-scale vigils in which thousands of participants held banners and chanted rhymed couplets in colloquial Arabic. One such protest included slogans such as "We want a decision, disaster beckons," "Mubarak, Mubarak, Dumyatis are awaiting your verdict," "Governor, tell the boss [Mubarak], Dumyatis are a good folk," and "If no one listens to our demands, we'll remove the factory with our own hands" (ibid.).[16] When Sheikh Muhammad Tantawi, head of al-Azhar, Egypt's leading institution of Islamic scholarship, gave a Friday sermon in Damietta to inaugurate new Islamic colleges, protesters received him with banners and protest chants against EAgrium. Sheikh Tantawi obligingly reminded the crowds that receiving commissions and bribes for contracts was illegal in Islam, alluding to a persistent rumor that Prime Minister Nazif and other officials had received kickbacks for the agreement with Agrium (El-Shazly and El-Kashef, "Dumyat: We Will Prevent Agrium...," 2008).

Damietta's activists also used neighborhoods, parks, and public squares for direct action, timing their use of these spaces with Egyptian holidays, Earth Day, and other commemorative occasions. For Sham al-Nasim, a popular holiday marking the arrival of spring and celebrated by Muslims and Christians alike, the popular committees asked residents of Ras al-Barr to display black banners inscribed with protest slogans from their apartments and villas. Thousands of Damietta citizens flocked to Ras al-Barr for the holiday, while children stood at the entrance to the area carrying a banner that read, "In sympathy with Ras al-Barr."

The popular committees and the Habi Center for Environmental Rights, an advocacy organization that seeks to help local communities organize, also staged an Earth Day celebration. They invited civil society organizations from across Egypt to participate under the slogan "Against Resource Drain and Pollution in Damietta...and No to Pollution of the Lands of the Peninsula Ras al-Barr." The celebration featured a march by children of Damietta carrying balloons, banners, and flowers (El-Kashef and El-Shazly, "March of the Children of Damietta," 2008). One such banner called on "President Mubarak and Mama Suzanne" to "Save Us from Agrium and Grant Us the Right to a Clean Life" (El-Kashef and El-Shazly, "With Flowers and Masks: The Children of Dumyat Protest...," 2008).

The activists thus showed they could consistently summon significant numbers of supporters into the streets. While the popular committee leadership emphasized that vigils would be conducted in a civilized manner, the possibility of significant street protests made the governor and the regime uneasy. On April 30, for instance, an estimated 5,000 people marched from al-Sa'a Square to the governor's office, carrying black banners. The governor, Fathi al-Barad'i, left his office to appeal to them to disperse, but they refused, prompting him to assure the crowd that "the factory would not be located on the land of Damietta without the approval of the people of Dumyat." "I am responsible before God for the ruling," he told the crowds. "The factory will be moved to Suez... Damietta is in the heart and mind of the president" (Salah Al-Din *et al.*, 2008).

Although an appointed official of the Mubarak government, al-Barad'i thus sought to portray himself as respecting the wishes of the residents of Dumyat, thereby reinforcing key themes of the activist campaign: that the central government was acting against local interests and that the protesters did indeed speak for "the people of Damietta." The fear that "the people" would continue to engage in sustained protest informed the governor's multiple appeals to the protesters to maintain their "civilized" (*hadari*) conduct and demonstrate self-control. He canceled holidays, such as Damietta's "National Day," in an effort to disrupt planned protests, arguing that while he personally opposed EAgrium, the government needed time to negotiate with EAgrium to find a solution (El-Shazly and El-Kashef, "National Holiday Festivities Suspended...," 2008).

As al-Barad'i had reminded the crowds, Mubarak had reportedly asked the Cabinet to explore the views of the people of Damietta vis-à-vis the proposed factory and then assuage their concerns (El-Sayed, 2008). Activists, in turn, asserted that Mubarak had promised that the factory would not be built without the approval of the people. They returned to this theme time and time again in calling upon the government to cancel the contract or move the plant elsewhere.

The assertions by al-Barad'i and others that Agrium could find an alternative site in other industrial free zones, such as those in Port Said or Suez, prompted immediate protests in those cities also, with several new popular committees emerging to coordinate campaigns that echoed the organization and tactics of Damietta. In the densely populated Cairo district of Shubra al-Khayma, for example, activists organized a popular committee to coordinate a campaign against a proposed petrochemical factory in close proximity to residential areas (Elmusa and Baraka, 2009).

The Nazif government received a major setback in promoting EAgrium when the Majlis al-Sha'b voted unanimously against the EAgrium project on June 19. Although parliamentary decisions were hardly binding in Egypt's executive-dominated political system, it was widely—and accurately—predicted that the government would be hard-pressed to pursue the project now that the NDP and opposition parties together had soundly rejected it. Damietta residents celebrated through the night once the vote was announced, in popular marches characterized by fireworks and a carnival atmosphere (El-Kashef and El-Shazly, "Carnivals and Fireworks and Popular Marches in Damietta Celebrating the Departure of Agrium," 2008). The following day, Agrium announced that it was studying two options put forward by Prime Minister Nazif, whereby the government would either directly purchase the company's investment or offer Agrium a significant equity stake in the adjacent MOPCO plant. With government assurances of additional urea production capacity by 2011, the equity deal went forward and Agrium was awarded a 26 percent stake in MOPCO (Bryner and Alperowicz, 2008).

In terms of forestalling expansion of fertilizer production in the city, the success of the Damietta campaign turned out to be limited. The government continued to supply the new MOPCO with natural gas at US$1 per Btu (Zalat *et al.*, 2008). The government also agreed to cover any outstanding loans obtained for the EAgrium complex (Fikry and Shalabi, 2008). Most importantly, however, the government helped to facilitate approvals for an expansion of the existing complex that tripled its production capacity, reported as an additional 1.35 million t/y of urea (Bryner and Alperowicz, 2008).

State-owned and private banks proved eager to finance this expansion, as high fertilizer prices, cheap natural gas inputs, and growing international demand made for guaranteed profits. Banks provided a US$1.05 billion loan for the MOPCO expansion—those participating included Banque Misr, the National Bank of Egypt, Bank Audi, Credit Agricole, the Greek National Bank, the National Bank of Abu Dhabi, Commercial International Bank, the National Bank of Development, and the United Bank. This keen interest on the part of banks also reflected the assurance of state participation, as MOPCO's largest shareholder was the national oil company, Egyptian General Petroleum Company (EGPC). Additional Egyptian state-owned shareholders included the Nasser Company for Petroleum, the National Investment Bank, the Nasser Social Bank, and Misr Insurance Company.

Thus, rather than a majority-owned private consortium as envisioned for EAgrium, MOPCO gave Damietta an expanded state-owned operation. As argued in Chapter 3, it is particularly difficult for environmental authorities and local activists to pressure state-owned enterprises. In terms of environmental risk, the MOPCO site was similar to the one in Ras al-Barr. Located directly across a small navigation canal, it was no greater distance than the EAgrium site from either the peninsula of Ras al-Barr or the city of Damietta. The MOPCO site, however, was classified as part of the Damietta Free Zone, not part of Ras al-Barr.

The MOPCO expansion epitomizes some of the problems that plagued the Mubarak regime's development strategy, which the post-revolutionary interim military council has shown little desire to reconsider. A major reason why public–private ventures such as MOPCO are protected from political pressure is that revenues from these plants accrue not only to private shareholders and banks, but also to an array of state-owned authorities involved in the extraction and processing of fossil fuels.

MOPCO exports the majority of its urea and ammonia abroad, particularly to Europe and the United States, where it is more difficult to site fertilizer plants. There is no provision for revenue sharing with governorates or municipalities, and no offset funds are required of the consortiums for investment in local schools, training, parks, clinics, roads, or other infrastructure that local communities wish to improve.

MOPCO uses the latest production technologies, installed by world-class multinationals. These plants are therefore much less polluting than older industrial facilities, but they are also highly capital intensive. The rapid expansion in fertilizer production has done little to address unemployment or support the upgrading of Damietta's traditionally strong manufacturing sector in wood and furniture. Furniture manufacturing is highly labor intensive, as production is concentrated in privately owned small and medium-sized workshops. Small and medium-sized workshops in Damietta, for example, accounted for approximately 65 percent of the governorate's furniture production and 23 percent of its output in the wood sector in 2005 (Ministry of State for Environmental Affairs *et al.*, 2005).

The protest campaign helped create a cadre of experienced activists in Damietta who have little intention of giving up. Damietta's activists were also caught up in the upheavals and activism of the 2011 uprising. As in other Egyptian cities, Damietta's workers, professionals, and citizens staged numerous strikes and protests, not simply in the momentous months of January and February 2011, but throughout the spring and summer. In the fall of 2011, renewed protest against MOPCO broke out. This upsurge in environmental mobilization and its linkages to the 2011 uprising are analyzed in the concluding chapter of this book.

## Conclusion

Comparing environmental campaigns in Alexandria and Damietta illustrates how activists overcame legal restrictions designed to limit political participation in authoritarian Egypt. In both cases, networks of activists and academics made persuasive discursive claims by highlighting local environmental and public health risks and questioning the role of foreign donors and foreign investors in the domestic political economy. They also appealed to citizens to preserve the distinctive historical identities and economic foundations of their cities. The strategic use of the media—and the media's interest in covering controversy—was pivotal in publicizing the campaigns and thereby raising the stakes for decision-makers.

A key discursive element in these environmental campaigns was the linkage between "local" pollution problems and the dysfunction of national decision-making. Provincial cities and their inhabitants felt they were peripheral to the calculations of centralized, opaque circles of decision-makers, as indeed they largely were. Writers such as Wahba and activists in Damietta argued that exclusionary and corrupt forms of governance prioritized the preferences of foreign investors and international donors over the health and economic wellbeing of inhabitants in the provinces.

The ability of the Damietta campaigners to create a truly popular campaign, in comparison with the more elite-centered network that emerged in Alexandria, reflected both the nature of the environmental issue and the changing conditions underpinning civic activism. Activists in Alexandria simplified the question of the design of the sanitation network into whether treated effluent should be disposed of on land or at sea, but either option, adequately implemented, would have improved public health conditions in the city itself. Both options were highly technical, and the complexity of the proposed solutions did not lend itself to the simple rejectionist stance found in Damietta. That is, no one in Alexandria was against improving the sewage system, and there was no real difference of opinion between the regime, committed to promoting land reclamation through reuse of wastewater, and the professors, engineers, and journalists who so ardently advocated land disposal.

In Damietta, on the contrary, the campaign involved local provincial elites who opposed the center's project of transforming Damietta—or part of it—into the "Mubarak Complex for Natural Gas and Petrochemicals." Neither the central government nor EAgrium sought to establish clear incentives and benefits to promote local acceptance of large-scale fertilizer factories. The campaign had at hand a clearly articulated alternative vision of development, sanctioned by the governor's investments and the reports of environmental experts who endorsed tourism. Indeed, the centrally appointed governor al-Barad'i found himself publicly siding with the activists even as he upheld the authority of Cairo. Egypt's fragmented system of legal authority allowed Damietta activists to make claims in multiple state institutions, filing court cases at different levels and formal inquiries with various ministries. These actions served to legitimate the grievances of the campaigns by legalizing them, that is, making the consideration of their claims part of the routine business of the state apparatus.

The decade that separated the two campaigns also mattered, as the structural conditions for collective action were more favorable in Damietta. In Damietta, a lively private sector centered on small and medium enterprises in tourism, fisheries, agriculture, furniture, and wood manufacturing supported alternative development strategies and provided a broad swath of society concerned about the impact of large, potentially hazardous industrial facilities. The regime's acceptance of new, privately owned media outlets allowed journalists to follow local stories consistently and often sympathetically.

Damietta and Alexandria face many other environmental problems that have not been the focus of collective action and popular mobilization. Rapid and poorly planned expansion along the Mediterranean coastline and around the coastal lagoons of Lake Maryut and Lake Manzala has accelerated beach and coastal erosion, produced rising groundwater tables and increased contamination of coastal aquifers, and degraded coastal habitats and marine water quality (Ministry of State for Environmental Affairs *et al.*, 2005). Like other cities of the Nile Delta, Alexandria and Damietta have endemic problems with water-borne diseases, water quality, and disposal of solid waste. Rapid urbanization on the peripheries and dense infilling of existing neighborhoods continue to strain the governorate resources for adequate extension of sanitation networks and the expensive treatment infrastructures that these networks require. Located at the terminal end of the Delta and the irrigation system, water quality in canals is poor, with the water often contaminated and highly saline.

Increased popular mobilization may well work to increase pressure on governmental authorities about those environmental issues that, like industrial plants, pose visible threats to health and livelihoods. Other environmental issues, however, such as salinity, cannot be addressed through the efforts of activist networks alone but require sustained institution building by managerial networks. One such policy issue is conservation and habitat protection, explored in the next chapter, where both experts and activists have been actively engaged in seeking to influence both formal state policies and environmental outcomes on the ground.

# 5  Natural heritage, mass tourism

## Conservation networks and coastal land use conflicts

In the span of a few decades, Egypt's coasts have been transformed. Strings of holiday villages, secondary luxury homes, and resorts—many left half-constructed by absentee investors—cover vast swaths of coastline, from the Mediterranean to the Red Sea. The coasts of the Red Sea and Sinai Peninsula host some of the most spectacular coral reef systems in the world, as well as stunning desert landscapes and rich historical–cultural attractions. These attributes, combined with extensive state incentives for land development, produced a boom in coastal tourism during the 1990s and 2000s. By 2002, the Red Sea and South Sinai governorates accounted for approximately half of all tourism receipts to Egypt, and half of all tourist arrivals in the country (Meade and Shaalan, 2002: 3–4). Most of these tourists came for sun, diving, and snorkeling, instead of the country's traditional tourism brand of antiquities. Rather than traveling down the Nile Valley from Cairo to Aswan and Abu Simbel, tourists increasingly flew directly from Europe, Russia, or Cairo to small airports along the coasts, including those in the towns of Hurghada, Sharm el-Sheikh, Marsa 'Alam, and Taba.

Not surprisingly, the building out of Egypt's shorelines severely impacted coastal ecologies. As Egypt's First National Report to the UN Convention on Biological Diversity noted in 1997, "The loss of coastal habitats should perhaps be Egypt's primary conservation concern" (National Biodiversity Unit, 1997: 27). Beginning in the early 1980s, conservation experts had sought to build a network of protected areas in Egypt, particularly in coastal areas. These experts viewed protected areas as the most practical way to conserve biodiversity in the face of rapid real estate and tourism development. A small in-country network of local and resident expatriate experts provided continuity in personnel and institutional memory through a series of donor-funded projects to build a protected area network. They served as project managers, consultants, and field scientists for the Nature Conservation Sector of the Egyptian Environmental Affairs Agency. The continued engagement of network participants helped ensure that the many "outputs" of these projects—reports, studies, ecological surveys, business plans, integrated management plans, tourism assessments, maps, and databases—informed a consistent vision for the evolution of Egypt's protected areas.

The results were, in many ways, impressive. Between 1982 and 2001, Egypt promulgated laws designating twenty-seven protected areas, covering 15 percent of the country. From 1991 to 2008, Egypt's protected areas expanded by more than 2.3 million hectares (Global Environmental Facility Evaluation Office, 2009: 55). However, areas critical to preserving biodiversity—coastal zones, estuaries, mountain ranges, bays, and lagoons—were often the same places that generated significant profits from tourism, fisheries, land reclamation, and conversion to urban uses. With the expansion of acreage under protected area status, the conservation network encountered an increasing number of conflicting economic interests and land uses. These included influential investors closely tied to the Mubarak regime; the military sector, accustomed to free rein in remote frontier areas; centrally appointed governors with executive authority over land use; and local communities seeking access to resources. Even in seemingly remote desert interiors, protected area managers encountered actors involved in mining, quarrying, infrastructure development, military installations and exercises, and energy extraction.

This chapter analyzes how a managerial conservation network sought to engage these actors by building discursive, legal, and infrastructural forms of authority. Conservation experts framed habitat protection not only in terms of conserving biodiversity but also in terms of contributions to the national economy and national security. Protected area managers sought to build linkages to tourism investors by providing environmental assessments and recommendations. They further filed court cases to sanction violators. As importantly, protected area managers sought to build infrastructural authority directly within and around protected areas, seeking cooperative relations with local Bedouin tribes and channeling central resources to hiring rangers to monitor protected areas. At the national level, the relatively small managerial network repeatedly proposed creating a financially and legally autonomous protected area authority distinct from jurisdiction of the national environmental agency.

The politics of conservation in Egypt has involved more players over time as the tourism sector has expanded and conflict over the rents generated from land and marine resources has intensified. The last sections of this chapter analyze the advent of activist networks into conservation activities. These include diving and tourism operators with an interest in safeguarding their livelihoods through improved reef conservation, and advocacy organizations seeking to use the strong legal framework for protected areas to address land use conflicts in more populated rural and urban areas.

## Establishing early protected areas in Sinai

Egypt's first protected areas were established in the Sinai Peninsula in 1983 following Israel's withdrawal, as stipulated by the Camp David Accords signed between Egypt and Israel.[1] Wars between Israel and Egypt, and Israeli occupation after 1967, had kept Sinai in a state of political and economic uncertainty, preventing large-scale tourism investment. Under Israeli rule, resort development of the 'Aqaba coast began in Na'ma Bay, near Sharm el-Sheikh, and several other small towns, notably Nuweiba and Dahab. Between 1967 and 1981, Israel also zoned protected areas in parts of the 'Aqaba and Suez coasts, the Straits of Tiran, the southern mountains around St. Catherine's monastery, part of the northern Sinai coast, and parts of Lake Bardawil in the north.

With Israel's withdrawal, Egyptian government ministries and international donors lost little time in preparing ambitious development and settlement plans for Sinai. With funding from USAID, the US consulting firm Dames and Moore prepared a seven-volume investment plan for Sinai. The plan emphasized mineral extraction, land reclamation, and industry for northern Sinai, while for the southern region, oil on the Gulf of Suez, fisheries, and tourism figured prominently. The Egyptian government's 1987 five-year plan thus allocated 81 percent of planned expenditures in Sinai for loans for new settlements and for the building of basic infrastructure, including roads and utilities (Academy of Scientific Research and Technology, 1986: 1).

The Egyptian government viewed tourism development in Sinai through the prism of money and security. Tourism has long been a pillar of Egypt's economy, generating foreign currency reserves and employment for large numbers of Egyptians. Tourism receipts remain the largest source of foreign exchange, helping the government balance its otherwise chronic imbalances in the current and trade accounts (Richter and Christian, 2007). Yet the tourism sector is also notably volatile, with tourist arrivals fluctuating in light of regional wars, terrorist attacks, and global economic downturns. Egyptian tourism receipts plummeted after the Gulf war in 1990–1 and attacks by Islamist militants in November 1992. Further militant attacks in 1997—in front of Cairo's Egyptian Museum and near the Valley of the Kings at Luxor, where sixty-two people (mainly tourists) were massacred—only deepened the government's commitment to reduce disruptions in foreign exchange receipts by diversifying tourism offerings out of the Nile Valley.

The Ministry of Tourism thus sought to promote "non-traditional" tourism (*siyaha ghayr taqlidiyya*) and "recreational" tourism (*siyaha riyadiyya*) on Egypt's Sinai and Red Sea coasts, far from militant activities and urban conglomerations (Awad, 1998: 22). The government and international tourism operators increasingly marketed coastal tourism separately from the traditional antiquities-based Egyptian tourism. Promotional materials produced by the Ministry of Tourism emphasized not simply sun and sand, but safaris, windsurfing, and diving, reflecting worldwide trends toward adventure and recreational tourism.

In addition to diversifying tourism options, the government specifically wanted to increase the number of people living in Sinai, to settle the area as a buffer zone with Israel. Tourism was seen as a labor-intensive sector that could attract people from the Nile Valley. As a top official at the Tourist Development Authority observed to the author in 1999, "We were trying to find an activity to get people to move. We want to inhabit Sinai, for keeping it vacant makes it another arena for war."[2]

*Discursive authority: preserving biodiversity, attracting tourists*

In light of these pressures for development, local conservation scientists and inter-national organizations began to organize to protect the coral reefs of the Gulf of 'Aqaba and the religious and archeological sites in the southern interior moun-tains. The monastery of St. Catherine and Gabal Musa (Mount Sinai), where Moses reportedly received the Ten Commandments, were a well-established basis on which to argue for historical preservation measures. Yet it was the ecological attributes of South Sinai that attracted a range of international advocacy groups working on migratory birds and wetlands preservation, coral reefs and marine habitats, and endangered wildlife and desert ecologies.

Conservation advocates were particularly concerned about safeguarding bio-diversity in the Gulf of 'Aqaba and Red Sea coral reefs. The first marine research center in the Red Sea and Indian Ocean was established on Egypt's Red Sea coast at Hurghada in 1931, followed by the Heinz Steinitz Marine Laboratory in Eilat. In addition to producing numerous scientific studies detailing the marine life and ecosystems of the areas, internationally recognized marine scientists popularized the unique ecologies of the area through such venues as *National Geographic* (e.g. Arden, 1982). One such account was by the world-renowned shark expert Eugenie Clark. Clark worked with the US Fish and Wildlife Service in the Red Sea area and had studied as a graduate student in the Hurghada marine station. She later founded the Mote Marine Laboratory in Sarasota, Florida. For the readers of *National Geographic*, she depicted the Red Sea as "a world apart—geographi-cally and ecologically," as it had the highest salinity of any sea and harbored volcanic hotspots. This confluence of geologic and climatic factors produced the northernmost reef systems in the world, a rich "incubator" for a multitude of species, 15 percent of which were estimated to be found nowhere else (Clark, 1975: 341).

Much as Darwin's account of the Galapagos Islands popularized the place itself as much as his understanding of it, these accounts created another mystique of place. This mystique no longer had its roots in Sinai's religious or archeo-logical heritage but in the newly emerging global understandings of biodiversity and ecological interrelationships. By 1982, an informal coalition of interna-tional environmental organizations interested in Sinai's natural heritage included Friends of the Earth, the World Wildlife Fund, the Near East Division of the State Department, the Smithsonian Institution, the US Fish and Wildlife Service, the Holy Land Conservation Fund, the Sierra Club, and the National Wildlife Refuge Association. In Great Britain, several voluntary associations—including Birds of Egypt, Friends of the Red Sea, and the Sinai Conservation Group—sponsored additional field surveys on migratory wildlife and reef ecology. Societies focusing on bird migration, such as the International Council for Bird Preservation and the Ornithological Society of the Middle East (both British groups), compiled lists of rare and endangered birds and their migration patterns (Holy Land Conservation Fund, 1989). Belatedly, the Egyptian government also announced the formation of the Association for the Protection of Sinai, a government-sponsored association headed by the then-Minister of Agriculture, Sayyid Marʻi, which played little practical role in promoting conservation.

Prominent Egyptian conservation scientists, such as the botanist Mohamed Kassas, were acutely aware of the national security and economic imperatives driving the Egyptian government's plans to develop Sinai. He and other Egyptian scientists focused their efforts on coordinating with international conservation networks to bring outside pressures on the political leadership. During his tenure as the head of the International Union for the Conservation of Nature (IUCN), the IUCN Annual Congress adopted a general resolution that called on member commissions to provide financial and technical assistance to Egypt to conserve designated areas of Sinai. "This was ironic," he later noted, "because at the time, in 1981, we had no protected areas. We had only laws under the Ministry of Agriculture protecting some specific species."[3]

Discursively, Egypt's conservation experts worked to make international concerns viable domestic policy choices by emphasizing the developmental benefits of protected areas. Reports by Egypt's scientific and educational institutes argued that protected areas should "realize national goals…considering a core goal in the process [is] attracting settlements" (Academy of Scientific Research and Technology, 1986: 1). Conservation scientists thus proposed that different kinds of natural reserves, with different levels of protection, be established. Drawing upon a variety of park models employed throughout the world, the 1981 report called for establishing "natural parks" (*mutanazzahat tabiʻiyya*) open to tourism, as well as "natural protectorates" that would be closed to tourism but open for scientific study. Although the tourism park model was predominant in the United States and Africa, the authors noted that the scientific preserve was used extensively in Western Europe (National Committee to Preserve Nature and Natural Resources, 1981: 7). By shielding protected areas from development, conservation scientists hoped that protected areas would safeguard the country's "natural inheritance" (*taʼmin al-wiratha*, discussed in Chapter 2) at the same time that they served as tourist attractions. Protected areas would also sustain critical natural resources and food production, such as fisheries (Academy of Scientific Research and Technology, undated).

A National Committee to Preserve Nature and Natural Resources was convened in 1981 and charged with drafting a national action plan for a network of protected areas (National Committee to Preserve Nature and Natural Resources, 1981). The committee provided an extensive list of potential protectorates in addition to those proposed in Sinai, listing the Gabal ʻElba region on the southeastern border with Sudan; the Red Sea mountains; Red Sea coastal areas with coral reefs; the northern Delta lakes; the arid Gilf Kabir plateau in the southwest; parts of the manmade Lake Nasser; parts of the Mediterranean coast; an oasis in the Western Desert; and a wadi in the Eastern Desert (ibid.: 9). This blueprint for establishing a formal network of protected areas changed remarkably little in the two decades following its circulation, except for the addition of small, compact sites near urban areas and Nile islands threatened by tourism development.

Existing Israeli-designated protected areas in Sinai made the Egyptian regime particularly sensitive to scientific and international criticism about the environmental costs of future development in Sinai. In citing legal and organizational precedents for establishing Egyptian protected areas, Egyptian scientists did not focus on existing Israeli protectorates but instead cited as precedents domestic initiatives regarding nature conservation. These included a 1980 directive issued by President Anwar al-Sadat on nature protection, Egypt's signing of the International Ramsar Convention on Wetlands, and a number of research reports on conservation carried out by specialized national committees (ibid.: 8).

Conservation scientists also enlisted prominent international scientists and personalities to make direct personal appeals to the then-President Sadat. Eugenie Clark was asked to petition President Sadat to declare Ras Mohamed, at the southern tip of Sinai, Egypt's first national park, which she did.[4] Similarly, in 1984, Kassas enlisted Britain's Prince Philip, in his capacity as president of the World Wildlife Fund, to ask President Sadat to declare Gabal 'Elba on the Red Sea Coast a protected area. The Gabal 'Elba petition itself was the culmination of earlier work done by a range of international, Egyptian, and Sudanese scientific teams under the sponsorship of the World Wildlife Fund. Consonant with conservation scientists' efforts to market the tourism potential of protected areas, the Gabal 'Elba petition noted that the area adjacent to the proposed protected area was "especially timely for tourist development in view of the completion of the new coastal highway by the Red Sea" (Kassas, 1984).

By the 1990s, conservation scientists began to frame the need for protected areas in terms of conserving natural "heritage" (*turath*). Egypt's first National Report to the Convention on Biodiversity in 1997 explicitly sought to redefine the notion of "heritage" to include natural resources:

> Egypt is endowed with a rich natural heritage as valuable as its cultural heritage; ranging from breathtaking desert landscapes, colorful coral reefs, spectacular untouched wilderness, pristine coasts, a rich and fascinating wildlife, unique geologic formations, and a high diversity of biological components and eco-systems. However, given the current rapid rate of development in Egypt, many unique ecosystems, landforms, biological components, and other natural heritage resources, are swiftly being lost and irreparably degraded... This waste of the country's irreplaceable natural heritage is often unjustifiable, occurring mainly due to ignorance, severe undervaluing of these resources, and limited enforcement of measures to control and monitor development activities.
>
> (National Biodiversity Unit, 1997)

Egypt's 1998 Biodiversity Action Plan and the 2001 National Environmental Action Plan further positioned protected areas as the principal mechanism for conserving natural heritage and biodiversity in the country (Ministry of State for Environmental Affairs, 2001b; National Biodiversity Unit and EEAA, 1998). Through field surveys and taxonomy studies, Egypt's conservation experts refined their claims about where this natural heritage was most concentrated and how protected areas would contribute to maintaining species and ecosystems (Kassas, 1995; Baha El Din, 2006). As these scientists noted, many indigenous flora and fauna had largely disappeared or were threatened with extinction. Egypt's remaining biodiversity was found in relatively few locations, making habitat conservation critical.

### Building infrastructural authority in the South Sinai protected areas

By the early 1980s, the efforts of international environmental advocacy networks and local scientists resulted in the passage of Law 102 (1983), which demarcated several areas in South Sinai as Egypt's first protected areas. As discussed in Chapter 2, the law was exceptional in that it vested executive authority for implementation and oversight of these areas to the Nature Conservation Sector within the Egyptian Environmental Affairs Agency (EEAA), although the agency as a whole was only authorized to coordinate between existing government ministries. Law 102 also provided a long-term funding mechanism, through the creation of an Environmental Fund to collect park entrance fees and levy fines for violations, such as damaging coral reefs and oil spills. The executive regulations specified that the EEAA would have control over this fund, and that part of the proceeds would go towards improving the reserves and providing compensation for whistleblowers as necessary. Law 102 further gave the Nature Conservation Sector (NCS) authority not only over protected areas, but also over coastal setback areas, in practice considerably expanding its spatial jurisdiction.

Multilateral and bilateral donors played a significant role in helping to transform selected protected areas from legally designated "paper parks" without infrastructural authority into parks with an institutional presence on the ground. The EU supported institution-building at the first national parks in South Sinai, while the United States Agency for International Development (USAID) worked along Egypt's Red Sea coast, and the Italian cooperation agency focused on protected areas in the Fayoum oasis near Cairo. By the 2000s, the World Bank's Global Environmental Facility channeled funds through the UNDP to establish management plans for the wetland protectorates of the northern Mediterranean coast and to help establish a more autonomous, capable conservation sector at the national environmental agency.

EU-funded projects for the South Sinai protected areas began in 1989. Focused initially on Ras Mohamed National Marine Park, these projects soon expanded to cover the St. Catherine, Nabq, and Taba protected areas in southern and central Sinai. The EU recruited expatriate managers with significant experience managing protected areas in the Middle East and Africa. Several of these individuals became an integral part of Egyptian managerial conservation networks as they stayed in the country to work on a series of donor-funded conservation projects. For example, the program manager for the Gulf of 'Aqaba protectorates, Michael Pearson, lived in Egypt for over a decade after a stint working on protected areas in Tanzania.[5] The project manager for Ras Mohamed, Alaa D'Grissac, had previously worked in thirty-two countries on protected areas, and had prepared portions of the Mediterranean Action Program related to protected areas.[6] John Grainger, the project manager for the St. Catherine protected area from 1996 to 2003, had previously worked in the development of protected areas in Saudi Arabia, Ghana, Sri Lanka, and Kuwait. After his work at St. Catherine, he worked as an adviser for the USAID-funded Wadi al-Gamal National Park on the southern Red Sea from 2003 to 2004, served as the IUCN team leader for the Nature Conservation Sector Capacity Building Project, and then worked as a freelance conservation consultant in Egypt from 2007 to 2010.[7]

These managers sought to create infrastructural authority for the Sinai parks by fostering cooperation with local stakeholders and building institutional capacities in the field. In contrast to the standard hiring practices within Egyptian government agencies, EU project managers directly controlled expenditures, allowing them to make their own decisions about staffing and operations. The Nature Conservation Sector and the EU projects in South Sinai obtained exemptions from public-sector hiring rules, which typically required government agencies to hire laid-off older public-sector workers, in order to hire young, well-trained, and committed graduates. In the late 1990s, EU-supported salaries for the protectorates division were competitive enough that several park rangers returned to employment in Egypt from the United States or Canada.[8] These practices, however, persisted only as long as the external donor-funded projects lasted, creating significant challenges for retaining skilled employees once the projects ended.

The two most important governmental stakeholders for the emerging protected areas regime in South Sinai were the Egyptian military and the provincial governors appointed directly by the president. Although the Camp David Accords between Israel and Egypt set limits on the numbers and kinds of military forces stationed in the peninsula, the military retained use rights to large tracts of land in Sinai, and internal security forces manned a number of checkpoints. Protected area managers also had to work closely with military appointees to the Nature Conservation Division at the environmental affairs agency. The Mubarak regime appointed a number of former military and internal security officials to top administrative positions at the Nature Conservation Sector as many protected areas were in strategically sensitive border zones near Sudan, Israel, and Libya. The first appointed CEO of the EEAA, Muhammad 'Eid, was an ex-general from the army's division of chemical warfare. He appointed another retired general, Ahmad Shahata, as the project liaison between the Nature Conservation Sector and the EEAA. He also appointed another former member of the division of chemical warfare as the Egyptian manager of Ras Mohamed National Park. This official was also the brother-in-law of the then-Minister of Defense, Muhammad Husayn Tantawi. Tantawi later served as the acting president of Egypt and head of the Supreme Council of the Armed Forces (SCAF) in the wake of the January 2011 uprising.

Protected area managers referred to their interactions with military personnel and appointed governors as "educating the state."[9] Several military appointees became convinced of the importance of protected areas, and helped facilitate basic infrastructure and enforcement activities. In Ras Mohamed National Park, rangers and the coast guard conducted joint land and sea patrols in the early years after the park was founded. But this cooperation was contingent on recognizing the first claim of the military and security forces to land use and service provision. For instance, the military built the water supply lines in Ras Mohamed, under a service division charged with providing water and electric lines to rural areas.[10]

Working relationships between park managers, military appointees to the NCS and the EEAA, and the local military officials in South Sinai facilitated extensions in the boundaries of the South Sinai protected areas. Ras Mohamed National Park was expanded in 1989 and 1991 to include coastal zones up to the highest equinox tide line. In 1992, two "multiple-use" areas were designated on the Gulf of 'Aqaba. With the creation of the St. Catherine's Protected Area, which encompassed much of the interior southern mountains, over a third of the territory of the South Sinai governorate was under formal protected status. The entire system of offshore coastal reefs was declared protected when the 1994 Environmental Law required a review of any development less than 200 feet from the highest tide line.

As the protected area network expanded, provincial governors played an increasingly prominent role in facilitating or constraining the infrastructural authority of the South Sinai protectorates. Appointed directly by the regime in Cairo, provincial governors controlled the issuing of all sorts of permits and licenses. Cooperative relationships with the governor simplified implementation of protected area management schemes, while conflicted relations could stall everything from housing construction for rangers to obtaining land for solid waste sites. Protected area managers thus sought to educate successive governors about the economic value of protected areas through field visits, formal and informal presentations, and providing public services, such as supplying a health clinic for local residents.

Governors, however, were often more interested in the direct financial benefits of resource exploitation from quarries, mines, and real estate development than in conservation. As regime appointees, they wanted to demonstrate meeting central plans and targets. For instance, the South Sinai governor wrote directly to the Minister of State for the Environment in 1998 to argue that attempts by the protected area managers to control quarrying in the St. Catherine protectorate were hindering mineral exploitation, blocking development, limiting employment, and leading to the depopulation of Sinai in the name of nature conservation (Pearson, 1990: 3).

As the network of protected areas consolidated itself across the landscape of southern and central Sinai, park managers also began to establish initiatives with Bedouin tribes in and around the parks. This was in stark contrast to the customary treatment of locals by the central government. The regime in Cairo had excluded Bedouin tribes from any significant participation in both central and provincial administrations; development plans focused on attracting elite investors and migrants from the Nile Delta rather than promoting tribal interests (International Crisis Group, 2007). The central government also appointed tribal sheikhs as intermediaries, restricting the mantle of tribal leadership to those approved by the regime.[11] Not surprisingly, therefore, field surveys conducted by the Nature Conservation Sector in 1996 found that "the relationship between Sinai Bedouin and Egyptian authorities is poor now, and communication is almost nonexistent" (Hobbs, 1996).

In contrast, the Nature Conservation Sector sought to build cooperative relationships with Bedouin tribes by providing employment and services, and by explicitly recognizing Bedouin land uses in protected areas. The two multiple-use areas of Nabq and Abu Ghalum recognized seasonal Bedouin settlements and traditional fishing areas, in contrast to the land use maps drawn up by the central ministries in Cairo. These multiple-use areas were also zoned to allowed limited tourism, while seeking to insulate the most sensitive ecosystems, such as mangroves, dune systems, and coral reefs, from development. In the Abu Ghalum protected area, for instance, about 20 percent of the area was zoned for tourism development, and traditional fishing was allowed along most of the offshore reef (Egyptian Environmental Affairs Agency and the European Union, 1993).

In the St. Catherine protected area, an estimated 7,000 Bedouin lived in and around the park in 2006 (Nature Conservation Sector, 2006). The St. Catherine protectorate employed forty-eight Bedouin out of its sixty-six employees by 2002, including thirty community guards. The protected area project helped establish a handicraft collective, FanSina, owned by its 300 Bedouin women employees, and also supported a veterinary clinic, a mobile health clinic, and an eco-lodge owned by twenty-seven Bedouin families (ibid.: 41).

Rangers also received training on community-based management of protected areas. One ranger recalled that spending three months in South Africa's Kruger National Park "changed my way of thinking about local communities. I learned how to talk with them and consult them."[12] While serving as the manager at the Taba protected area for seven years, he convened an informal steering committee of tribal leaders from local Bedouin tribes to provide input on park management decisions. Their input was influential in altering some park plans, such as the decision not to build a paved road to bring in more tourists by outside operators, but rather upgrade the existing camel path by which Bedouin transported tourists by jeep and camel. "We saved a lot of money on the road and we also helped the local community keep an important source of income," observed the ranger.[13]

## Liberalizing tourism and limiting conservation on Egypt's coastlines

Success in conserving portions of South Sinai through a network of protected areas was soon challenged by state promotion of coastal tourism development. State and donor interventions focused on liberalizing the tourism sector to encourage private investment in tourism services, infrastructure, and land development (Sakr *et al.*, 2009: 29).

Following an institutional blueprint supplied by USAID and the World Bank, Presidential Decree No. 274 for 1991 established the Tourism Development Agency (TDA) as a legally autonomous "economic authority" authorized to distribute vast tracts of coastal land (Ministry of Tourism, undated). Using property maps drawn up by the Ministry of Defense and Military Production, the TDA was allocated most desert land outside of municipal boundaries, protected areas, and military zones for tourism investment.[14] Under Egyptian law, all land not located within municipal boundaries or registered as private agricultural land is claimed as state property (*malakiyya khassa lil-hukuma*), and thus no legal provisions were made for customary and seasonal land uses.[15]

To encourage investment, land prices were set extremely low, ranging from US$1 per square meter along the Sinai coastline, whose offshore reefs are some of the most spectacular in the world, to US$10 per square meter near St. Catherine's monastery and Mount Sinai (Sowers, 2003: 225). Land was similarly priced along the Red Sea coast. The TDA allocated land on the basis of a nominal application, to be followed within three years by unspecified substantive improvements to the site. Investors enjoyed payment schedules of ten years, and 10–25-year tax holidays.[16]

This system of land allocation promoted speculation in land and a shift in land-holdings to large conglomerates. Cheap land costs combined with large minimum plot sizes encouraged large investors to buy extensively. Investors reported it was easier to pursue real estate development in Egypt than in the surrounding countries of Greece, Italy, and Turkey, because large land parcels were available and environmental restrictions were not enforced. In addition, the three-year deadline for making tangible investments in their parcel provided ample time for investors to make small changes while the price of land increased. An Egyptian consultant for the Ministry of Tourism told the author, "Investors who have money may just wait to develop the land they purchase, so that the price increases in the meantime. The smaller ones do the same, but use bank loans to tide them over."[17] As the IMF noted in a critical review of these policies, delayed investment requirements and tax holidays merely restricted general state revenues and increased the tax burden on medium and small-sized firms unable to join the land acquisition rush (Goldrup, 1998; International Monetary Fund, 1998).

Reportedly, the TDA transferred a number of land parcels to ex-military and security officials as well as private investors, many of whom resold the land as prices escalated. In interviews, some businessmen were candid about their decision to diversify into tourism and land development. One, a well-known importer of Ford automobiles, observed, "We diversify to follow the profitable sectors. A few years ago this was land, bought from developers in Sharm el-Sheikh and the Red Sea. I own some, bought from a developer who owned huge tracts."[18]

Large investors typically combined tourism resort construction with investments in luxury secondary housing. The demand for coastal vacation villas and secondary apartments on the coast stemmed from several factors, including the paucity of secure investment vehicles for Egyptians other than land as well as increasing demand from the upper classes for holiday locations far from the crowded beaches of traditional holiday destinations, such as Alexandria, 'Agami, and Ma'moura. Most resort complexes built on the Red Sea and Sinai coasts therefore mixed hotels and holiday villages with villas, apartments, and/or timeshare sales. Many of the investors working on the coastlines also developed dedicated luxury gated communities around Cairo, such as Muhammad Farid Khamis in al-Shorouq, the Tal'at Mustafa Group in al-Rihab, and Ahmad Bahgat in Dreamland.

State policies and economic incentives thus combined to produce spectacular growth in Egyptian coastal tourism development during the 1990s and 2000s. Between 1993 and 2007, according to Egypt's Ministry of Tourism, the number of tourist arrivals increased from 1.5 million to 11.1 million, tourism receipts rose in value from US$1.9 billion to US$9.5 billion, and lodging capacity grew from 27,300 rooms to 190,200 (Sakr *et al.*, 2009: 4). Egypt's coastlines along the Red Sea and the Sinai Peninsula accounted for the bulk of this investment.

The list of developers involved in coastal real estate included the wealthiest business conglomerates and investors in Egypt. One scientist who had worked extensively in coastal zone management for the Red Sea told the author in 1999 that:

> Before, we used to say that the coastal tourism sector was the *hajj* [an older man] with the *lukanda* [small, non-luxury hotel] near the railway station, who then went to Hurghada (on the Red Sea) and built anything. But now it is only the tycoons.[19]

The "Charming Sharm Company," for instance, was a consortium of twenty-eight investors including Muhammad Farid Khamis, owner of Oriental Weavers and former head of the Egyptian Businessmen's Association. The consortium bought land in the Nabq protectorate development zone, ten kilometers north of Sharm el-Sheikh, for US$1 a square meter to be paid in ten-year installments with a three-year grace period on payments (Atraqchi, 1998).

El Gouna, a 9.93 million cubic meter parcel on the Red Sea developed and majority-owned by Orascom Development Holdings, contained fourteen hotels, two tourist villages, a golf course, several marinas, shopping malls, a vineyard, a bottling company, a brewery, and a hospital, in addition to 1,350 villas and 1,940 apartments (International Finance Corporation, 1997). For the *Financial Times*, El Gouna's "pastel-painted domes and turrets beside a manmade lagoon" were "the brashest symbol of the Egyptian private sector's relentless investment drive" (Huband, 1998). The International Finance Corporation (IFC), the private investment arm of the World Bank, invested not only in El Gouna, where it held a 5 percent stake, but also with the Farid Saad Group, developing the Red Sea resort of Abu Soma (Fiana and Partners, 1998: 224). Farid Saad was the former managing director of the Egyptian American Bank, as well as the import licensee for Nestle and Xerox in Egypt.

Not surprisingly, charges of corruption dogged investors and tourism officials long before the 2011 uprising brought formal charges against some of the most well-known figures in coastal real estate. Since the TDA wielded considerable discretionary powers to approve investment applications and collect revenues from land sales, top officials were frequently accused of wrongdoing. The first tourism minister to preside over the rapid allocation of coastal land, Fu'ad Sultan, resigned in 1994 over parliamentary allegations of corruption and favoritism. He later joined the board of directors of Orascom Development, one of the largest firms in Egypt and owned by the Suweiris family.

While elite business groups bought up land, local Bedouin communities were systematically excluded from the boom in coastal tourism. Beginning under the Israeli occupation of the Sinai Peninsula, Bedouin established small camps to service tourists, typically consisting of small huts, an open-air restaurant, a bathing area, and arrangements for diving trips and desert safaris. These operations, with low tourist densities and use of local materials, were local forms of ecotourism. As the real estate and tourism market saw an influx of Gulf and Egyptian investment along the Gulf of 'Aqaba during the 1990s, however, bulldozers and truckloads of soldiers forcibly displaced a number of existing small Bedouin camps established to service tourists (Bortot, 1999).

Government agencies at all levels proved hostile to Bedouin land claims and few Bedouin successfully entered the expanding tourism sector. The only Bedouin to own a hotel and dive operation in Sharm el-Sheikh recalled the many difficulties he faced in an interview in 2011:

> I acquired a fishing boat and a local fishing license near Sharm el Sheikh in 1981. The Egyptian navy soon caught me near Tiran Island with an American photographer and his Israeli assistant, and told me that I was not allowed to take tourists without a permit for tourism, even though we Bedouin had done this when the Israelis were in control of the area, and we know the Red Sea very well. I went to prison in al-Tor, paid a fine, and then was released. A court eventually found in my favor, but still I had stopped work for three months.
>
> So then I tried to get a legal tourist boat—I called her Freedom I. I built the boat here myself. The Egyptian officials told me I could only get the boat license to be skipper in Suez. So I traveled to Suez, and then to Alexandria, but each time the authorities refused. I have a friend who works in Cairo for the Nile Water Police, so I also tried through the Water Police. Still no luck— the water police said I needed a LE6,000 radio before they would consider my application.
>
> Eventually I built a jetty, working illegally, here on the coast. I eventually was able to buy this land and legalize my jetty by finding a person from the government side to go in with me. I paid for the whole parcel but he got to take half of the land. The cost was LE5 per meter.
>
> My story is like thousands of other Bedouin. The Bedouin feel like rubbish; we are treated like garbage. The government always uses the excuse of "the bad Bedouin" to deny us access to land and work. What has been left for us?[20]

The Tourism Development Authority was no different than other Egyptian government authorities in their approach towards Bedouin land ownership in the tourism sector. In an ill-concealed attempt to justify displacement of local Bedouin from areas zoned for tourism, a glossy investor brochure produced by the TDA for the 'Aqaba coastline noted that:

The Om Mreikha Center [for Bedouin] was established in order to overcome the growing trend of Bedouin squatting in beach areas close to the borders of the Nuweiba city. This trend is quite dangerous and the establishment of the center would halt it and provide for a safer and more environmentally healthy region.

(Tourism Development Authority, undated)

## Social and environmental impacts of coastal tourism development

Rapid tourism development of Egypt's coastlines produced a number of social and environmental impacts. In South Sinai, the pace of land development from private investors and corrupt state officials soon overwhelmed government planning functions. By the EEAA's accounting, between 1982 and 1993 the general population increased by 66 percent in southern Sinai settlements (Gulf of 'Aqaba Protectorates Development Programme, 1997). While the total population increased from 28,929 people to 54,495 inhabitants between 1986 and 1996, far short of the Ministry of Planning targets for permanent residents, the numbers of tourism rooms far exceeded those set by the same ministry (Cole and Al-Turki, 1998: 11). In 1993–4, the numbers of tourist rooms set for the Ministry of Planning until the year 2017 were already exceeded in Sharm el-Sheikh by 60 percent (European Union and EEAA, 1998). The response of the Ministry of Planning was simply to repeatedly revise the targets for numbers of tourist beds upwards. The governorate followed suit: in the tenure of one governor of South Sinai, tourist bed ceilings for municipal land were repeatedly increased with no assessments of the consequences for municipal infrastructure.[21]

The TDA primarily sold linear coastal parcels with little development in clusters or townships to use land behind the direct coast. These parcels neglected to preserve such critical features as wadi flood zones, coastal access for investors behind the shoreline, or access for the public. This pattern of land allocation also discouraged economies of scale in infrastructure and public services that could have been achieved by grouping smaller parcels together in clusters. The TDA's marketing brochures for the northern 'Aqaba coastline, which it depicted as a new "Egyptian Riviera," exemplified the extensive, linear designs proposed for tourism resorts (Figure 5.1).

This "Egyptian Riviera" marketing campaign captured the dreams of tourism officials and the fears of conservation experts. Long denounced in planning circles as a model of overdevelopment, the French Riviera was hardly a model for conservation. The lack of awareness about the tourism potential of Egypt's reefs, in particular, among the top officials at the Tourism Development Authority in the late 1990s was striking. In an interview with the author in 1999, the head of the TDA lamented, "Here in Egypt, the marine attractions are not polished, they are not prepared. We have no Sea World, no aquariums, no sea restaurants."[22] This vision of tourism minimized Sinai's greatest tourism assets, namely ecosystems that in terms of diversity and beauty could not be matched by aquariums or constructed attractions. Most of the European tourists who made up over half of Red Sea and Sinai tourism in 1997 were attracted precisely to the rugged wilderness and stunning undersea vistas that neither the French Riviera nor Sea World provide. The TDA, however, continued to use the Riviera-themed marketing campaign to attract investors to the Red Sea coastline (Chemonics International, 2008: 5).

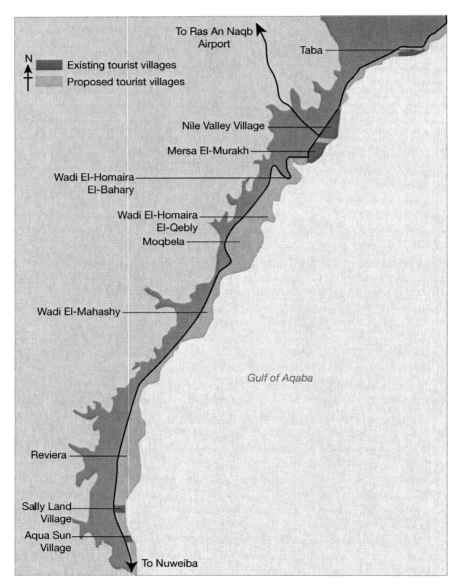

*Figure 5.1* Tourism Development Authority plan for "the Egyptian Riviera," northern Gulf of 'Aqaba

Source: Tourism Development Authority, 1999, promotional brochure

The TDA thus made little attempt to diversify tourism offerings to include ecotourism or low-impact forms of nature-based tourism. The tycoons and international hotel management chains alike generally strove to replicate the aesthetic and level of amenities found in luxury beach tourism elsewhere. In contrast to ideals put forth under the rubric of "eco-tourism" or vernacular architecture movements, which celebrate the unique aesthetics and materials of a particular location and culture, luxury secondary homes and hotels promoted the homogeneity of their products regardless of the singular attributes of place. Sinai had its own models of ecotourism, in local Bedouin camps and in such innovative small resorts as Basata (simplicity in Arabic), that conserved water, separated and recycled wastes, and used local materials and vernacular designs in resort construction. The TDA showed no interest in replicating or scaling up these kinds of tourism facilities. According to the head of the TDA, the government considered ecotourism a market niche that would not bring in the desired mass numbers of tourists.[23]

The impact of rampant tourist development quickly became clear. A 1998 field survey of thirty-one hotels compiled by the Sinai protectorate staff to monitor resort development in Sharm el-Sheikh found that almost every resort engaged in construction and operating practices that damaged offshore reefs (South Sinai Sector Staff, 1998). In addition, increasing numbers of desalination plants providing water for towns and resorts pumped concentrated brine effluent over the reefs.

Tourist development brought influxes of employees, tourists, and laborers to the region, with consequent increased demand for natural resources and municipal services, but with no mechanism for extracting taxes from private investors. Local governments and the NCS had little leverage to compel investors and central government ministries, particularly the Ministry of Tourism, to address the environmental and social "externalities" produced by the proliferation of enclave luxury resorts. Like other municipal authorities in Egypt, the South Sinai governorate and city budgets were centrally allocated, with no local accounting mechanisms for costs of services and needs assessment.

Water supply provided a striking example. Scarce water resources had long been decried by the government as the limiting factor to population expansion in Sinai, yet the boom in tourism development was decoupled from considerations of freshwater supply. A pipeline under construction to carry Nile water to southern Sinai was projected to use only half of its capacity due to limited supplies of Nile water. Generally hotels and resorts erected their own electricity generators and desalination plants, precluding economies of scale in utilities. Existing water, sewer, and power supplies did not perform to original capacity or specifications. The municipal water distribution in Sharm el-Sheikh, for instance, had estimated losses of 40 percent, while a nearby desalination plant built during the Israeli occupation had a desalination capacity of 1,750 cubic meters per day but by 1998 was only producing 400 cubic meters per day (European Union and EEAA, 1998: Annex 7: 11). Municipal sewage oxidation ponds were badly damaged and barely functioned, releasing untreated effluent into the water table. Since existing water systems did not meet municipal demand, water was increasingly trucked into towns and cities.

As water was trucked in or desalinated for ordinary household use, luxury hotel development, including golf courses and multiple outdoor swimming pools, consumed far more water than municipal usages. The average freshwater pool in South Sinai, given evaporation rates, required 25,000 liters daily, which was equivalent to the daily consumption of fifty guests in a five-star hotel, or the daily requirements of 300–400 urban residents in Sinai (ibid.: 5).

## Creating legal and infrastructural authority for protected areas in South Sinai

Drawing on their legal authority to review developments that impacted coastal setbacks, park managers asked tourism investors to submit environmental impact assessments (EIAs) and project designs in order to identify problems and recommend mitigation measures. Recalled one military appointee to the NCS, "Some of the EIAs submitted for the Red Sea projects were just one page, containing no useful information. So we went directly to investors or the TDA to discuss project plans."[24] During the late 1990s and 2000s, rangers thus found much of their time dedicated to monitoring development sites, trying to rectify or minimize mistakes already made by investors and construction companies.

The South Sinai protectorates operated under a political constraint to accept virtually all projects in some form; observed the program manager in 1998:

> We never apply the law in its strict sense, because if we did, the government would call us anti-development and shoot us down. So we don't reject a development, but we try to propose ways to mediate or prevent damage, and explain to investors why this is in their own best interest.[25]

Protected area managers offered investors input into the design of lagoons, marinas, construction works, setback use, and disposal methods and, in return, obtained information about investment projects otherwise unavailable to them.

This informal, personalized form of coordination was possible, however, only when the number of investors was small. The rapid growth in tourism investment overwhelmed the emerging institutional capacities of the protectorates to monitor coastal development. The TDA approved investment applications regardless of the status of environmental impact assessments, while the pace of construction soon strained the small numbers of protectorate staff qualified to monitor investor compliance. The TDA did not supply the protectorates with information on allocated properties nor did it inform developers of existing regulations (South Sinai Sector Staff, 1998). In addition, the authority allocated land deemed unsuitable for construction, located in flood areas, security zones, or within the coastal setback area, without seeking the required EEAA approval.[26]

As investment accelerated during the mid-1990s, protectorate managers shifted from personal negotiation with investors to litigation. Their aim was to call attention to indiscriminate land allocations and the increasing number of coastal violations. The EEAA prosecutor reported to the author in 1998 that he had filed over two hundred cases against investors on the Red Sea and 'Aqaba coasts, but that without a system of civil liability in place prosecutions were difficult.[27] The Egyptian legal system was perfectly capable of devising laws for environmental civil liability, as fines for reef damage had long been quantified and monetized.[28] No such system of civil penalties, however, existed for violations by tourism investors, meaning that the prosecutor could only file criminal charges, a much higher threshold for legal action, and the charges could be dismissed through the personal intervention of the president, any minister, or the centrally appointed governors. The prosecutor further reported that he was under pressure from his superiors not to file cases involving elite investors.

Nevertheless, the environmental agency's prosecutor was able to obtain convictions in several court cases against leading investors. In the case of the five-star Hilton Residence built in 1990 in Sharm el-Sheikh, the EEAA sued for illegal fill of the shoreline. The owner was eventually convicted, but assessed a mere LE1 fine and a one-year prison term, from which he was excused. Hussein Salem, one of the first business tycoons to be charged with corruption in the post-Mubarak era, claimed land inside a protected area in order to construct a presidential villa; the prosecutor's cases went to the highest court to stop construction.[29]

## Tourism and protected areas on the Red Sea

Along the Red Sea coast, developing legal and infrastructural authority for protected areas proved even more challenging than it had in the Sinai Peninsula. Whereas the protected areas regime began in Sinai prior to tourism development, along the Red Sea coast tourism development outpaced the development of protected areas management. The TDA was given jurisdiction to develop most of the Red Sea coastline, including a five-kilometer strip from the shoreline inland. In contrast to the Gulf of 'Aqaba, where a significant proportion of the coastline was eventually designated as protected and the coastal protectorates were territorially compact, terrestrial protected areas in the Red Sea consisted of two huge remote and rugged southern areas, Wadi al-Gamal and Gabal 'Elba, near the border with Sudan, as well as a number of offshore islands with fringing reefs. In these remote areas it proved much more difficult for the Nature Conservation Sector to establish an institutional presence on the ground, in part because the military viewed these areas through the prism of border security.

International donors, particularly USAID, funded several projects for environmental management on the Red Sea coast, beginning in 1998 and continuing throughout the 2000s. As in the EU South Sinai areas, Egyptian conservation experts staffed key positions in these projects, working with such well-known US firms as Chemonics International and Winrock International. USAID support was channeled in large part through the Egyptian Environmental Policy Project (1998–2004), in which a significant component was directed toward land use planning for the Red Sea, followed by the US$17 million LIFE Red Sea project (2005–8). In addition to direct budgetary support of the Red Sea protectorates, USAID projects sought to introduce what the agency termed "sustainable tourism development." The USAID-funded "Red Sea Sustainable Tourism Initiative" published best practices guidelines for coastal resort development, supported the creation of investor associations, and sought to create an environmental unit within the TDA itself. These initiatives reflected USAID's ongoing attempt to work with the "private sector" in the belief that, as one USAID project document noted, "the design and program of an individual property is a personal and private decision" (Tourism Development Authority and United States Agency for International Development, 1998: 7). This project orientation ran counter to attempts by protected area managers to more directly influence investor decision-making, as had been done in South Sinai.

Instead, USAID supported creating environmental tourism investor associations. Members of these associations, however, consisted almost exclusively of large investors. For example, the attendees at the 1998 founding meeting of the "Tourism Investors' Association to Protect the Environment" (*Jam'iyyat Mustathmari al-Siyaha lil-Hifaz 'ala al-Bi'a*) included Orascom Development's Samih Suweiris, the Minister of Tourism, the Minister of Environment, and the head of the Tourism Development Authority. The men convened under the banner that read, "Tourism is a friend of the environment" (*al-siyaha sadiq al-Bi'a*) ("The Ministers of Tourism and Environment...," 1998). The meeting highlighted the use of best practices and environmentally friendly tourism. Yet none of the investors present had invested in an ecotourism development, at least by the standards laid out in USAID's manual on ecolodges: low-density, unobtrusive designs, local aesthetics and materials, and limited impact on the surrounding environment.

Egyptian conservation experts knew that "the private sector," as an entity, would not take the lead on developing environmentally sensitive coastal developments, any more than "the state" had done so. These undifferentiated categories were of little value, in any case, for untangling the skein of land acquisition deals that unfurled during the 2000s as the TDA rapidly allocated coastal property.

One of the primary goals of USAID's Egyptian Environmental Policy project was thus the development of a comprehensive, binding land use plan for the Red Sea coast, to be officially agreed upon by the Ministry of Tourism, the Ministry of State for Environmental Affairs, and the Red Sea governorate. The land use plan was to secure designated protected areas and promote a diverse array of tourism offerings, including ecotourism. To encourage governmental authorities to participate, USAID offered lump-sum cash transfers (tranches) once the land use master plan was officially signed. The fate of this Red Sea master plan aptly illustrates the difficulties that managerial conservation networks faced in seeking to strengthen legal regimes for land use planning and conservation. Reflecting back on the master plan he had helped to devise, a leading Egyptian environmental consultant observed:

> The ministers finally signed the agreement, but then the map simply disappeared. A new minister at the EEAA, a new Red Sea governor, and a new tourism minister were appointed, and they never even knew about the map.

Everyone just pretended it didn't exist. The biggest mistake was that USAID transferred the lump-sum funds without any conditions for implementation. If USAID had tried to make the project more transparent from the beginning, however, the Egyptian governmental authorities would simply have said they didn't want it.[30]

The TDA thus continued to distribute land throughout the southern Red Sea as if there had been no laboriously agreed-upon master plan. When project managers complained that the plan was clearly overlooked in the rapid tourism development on the coast, newly appointed officials claimed ignorance of their predecessors' decisions.[31]

Managerial networks were somewhat more successful in leveraging donor assistance to build institutional capacities within the Nature Conservation Sector itself for the Red Sea zone. Between 1999 and 2003, the number of employees working in the Red Sea marine zone increased from twelve to fifty-four, most of whom were park rangers (Colby, 2002: 11). In 2003, USAID reported that it financed 95 percent of the Red Sea protected area unit's operating costs for the year, including employing three Egyptian conservation experts to staff the program management unit (Abdel Razek, 2003: 14). USAID's LIFE project also supported upgrading of tribal settlements in and around the southern Red Sea protectorates, providing training and marketing in local handicrafts, and the provision of basic services, such as generators and solid waste collection.

By creating a staffing and management presence in the Red Sea protectorates, donor funds helped the NCS attract centrally allocated budgetary resources. The EEAA expenditures on the Red Sea protectorates kept pace with USAID spending; between 1999 and 2003, USAID spent US$1.1 million on the Red Sea protectorates, while the EEAA spent US$1.2 million (Abdel Razek, 2003).

These investments, however, were not sufficient to meet the expanding needs of protectorates in trying to safeguard coastal habitats. As the only institutional presence responsible for enforcing Egypt's major environmental laws (Law 102/1983 and Law 4/1994), rangers were charged with a diverse and expanding set of tasks that included monitoring protected areas, reefs, and islands, enforcing no-fishing zones in cooperation with the Coast Guard, responding to visitor needs, liaising with local communities, and other tasks (Colby, 2002: 3). In 2002, the then-director of the Nature Conservation Sector, Mustafa Fouda, and a working group of Red Sea rangers estimated that, for the Red Sea protectorates to be managed adequately, total expenditures needed to increase from approximately US$1 million per year (shared between USAID and the EEAA) to US$4 million (ibid.).

Within the Red Sea protected areas, environmental experts working with the NCS and donor projects found the protectorates' legal authority over the land increasingly challenged by the military, security forces, and the TDA. For example, USAID's LIFE project enlisted well-known Egyptian conservation experts, such as the ornithologist Sharif Baha El-Din, to devise a coastal sensitivity mapping protocol for the Gabal 'Elba Protected Area, which borders Sudan on the southern Red Sea coast. Conservation experts wanted to devise a protocol that rangers could use to rank areas of critical biodiversity and ecosystem importance. As USAID contractor Chemonics International noted, "The activity was given high priority because coastal areas in the Elba PA [protected area] had been purportedly sold to developers by the TDA" (Chemonics International, 2007a). After an initial mission to the area, the joint team of Egyptian experts and park rangers were denied permission to return by the security services. Thwarted in their attempt to map the 'Elba coastline, the team instead conducted a pilot mapping in a section of the Wadi al-Gamal Protected Area that the TDA had sold to developers (Chemonics International, 2007b).

One of the greatest challenges to attempts to build management capacities in the Red Sea protected areas was thus the property claims of the TDA itself. For instance, USAID attempts to build a visitor center and ranger operation center in Wadi al-Gamal National Park provoked long negotiations with the TDA, which claimed it owned the land. The resolution of this inter-agency conflict confirmed the TDA property claim, as a report by a USAID contracting firm noted: "The TDA agreed to give the EEAA a ninety-nine-year concession to use the land, without charge, so the structures could be built" (Chemonics International, 2008: 10). The TDA further allowed resort development within the boundaries of the Wadi al-Gamal Protected Area itself. By 2011, the Gorgonia Beach Resort offered guests 350 rooms, three restaurants, six bars, a theater, a disco, four swimming pools, excellent sports facilities, and 700 meters of white sandy beach, all inside the protected area.[32]

As in Sinai, the social and environmental impacts of tourism development were not adequately addressed. Resort construction, intensive diving, and oil contamination contributed to a reduction in coral cover of up to 30 percent in some portions of the Red Sea reefs (Pilcher and Abou Zaid, 2000). In one of the first areas to be developed, the town of Hurghada (al-Ghardaqa) on the Red Sea coast, investors built forty-two major recreational resorts and seventy private or individual projects (Frihy *et al.*, 1996: 324). Egyptian marine scientists found extensive ill effects upon the coastal reef ecosystems, stemming from dredging, the construction of artificial beaches, lagoons, marinas, jetties that altered the coastline, and inadequate handling of solid and liquid wastes (El-Gamily *et al.*, 1997; Frihy *et al.*, 1996). The researchers concluded, "Irrational projects implemented with improper designs have progressively created deterioration of the coastal ecosystem" (Frihy *et al.*, 1996).

Also as in Sinai, local tribal land use claims were overlooked, tourism employment excluded local residents, and public services for expanding municipalities were entirely inadequate. In 2008, a USAID-funded report observed that "local residents made up only 3 percent of the tourism workforce industry in the Red Sea governorate" (Chemonics International, 2008: 21). Tourist establishments linked to the municipal network did not pay sewage costs, and resorts were not required to create or subsidize the construction of landfills. Municipalities faced serious budget constraints in establishing public services for trash collection and disposal, and resorts paid for private collection trucks that then dumped trash anywhere. Piles of trash, particularly plastics of all sorts, dumped in streets, wadis, and vacant lots in the backs of houses, was thus the most visible sign of failed public service provision. As one reporter wrote in 1997, "Lack of clean water, adequate housing, managed waste collection, and reasonable wages have locals bearing the brunt of tourism growth" (Marsh, 1997).

## Activist conservation networks in the Red Sea

Environmental degradation in and around Hurghada eventually sparked the creation of an activist conservation network based largely on the concern of dive operators to protect the reef systems on which their livelihood depended. A handful of resident foreigners and Egyptians that owned and operated dive centers and live-aboard diving boats thus founded the Hurghada Environmental Protection and Conservation Association (HEPCA) in 1990. Unlike most environmental organizations in Egypt, HEPCA drew upon fee-paying members to support its advocacy and activities. The organization accepts only institutional members that pay annual dues of LE1,200. As of 2011, members included dive centers and live-aboard diving boats, a few resorts, restaurants, international tourism operators, and the Suweiris' construction firm Orascom.[33] In addition, USAID and several Egyptian companies found funding the organization attractive as part of their broader efforts to promote environmental awareness in "the private sector."

HEPCA's first initiative was to install a mooring system for boats to safely anchor near coastal and island fringing reefs. Increasing numbers of dive boats had extensively damaged the reefs; without moorings in place, boats simply dropped anchor on the reefs. Supported by USAID and member dues, HEPCA had installed 1,064 moorings along the Red Sea coastline by 2011. It currently produces the moorings locally and has exported the product to other Red Sea states, notably Jordan and Saudi Arabia.

By 2004, the organization began experimenting with direct environmental advocacy. The TDA had awarded Italian investors an entire island, Giftoun, off the Hurghada coast, for tourism development. HEPCA coordinated the Hurghada diving community to go on strike, and launched several public street protests that received significant media attention. As in the popular campaigns against the fertilizer plant in Damietta, media coverage proved an effective means to capture the attention of the highest levels of the Egyptian regime. Shortly thereafter, Mubarak issued a presidential decree banning the sale of entire islands.

Emboldened, the organization began to take the TDA to court over its land use allocations, as the EEAA legal department had tried to do as well. As a member of HEPCA observed in 2011:

> there are 806 kilometers of fringing reef along the Red Sea coast and therefore there are 860 kilometers that the TDA is trying to develop. Just in the 200 kilometers between the cities of Quseir and Marsa Allam on the southern Red Sea coast, there are 3,200 rooms in TDA projects.[34]

The organization filed seventy-six cases against the TDA between its founding in 1990 and 2011. In its legal filings, HEPCA tried to establish that coral reefs constituted "productive public property" in order to extend protections present in Egyptian law for agricultural land.

In order to build infrastructural authority for conservation along the Red Sea coast, HEPCA initially sought cooperative relationships with the NCS. As noted by most environmental experts, however, during the 2000s the NCS, like the environmental agency as a whole, saw top staff positions increasingly drawn from the ranks of ex-military and internal security men. "The minister kicked out many of the scientists and brought in 'trustworthy' generals," argued a HEPCA representative. "We've seen the national park authority falling apart, so we have tried to step in where we can."[35]

To compensate, the dive operators' organization worked more closely with the existing managerial conservation network to undertake specific conservation initiatives along the Red Sea. HEPCA's 2011 advisory board reflected this mix of activists and experts. It included the former director of the NCS; the primary Egyptian consultant to USAID's Egyptian Environmental Policy Project; one of the leading businessmen advocating for ecotourism through newspaper and media work; two resident foreigners that founded early dive centers in the Red Sea; and an outspoken local entrepreneur who has developed two environmentally friendly dive resorts in the Red Sea.

As protected area managers had sought to do in Sinai, HEPCA's board tried to inform and educate governors on the economic value of marine conservation. In doing so, they were able to get official support for initiatives like an official decree banning the use of plastic bags in the Red Sea governorate. HEPCA also sought to build infrastructural capacities on the ground. The association purchased a few fast, small boats to conduct patrols of the coastline to supplement the woefully inadequate patrols conducted by the Egyptian Coast Guard and Navy. They hired ex-generals as consultants, to help navigate the rocky shoals of competing personal and bureaucratic interests of the Red Sea governorate, the Navy (responsible for Red Sea offshore islands), and the Coast Guard, with jurisdiction over the coastline to three miles out. They used the international and local press to publicize cases of environmental damage and violations. HEPCA also tried to provide direct support to rangers working in the Red Sea protectorate, bypassing the central environmental agency, just as the former head of the NCS had also tried to do. When rangers received more lucrative offers to work in the Gulf, for example, HEPCA found some of them alternative employment with the organization to keep them in Egypt. Lastly, HEPCA eventually also moved into providing solid waste collection and recycling to address the pressing solid waste problem in Hurghada. By 2011, HEPCA was the sole contractor with the Hurghada municipality for trash collection, separation, and disposal, employing 896 people in total.

For most of HEPCA's activities, governmental entities remained necessary counterparts even as they were often obstacles to implementing initiatives. As a HEPCA member observed:

You cannot simply get into a conflict with the government. You need to find someone in the government—one side of a triangle—to help neutralize objections from other parts of the government. You need to have at least one part of the government in the boat with you. So that when the conflict goes to the top, it is not a conflict between an NGO like ours, and the government, but between government agencies.[36]

HEPCA was thus a new kind of conservation interest group in Egypt, prompted by the interests of the diving business community in trying to slow degradation of Red Sea reefs. HEPCA's work highlighted how activist campaigns need not be restricted to the kinds of popular movements in urban areas analyzed in the previous chapter. The institutional members shared a clear economic stake in reef protection. Through coastal patrols, solid waste operations, autonomous financial resources, and an ongoing (if conflicted) relationship with governorate officials and generals, the association wielded some infrastructural authority to influence outcomes along the Red Sea.

## Activist campaigns for protected areas

HEPCA was not the first voluntary association to campaign on behalf of protected areas. Efforts by the EEAA legal department to litigate against violations in and around protected efforts were widely publicized and set a precedent for environmental associations to follow suit by the late 1990s. As the existence of protected areas (*mahmiyat*) became more widely known, the legal framework governing protected areas became increasingly recognized as an avenue to contest unpopular land uses in general. A letter in the government-owned daily newspaper *Al-Ahram* in 1998 provided a humorous example: the correspondent noted that since the ex-Minister of Tourism had allowed several villas to be built on the grounds of Alexandria's Muntaza Palace, supposedly a public park, the palace grounds should be declared as a protected area if they were to be salvaged (The "Green Man," 1998).

Several NGOs employed Law 102 to sue the environmental agency and provincial governors for mismanaging formally designated protected areas. In the case of Wadi Sannur in Bani Suwayf, the Land Center for Human Rights sued the environmental agency in 1997, claiming that the agency had not enforced restrictions on illicit quarrying in the protectorate's marble caves (Saber and Abu Zeid, 1998). The Land Center's network of lawyers and activists hailed from an array of leftist opposition perspectives; most had worked on human rights campaigns or in union and labor activism in the 1980s and 1990s.[37] The Land Center filed several cases on behalf of whistleblower rangers, injured workers, and the Bani Suwayf Local Council, citing the governor and the EEAA as defendants and seeking compensatory damages.

Another network of activists coalesced around threats to Wadi Digla, a canyon located on the outskirts of Ma'adi, the tiny suburb at Cairo's southeastern edge. After a campaign by the Tree Lovers' Association, a local group based in Ma'adi, whose residents used the geologically rich area for hiking and school trips, the wadi was declared a protected area in 1999. The head of the association report-edly enjoyed cordial relations with the regime, helping to usher the case through the EEAA to the Cabinet (Stanford, 1999). The EEAA hired several conservation experts to survey biodiversity in the area and propose boundaries for the new protectorate. Yet the maps and field studies produced were not used; instead, the protectorate was designated as a long and narrow area difficult to protect from encroaching land uses and illegal waste dumping.[38]

The Wadi Digla protected area directly abuts Shaqq al-Thu'ban, a complex of approximately 400 small-scale factories that represent 60–70 percent of all marble working in Egypt, employing up to half a million workers (Elmusa, 2009: 191). Existing workshops were grandfathered into the buffer zone of the protected area but, in 2006, new marble factories were licensed under a protocol between the EEAA and the Ministry of Industry (ibid.: 191). The protocol did not include pro-visions to contain or dispose of slurry and dust generated from quarrying, cutting, and transport, or the solid waste produced by the factories. Plastic bags and other trash from the factories, a nearby recycling center, and inadequate solid waste disposal blew into the wadi (ibid.: 192). As on the Red Sea coast, plastic waste proved a significant threat to local fauna and increasingly destroyed the aesthetics of desert landscapes. Despite ongoing activism on the part of the Tree Lovers' Association and other concerned citizens, Wadi Digla remained encroached upon and increasingly polluted.

In these local campaigns to protect specific protected areas, Egypt's mana-gerial conservation experts did not play a significant role. Some members of Egypt's conservation network eventually created their own association, Nature Conservation Egypt, which they formally registered with the government in the late 2000s. The group did not engage in significant activism until 2011, however, when risks from tourism investment in and around protected areas in the Fayoum oasis intensified and Egypt's January 25 uprising offered new possibilities for mobilization, as discussed in the concluding chapter.

## An autonomous authority for protected areas?

The erosion in top leadership and institutional capacity that characterized the EEAA during the 2000s, analyzed in Chapter 2, also impacted the EEAA's Nature Conservation Sector. President Mubarak's political appointees from the police, military, and security forces were widely regarded as ineffective advocates for conservation, and unable to counteract the political appeal and economic ben-efits associated with tourism development. The NCS found itself chronically underfunded, understaffed, and hampered by the standardized, cumbersome, and centralized procedures governing Egypt's governmental institutions.

At the same time, visitation rates to Egypt's protected areas had skyrocketed. Between 2003 and 2008, 1.6 million tourists visited Egypt's protected areas, with an annual average increase of 9.5 percent (Global Environmental Facility, 2010: 14). Of these visitors, 47.1 percent went to the Red Sea, 22.1 percent visited the reefs at Ras Mohamed, and 20.1 percent headed to the South Sinai interior of St. Catherine (ibid.). During the same period, the protected areas generated LE17.3 million in entrance fees, even though entrance rates were kept at a mere US$3–5 for foreigners and LE2–5 for Egyptians (ibid.: 15).

Yet little of the money generated by entrance fees was reinvested in the protected area network. Investments in the entire Nature Conservation Sector from the state budget in 2006 did not amount to even half of the revenues generated from the South Sinai protected areas (Child, 2006). In 2006, Egypt spent approximately US$19 per square kilometer on its protected areas; in contrast, mean expenditures for all developing countries in 1999 averaged US$157 per square kilometer, while in the Middle East and North Africa region, the equivalent figure was US$74 per square kilometer (ibid.: 7). As one report noted, "In order to reach the regional, or developing country, norms, Egypt would need to invest between $7.4 million and $15.7 million annually in its national protected area system—a four- to nine-fold increase in current levels of expenditure" (Nature Conservation Sector, 2006). Protectorate staffing levels were correspondingly low relative to the global mean of twenty-seven employees per 1,000 kilometers; in 2006, the NCS employed 512 persons, while to perform at the global mean it would have needed to employ 2,700 (ibid.).

For Egypt's most visited parks, the discrepancies in use and reinvested funds were even greater. Ras Mohamed Marine Park generated US$1.972 million in 2004–5, of which only US$200,000 was reinvested in the park (Harper, 2006: B-69). In contrast, the recreational value to the Egyptian economy of the Ras Mohamed coral reefs for the Egyptian economy was estimated at between US$142 and US$191 million per year, not including ecosystem services or tourism-related employment (Tawfik, 2004). For some within the protectorate authority, the culmination of governmental underfinancing was the deaths of four rangers within a six-month period in the mid-2000s in several of the more isolated protected areas, incidents marked by equipment failures and inadequate training.[39]

A rapid assessment of protected area management effectiveness carried out in 2006 highlighted some of these challenges (Nature Conservation Sector, 2006). The first such exercise in the Arab world, and a very rare one in any Egyptian state agency, the assessment asked lower and mid-level employees to assess management effectiveness and pressures on the protected area in which they worked. Egyptian experts adapted a questionnaire devised by the World Wildlife Fund for use in Egypt. In two days of workshops, seventy-two rangers and managers gave their views on the extent of illegal activities in their protected area, the role of police and other state authorities, the extent of corruption and pressures to exploit resources, difficulties in recruiting and retaining staff, levels of staff and resources, the extent to which the protectorate safeguarded biodiversity, legal protections, conflicts of use, boundaries, and property rights, and adequacy of environmental impact assessment procedures, among other issues.

The assessment asked protected area personnel to rank the greatest threats to their reserve. The principal challenges were reported as land use conversions, tourism and recreation, and hunting (ibid.). As shown in Figure 5.2, protected areas on the Red Sea coastline, St. Catherine in South Sinai, and Wadi al-Assuti in the upper Nile Valley scored as the areas facing the most significant threats and pressures. Employees felt that these threats persisted because of severe shortages and delays in government funding, a low level of political support, insufficient staffing, a lack of staff training opportunities, low salaries, scarce opportunities for promotion, inadequate infrastructure and field equipment, dependence on foreign donor funding, unstable long-term financing, centralized decision-making in the NCS and the EEAA, and lack of participation from local communities in managing protected areas. Staff reported that these conditions allowed the encroaching forms of land use (legal and illegal) that threatened the viability of protected areas and jeopardized the primary goal of conserving biodiversity through a network of protected areas (ibid.: 65).

To address these mounting problems and budgetary shortfalls, Egypt's managerial conservation network proposed establishing an autonomous Nature Conservation Sector, along the lines of the US Park Service. Such an authority would be either legally separated from the EEAA or at least endowed with executive authority over its budget, staffing, and decision-making. Through a series of projects and consultancies funded by the UNDP, the Egyptian–Italian Environmental Cooperation Program, the IUCN, the Global Environmental Facility (GEF), and USAID, this expert network identified significant opportunities available for strengthening revenue generation from protected area entrance fees and from concessions.

Discursively, conservation experts framed the challenges facing the protected areas not in terms of institutional autonomy, but in terms of the less politicized issue of establishing the financial sustainability of the protected area system. Through surveys, the expert network showed that the principal source of revenue from the protected area network was entrance fees charged at a few protected areas. The managerial network argued that Egypt's protected areas could become self-supporting if the Egyptian government would allow the NCS to diversify revenue streams, reinvest larger proportions of revenue generated, and expand revenue collection systems to other protected areas outside of the handful of operational parks. Proposed means of revenue generation included higher entrance and user fees, adequate concession arrangements, and debt-for-nature swaps with international environmental organizations and financial institutions (Global Environmental Facility, 2010). They also mapped out the legal and administrative reforms needed to strengthen the legal and regulatory capacities of the NCS.

Proposals to allow the NCS to become financially self-sustaining, however, encountered significant resistance from a variety of other government authorities, particularly the Ministry of State for Environmental Affairs itself. Revenues generated by the protectorates went directly to the EEAA's Environmental Protection Fund, which was used to fund a variety of environmental initiatives prioritized by the Minister of Environment or the CEO of the EEAA. Similarly, sectoral ministries obtained royalties from concessions for resource extraction (such as oil, quarrying, mining, and fisheries) conducted in protected areas. Concessionaires refused to pay royalties to both sectoral ministries and the NCS, leaving protected area entrance fees subsidizing other governmental activities. Proposals to make the NCS an autonomous agency were introduced as far up as the Cabinet and the Prime Minister's office, but there the proposals languished.[40]

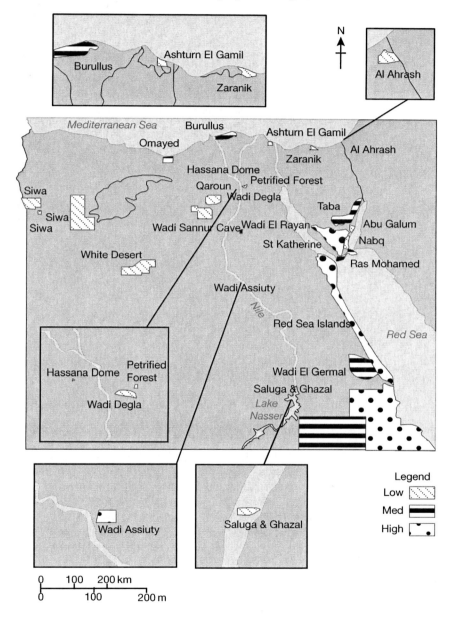

*Figure 5.2* Geographic distribution of pressures and threats identified for the Egyptian system of protected areas

Source: Fouda *et al.*, 2006: 35

While putting forward proposals for substantial institutional reorganization, Egypt's managerial network also sought to engage in smaller-scale interventions to bypass the EEAA and other government ministries. Recalled a long-term manager of the NCS:

> We had to maintain a long-term vision because we had to work with corrupt and ignorant officials without confrontation. We were frustrated about the lack of autonomy, but I thought, let's go from the bottom up. We didn't always get our money officially. We tried to find whatever we could to hire people or buy equipment. I learned to create networks and lobbies, to bargain and negotiate even if all we got was 5 percent of what we needed. Because next time it might be 10 percent. You have to build capacity, but within the framework of local conditions.[41]

Conservation experts focused on obtaining smaller, more flexible grants from donors that could be directly administered by protected area staff or by local environmental organizations. The GEF's Small Grants Programme provided one such vehicle. Between 1994 and 2008, according to the GEF, Egyptian environmental associations administered 224 small grant programs. Of these, thirty-one grants were classified as biodiversity projects. Most of the projects involved local associations embarking on tree planting in and around protected areas, conducting surveys of flora and fauna in various areas of Egypt, developing community participation and management plans for protected areas, or devising strategies to protect medicinal plants (Global Environmental Facility Evaluation Office, 2009: 147–57).

These small-scale projects, however, hardly addressed the larger structural challenges facing Egypt's protected areas. Amidst the turmoil unleashed by the 2011 uprising, the former head of the NCS and several other environmental experts quietly resubmitted a large-scale project request to the GEF to support creating an autonomous Nature Conservation Sector that would control its own financial resources. They did so after gaining formal approval from the EEAA and the Ministry of State for Environmental Affairs to allow a progressively larger share of funds generated by the protected area network to be reinvested. They were able to reach agreement since the GEF project put forward reforms to increase total revenues generated by protected areas, leaving some funds to be used as side payments to the EEAA and other governmental authorities.

This chapter focused on the challenges to conservation posed by rapid tourism development and inadequate investment in the protected area regime. Other pressing coastal conservation challenges include pollution, solid waste disposal, and the effects of climate change on coastal ecosystems (for press accounts, see Marroushi, 2011b; Sarant, 2011). To begin to address these challenges, conservation networks will need to strengthen infrastructural, on-the-ground forms of authority and find new discursive framings that appeal to more popular constituencies, as well as gain legal recognition for a more autonomous parks authority. In this effort, managerial networks are likely to increasingly explore activist tactics—litigation, publicity campaigns, and direct action—as well as working with groups in the tourism sector with direct stakes in preserving coastal habitats and coral ecosystems. These and other trends emerging in conservation politics in post-Mubarak Egypt are explored in the concluding chapter.

# 6  From *masqa* to ministry

## Managerial networks and integrated water management

On November 4, 2011, protesters from a village in the southern governorate of Luxor occupied the main railroad line connecting upper Egypt to Cairo. They refused to depart until the government promised to provide drinking water to their village (Pollick, 2011). Later that month, the Supreme Council of the Armed Forces (SCAF) appointed Kamal al-Ganzouri, a Mubarak-era politician who had served as prime minister from 1996 to 1999, back to his former position. As Prime Minister, al-Ganzouri had championed several controversial large hydroengineering projects to divert Nile water for land reclamation projects in Egypt's deserts.

Not enough water to drink in a village in southern Egypt, so much water that it can be diverted to large-scale irrigation projects. This contrast between too much and too little hints at the complex politics of water in Egypt.[1] Egypt's irrigation and drainage systems are among the most extensive in the world and depend almost entirely upon the Nile River and its renewable aquifer. Egypt's seemingly Malthusian combination of relatively fixed water supplies, a growing population, and increasing consumption have long attracted international attention and domestic intervention in the water sector.

Managerial networks have sought to restructure the governmental and social institutions that govern flows of water in line with global trends in water management. Neoliberal reforms adopted in the agricultural sector in the 1980s deepened expert and international engagement in pushing for restructuring of the water-agricultural sector. Since then, Egyptian water experts and international donors have increasingly employed discourses emphasizing demand-side management, efficiency and conservation, and increased participation of agricultural users in the management of water supplies. By the 2000s, these various policy approaches were increasingly subsumed into an expert discourse of integrated water resource management (IWRM).

To a greater extent than other policy domains analyzed in this book, managerial networks have envisioned remaking Egypt's irrigation and drainage systems in their entirety. Managerial networks sought to implement new paradigms of water management through a series of donor-funded projects that combined investments in physical infrastructure and technology with new forms of social organization, such as users' associations, and institutional restructuring of the governmental bureaucracies involved in water distribution and treatment. These projects, implemented over several decades, translated generic discourses about demand management, water conservation, and integrated resource use into geographically and administratively specific pilot areas that have been gradually expanded outwards. In implementing these long-term interventions, water experts gained concrete information about how complex systems of water use and reuse are used in practice. Often gathered in hindsight, these findings showed a consistent mismatch between many of the informational assumptions and administrative routines employed by central government ministries, on the one hand, and the coping mechanisms of diverse water users, on the other.

Drawing on this consistent mismatch between existing practices of users and the policy prescriptions of experts, I argue that one of the central conundrums encountered in attempts to remake Egypt's irrigation and drainage is a lack of infrastructural authority, that is, a lack of cooperative and trust-inducing linkages between local state representatives and small-scale cultivators. National water institutions are preoccupied with generalized water scarcity and managing the water system as a whole in a centralized fashion, while most small-scale farmers are left to access flows of water that may or may not be adequately supplied by the Ministry of Irrigation (Hopkins, 2005: 4). The result, as Hopkins argued, is two parallel systems of water management—the official, governmental realm of national planning, to be implemented by irrigation and agriculture officials at a variety of scales, and the often unofficial, customary, and widely recognized practices used by many small-scale farmers to ensure adequate supply (Hopkins, 2005).

Managerial networks of water experts have further been unable to counter the influence of privileged water users in agribusiness, tourism, and industry. These actors create demands that central water institutions are forced to satisfy in a reactive manner. While managerial networks have embraced discourses of decentralization, conservation, and efficiency, many governmental initiatives and priorities work in the opposite direction. These include a focus on large-scale land reclamation and domestic subsidies on various crops.

These developments are analyzed as follows. The next section provides an overview of Egypt's water situation, focusing on the supply and demand for freshwater, sources of pollution and contamination, and the regional and domestic constraints on further increasing Nile extractions. I then turn to the evolution of discursive framings about water management, exploring how the liberalization of Egypt's agricultural sector in the 1980s prompted managerial networks to advocate for user participation, cost recovery, and new methods of distributing irrigation supplies. By the 2000s, many participants in managerial networks had subsumed these approaches into the idea of IWRM. Egyptian water experts were active participants in diffusing the idea of IWRM in domestic planning documents and regional fora, but faced significant difficulties implementing these ideas within the Ministry of Irrigation or across government ministries. The limits of applying IWRM to Egyptian governmental planning are aptly illustrated through a discussion of the Mubarak regime's promotion of large-scale land reclamation projects.

The last sections of the chapter examine the disconnects between top-down interventions to decentralize resource management and the realities of how most cultivators experience and react to these central directives and interventions. I focus here on attempts by water experts to limit the amount of rice cultivated in the name of conserving water, on initiatives to create user associations, and on the creation of integrated water management districts. In all three cases, infrastructural authority proved lacking to various degrees, as did enabling legal frameworks and discursive framings that would mesh with the needs and experience of small users.

## Overview of Egypt's water situation: distribution, pollution, and scarcity

While Egypt's water situation is often reduced to a discussion of water scarcity and population growth, the water sector is more accurately approached in terms of evolving, complex systems of distribution, use, reuse, and contamination, operating within an overall constraint of limited physical supply, a changing economic structure, and increasing population. Egypt's water sector is also more correctly a water-agricultural sector. As in most countries, agriculture is the largest sectoral consumer of water, accounting for 86 percent of total water distribution, with 6 percent consumed by municipalities and 8 percent by industry (Ministry of Water Resources and Irrigation, 2005b: 10).

Water experts at the Ministry of Irrigation face an intricate political problem of how to distribute and treat flows of water amidst multiple demands and myriad sources of pollution. The irrigation system delivers Nile water through 31,000 km of state-owned canals and 80,000 km of privately owned field channels, supplemented by groundwater pumping from renewable and non-renewable groundwater aquifers, to cities, fields, and industries (Abu Zeid, 1995: 39). An equally extensive system of 18,000 km of drainage canals and 450,000 km of subsurface drainpipes carries agricultural wastewater out to the northern lakes and the sea (ibid.).

The management of this irrigation-drainage system has long been the purview of Egypt's Ministry of Irrigation.[2] Distribution of irrigation water was based primarily upon water quotas distributed hierarchically downward through a series of delineated geographic-administrative areas, from irrigation directorates, to inspectorates, to districts (Khouzam, 1994: 3.3–3.4). As the country was divided into irrigation districts, cultivated areas were also mapped onto distinct drainage districts. Drainage networks provide another source of water for farmers to access water when freshwater supplies are late or inadequate.

Renewable water resources constitute 96 percent of Egypt's total water resources and are largely limited to the Nile River and aquifers recharged by the Nile. The 1959 Sudan–Egypt water sharing agreement for the Nile granted Egypt 66 percent of the annual Nile flow and Sudan 22 percent, with the rest consumed by evaporation in Lake Nasser and the need for sufficient flow for navigation, power, and ecosystem functions. Egypt fully uses its share of Nile water, and the Nile Valley and Delta are considered a closed river basin, with very little unused freshwater reaching the sea. During periods of high rainfall in the Ethiopian highlands, and amidst ongoing civil strife in Sudan and Ethiopia, Egypt has been reportedly able to use an additional amount of Nile water, estimated to range between 3 and 5 billion cubic meters.[3]

*Table 6.1* Water in Egypt: consumption, renewable resources, and resources per capita

| Annual water consumption (billions of cubic meters) | Nile River, annual renewable resources (billions of cubic meters) | Renewable groundwater aquifers, Nile Valley and Delta (billions of cubic meters) | Per capita water resources (2006, cubic meters/ cap/y) | Per capita water resources (projected 2025, cubic meters/ cap/y) |
| --- | --- | --- | --- | --- |
| 73.10 | 56.8–57.8 | 6.1 | 773 | 600 |

Sources: Compiled from FAO AQUASTAT; World Bank 2007; World Development Indicators 2006; Ministry of Irrigation, "Integrated Water Resources Management Plan 2005"; and Abaza *et al.*, 2011: 56

As shown in Table 6.1, Egypt's annual consumption has exceeded its annual renewable freshwater supplies for some time. A significant proportion of current water consumption is met by imports of staple cereals, a source of virtual water (Allan, 2001). Egypt's Ministry of Irrigation estimated the virtual water embedded in food imports in 2005 at 18.9 billion cubic meters, a source of water that far exceeds all other supplementary sources of supply (Ministry of Water Resources and Irrigation, 2005a). Climatic disruptions and drought led food-exporting countries to impose export bans on rice and wheat during the mid- and late 2000s, leading to escalating food prices on the global market and raising new fears about food security in Egypt and other Middle Eastern countries (Sadik *et al.*, 2011: 2; Woertz, 2011).

Per capita freshwater resources will continue to decline as Egypt's population is projected to increase from 75.4 million in 2006 to between 94 million and 106 million in 2025.[4] Combined with increased water demand from all sectors, Egypt's per capita water availability is estimated to decline from 773 cubic meters per person per year in 2006 to 600 cubic meters per person per year in 2025. Additional supplementary sources of supply include reusing water and limited exploitation of non-renewable groundwater. Significant reuse by farmers goes unrecorded. The government has formally embraced reuse of wastewater to augment water supply, building plants to mix agricultural drainage water with freshwater for irrigation purposes and expanding plans to reuse treated municipal wastewater.

Water pollution constitutes the most immediate problem for most Egyptians as well as for water planners, as it makes water less usable and thereby contributes directly to scarcity. Pollutants, pesticides, fertilizers, and salts accumulate as users reuse water downstream through multiple access points (Elarabawy and Tosswell, 1998: 172). The most significant contributing factor to contaminated water is raw sewage, followed by industrial wastewater, agricultural runoff, and trash thrown in waterways (World Bank, 2005a: 40–1). As a result of inadequate sanitation and increased reuse, water quality in surface canals and shallow underground aquifers diminishes significantly as water moves downstream toward the Mediterranean.

Water pollution has already limited government investment in increasing water reuse in agriculture. By 2004, at least five of twenty-five mixing stations constructed in the Delta to mix drainage and freshwater were unable to be used because of severely polluted drainage water (International Resources Group *et al.*, 2002a: 19). Investment in sanitation systems thus prioritizes cities and towns that discharge directly into surface waters or the upper reaches of drainage canals, in order to maximize possibilities for reuse downstream.

As elsewhere in the Middle East and North Africa, high official coverage rates for potable water and sanitation to the population underreport grave problems with service quality, accessibility, and affordability (Zawahri *et al.*, 2011). Despite significant investments in extending potable water systems, these networks are not adequately maintained, resulting in significant water losses in the distribution networks and contamination of supplies. Periodic water shortages and loss of pressure are experienced in Cairo's wealthy suburbs as well as in informal areas (Reem, 2008). Drinking water in rural and peri-urban areas is often reported as unusable or contaminated; 20 percent of all childhood deaths in Egypt are attributed to diarrheal diseases caused by inadequate or contaminated water supplies (World Bank, 2005a). Households also report a variety of illnesses from coming into contact with irrigation canals, particularly when these are used as informal solid waste dumpsites (Pollick, 2011). The extensive informal use of drainage water for cultivation, to compensate for periodic water shortages, poses additional public health threats (Salem *et al.*, 2009).

Egypt further faces increasing pressure from upstream riparian states regarding its historically dominant Nile allocation. Ethiopia, Uganda, Rwanda, and Kenya signed a new Nile sharing agreement on May 15, 2010, over the objections of Sudan and Egypt. Upstream states also filed a case with the International Court of Justice to annul the 1959 agreement (Othman *et al.*, 2011: 1935). In the face of increasing pressure from upstream states and rising demand in Egypt, it is likely that discussions will eventually resume on infrastructure projects to harness Nile flow upstream in riparian states.

Demographic pressures, deteriorating water quality, and upstream withdrawals mean that eventually Egypt will have to allocate less water for agriculture. Agricultural production in Egypt largely depends upon reliable supplies of irrigation water and groundwater pumping to access renewable aquifers that are recharged by the river and by "loss" of water from the irrigation and drainage networks. Fully 98 percent of Egyptian agriculture is irrigated with Nile water or pumped from aquifers renewed by the Nile River flow (International Bank for Agricultural Development, 2005: 3). The remainder, as in the oases of the western desert, depend upon pumping groundwater, often from fossil (non-renewable) aquifers, such as the Nubian Sandstone Aquifer System that lies underneath parts of Chad, Sudan, western Egypt, and Libya. It is likely that, as water becomes scarcer, allocations of water will eventually be forced out of agriculture to meet municipal and industrial demands. Yet this shift is socially, politically, and economically costly for many. As we shall see, attempts to "conserve" water in agriculture for other uses often entail significant social costs, which have not been accompanied by compensatory policy interventions in rural areas, such as social insurance or employment schemes.

# Water reform initiatives

## *Liberalizing the water-agricultural sector*

The neoliberal restructuring of Egypt's agricultural sector during the 1980s and 1990s was a major impetus for significant restructuring of the water distribution and drainage systems. Market reforms in the agriculture sector rendered existing systems of irrigation management problematic and, in the view of managerial networks, obsolete. Between 1986 and 1994, the Ministry of Agriculture removed crop area allotments and abolished fixed procurement prices (with the exception of cotton and sugar cane). The ministry stopped issuing centralized directives that dictated what farmers could grow, and at what price, with the exception of several important export crops, such as cotton, rice, and sugarcane. The government also reduced non-tariff barriers to imports and exports, and privatized many state-owned farms. Alongside macro-level policy reforms, the government supported intensification of cropping on existing arable land, disseminating high-yield varieties and subsidizing diesel used in pumping irrigation water to fields.

The liberalization of Egypt's agricultural sector deepened in the late 1990s with the elimination of Nasser-era property right protections for small-scale and tenant farmers. Rent ceilings on land were lifted, allowing larger landlords to charge what they considered to be market value for their land. While price liberalization policies generally benefited farmers, removing property right protections for small and tenant farmers made sustaining livelihoods difficult for many small and medium-sized farmers (Bush, 2004, 2007).

Average yields on most crops rose significantly as a result of the policy reforms in the agricultural sector (Sadik *et al.*, 2011: 32). For several crops, Egypt already had among the highest cropping intensities and highest yields in the world (International Bank for Agricultural Development, 2005: 3). Rising yields reinforced the government's commitment to continued agricultural liberalization. Egypt's experience with the Green Revolution led to similar problems with water pollution, soil exhaustion, and salinization that emerged elsewhere in the world. Government and donors alike, however, continued to hold up agricultural liberalization policies as a model of successful policy reforms.

A liberalized agricultural sector, in which farmers largely chose which crops to grow and prices were market-determined, required a simultaneous liberalization of water, in which farmers would have some say in how much water to consume and when (Hvidt, 1998). As one consultant concluded:

> The studies available to us show that control over irrigation water is insufficient to provide farmers with adequate, reliable, and fair water distribution, and this places a significant constraint on farmer water management. The rigidities of the present system, for example, do not allow for satisfying different water demands for different crops, and do not allow for the precise control of water, a prerequisite for the adoption of state-of-the-art agricultural technologies.
>
> (Ibid.: 3)

Managerial networks thus argued that overarching institutional reform of the water distribution and drainage systems was needed to sustain gains in agricultural productivity, enhance cost recovery for the irrigation and drainage network, and promote water savings. Cost recovery—that is, shifting some of the costs to farmers for operating and maintaining the lower levels of the irrigation system—was particularly important to Egypt's water managers. Public financing for operation and maintenance for the irrigation sector amounted to 4 percent of total public expenditures, an amount entirely inadequate to service-deferred investments in rehabilitation, repair, and upgrading of the irrigation and drainage networks. Inadequate investment and funds for operation and maintenance meant extensive water loss in the conveyance and drainage system (World Bank, 2007: 14).

Beginning in 1981, USAID and the Ministry of Irrigation undertook the Irrigation Improvement Project (IIP) in selected areas of the Nile Delta, focused on upgrading the physical infrastructure and the social organization around the tertiary, privately owned canal (*masqa*) that delivers water to fields from a secondary (or branch) canal. This intervention was based upon field studies of irrigation problems in pilot sites in upper, middle, and lower Egypt (International Resources Group and Development Alternatives Inc., 2003: 5). With the goal of increasing equity in water deliveries and allowing farmers more control over water distribution, the IIP promoted a package of technical and social changes. These included changing the distribution of water from an on/off water rotation, controlled by the ministry's district irrigation engineer, to a continuous but lower volume in branch canals, controlled by automatic floating gates at the entrance to selected canals; lining and raising the *masqa* above field level so that each farmer was not required to pump water up into each field (a previous technical intervention had been to "lower" the *masqa* to make it more costly for farmers to access water and therefore conserve it); and the provision of a single pump to "lift" water from the branch canal at the head of the *masqa* (Hvidt, 1998).

Along with these changes in physical infrastructure, the project created user associations to own, operate, and maintain the new pump and raised *masqa*, to schedule irrigation deliveries and manage potential conflicts among users. While not formalized, the "old" system of irrigation already had user associations, "circles" of farmers who rotated access to diesel pumps to lift water from the *masqa* to their field ditches (Mehanna *et al.*, 1984). Nevertheless, donors and water experts widely viewed the new *masqa* associations, which included up to 200 farmers, as improving both the efficiency and equity of irrigation water delivery (Institutional Reform Unit *et al.*, 2005: 20). This package of technology improvements paired with the establishment of local user associations was later expanded to other areas of Egypt using World Bank funds, and remains ongoing.

A number of other water-related projects were pursued as part of USAID and other donor supports. All of these projects used the model of tranche funding, where USAID released direct cash transfers to Egyptian governmental authorities when specific policy objectives had been met. The Water Policy Reform Project, one subsector of USAID's Agricultural Policy Reform Program that ran from 1997 to 2002, for instance, had a budget of US$245 million for cash transfers. The process of developing and certifying specific policy benchmarks to trigger tranche releases was a negotiated process with Egyptian governmental agencies (Keith, 2003). For each programmatic focus, the projects convened working groups of experts and government officials ("policy champions" in the language of USAID's assessments) to build political consensus around what constituted reasonable benchmarks and feasible implementation plans in the form of small pilot projects (Tczap, 2002). The process of carrying out pilot projects produced a number of suggested modifications for scaling up to larger areas (Ender, 2003).

In addition to project-specific working groups, managerial networks of experts and donors established semi-autonomous units to promote organiza-tional restructuring. These enclaves of reform included an Institutional Reform Unit (funded by the Netherlands) and the creation of the Irrigation Advisory Service (funded by USAID), both within the Ministry of Irrigation. The Irrigation Advisory Service was later transformed into a regular directorate at the ministry charged with overseeing the creation of user associations. The Netherlands also funded a new Groundwater Sector and a Water Quality Unit, to incorporate groundwater resources planning and water pollution issues more fully within the purview of the ministry (International Resources Group *et al.*, 2002b: 11–12).

### *Integrated water resource management*

By the 2000s, managerial networks increasingly portrayed efforts to restructure water institutions in terms of IWRM. Under IWRM, water is to be valued by multiple criteria: as a social necessity, as an economic good, and as an ecological resource. In other words, management institutions need to consider how to bal-ance the imperatives of consuming water for people, for food, for nature, and for other uses (Jønch-Clausen, 2004: 7). Balancing these needs is to be accomplished through cross-sectoral, coordinated planning at the level of state institutions; involvement of multiple stakeholders in water decisions; and the promotion of participatory, decentralized systems of water management.

Over the past two decades, IWRM has become the dominant approach to water management among professionals, development agencies, international donors, and government ministries (Conca, 2006). Adopted by participating countries at the Johannesburg World Summit on Sustainable Development in 2002, IWRM was seen as the new paradigm for water management, even though many of the central ideas had been in circulation for two decades. Nevertheless, as Conca noted, by the time of the summit "a large professional community of water knowledge experts had crystallized around the concept, promoted it vigorously, and enjoyed increasingly robust transnational linkages in doing so" (Conca, 2005: 450).

Top officials at the Ministry of Irrigation emerged as the principal exponents of IWRM in Egypt during the 1990s and 2000s. With the appointment of Mahmoud Abu Zeid as Minister of Irrigation in 1997, a post he held until 2009, the pace of administrative decrees pushing forward various aspects of IWRM accelerated (International Resources Group *et al.*, 2002a: 26). Egyptian experts promoting IWRM argue that Egypt's freshwater should be reserved for uses that extract the highest value per unit of water.[5] Faced with constant requests to allocate Nile water for new activities, managerial networks would like government ministries to evaluate new industries, cities, and economic activities in terms of potential water demand.[6] These experts envision requiring new development activities to employ water conservation measures and be required to provide their own supplemental water supplies (through water harvesting, desalination, and other means). From the perspective of other governmental ministries, however, IWRM further reifies the important distributional and planning role of the Ministry of Irrigation vis-à-vis other governmental authorities, and gives water experts a more decisive role in development decisions.

By 2005, the discourse of IWRM was formally adopted as the basis for Egyptian water planning. The Ministry of Irrigation issued an "Integrated Water Resources Management Plan," formulated with the assistance of the World Bank (Arab Water Council *et al.*, 2005; Ministry of Water Resources and Irrigation, 2005a). In the Arab world at the time, only Jordan, Tunisia, Yemen, and Palestine had similar plans, also devised with international assistance (Arab Water Council *et al.*, 2005: 2–3). Attempts to integrate water resource planning were also undertaken at the subnational level; with support from the EU Commission, the Egyptian organization CEDARE undertook an integrated water plan for the city of Alexandria.[7]

### *Regional diffusion of IWRM*

While seeking to promote IWRM through national planning documents, Egyptian water experts also diffused notions of IWRM through regional and transnational fora. Egypt's Ministry of Irrigation was one of three organizations that founded the World Water Council in 1996, along with the Canadian International Development Agency (CIDA) and the multinational firm Suez-Lyonnaise des Eaux (Conca, 2005: 452). The World Water Council was to serve as a forum for networks of water experts to influence policymaking and international debates. As of 2011, the Council counted 300 organizational members from fifty countries.[8] Egypt and the Arab states more generally are well represented in the governance structure of the Council. Of the thirty-one elected members of the Board of Governors in 2011, seven were water experts from the Middle East; in comparison, the United States had four representatives. Egypt's former Minister of Irrigation, Mahmoud Abu-Zeid, served as the elected President of the Council up through the World Water Forum in 2000.

IWRM was further spread in the Arab world through multilateral institutions such as the World Bank and the UNDP. The UNDP, from its regional office in Beirut and country offices in nineteen Arab countries, sponsored a regional support program to promote the principles of IWRM in the Arab world (Arab Water Council *et al.*, 2005). Abu Zeid and others further established the Arab Water Council in 2004, a regional forum structured along similar lines to the World Water Council and endorsing a similar technocratic approach, to promote IWRM in the Arab world. This regional council emphasized maintaining "a multi-disciplinary, non-political, professional, and scientific manner," as noted on its website.[9] It held meetings, generated publications, and undertook project work. In 2008, the council sponsored the Arab Water Academy, a regional executive training center on water issues headquartered in Abu Dhabi's Environment Agency. Funded in part by the World Bank, USAID, and the Islamic Development Bank, the academy's goals were to "accelerate the shift from a focus on water supply augmentation and direct service provision to integrated water management and service regulation."[10] As of 2011, the Arab Water Council's executive committee remained dominated by a handful of Egyptian water experts. Mahmoud Abu Zeid served as its president, Muhammad 'Abd al-Da'im as secretary-general, and Khaled Abu Zeid, Mahmoud's son and a water engineer, as treasurer, while one of the executive committee members was the current Minister of Irrigation in Egypt, Husayn al-'Atfi.[11]

Egyptian water experts, along with international donors, have thus been at the forefront of promoting IWRM in international fora and at home. Yet as Conca has argued, the technocratic precepts of integrated water resources management belie the fundamentally contentious nature of water management (Conca, 2006). As a set of generic policy prescriptions, the discourse of IWRM offers little guidance for actors tackling the profoundly political task of restructuring water management. The participants in Egypt's managerial water networks are typically irrigation engineers. Their background and training prepares them to think about water management in terms of physical infrastructure, and they view implementing integrated resource management as a top-down exercise in reconfiguring constituent parts of a system.

The director of the Ministry of Irrigation's institutional reform unit, whom I interviewed in 2008, typified the engineering background and technical Weltanschauung (worldview) of participants in managerial water networks. Hired in his retirement as a consultant to promote IWRM within the Ministry of Irrigation, his career spanned the principal areas of focus for managerial networks in the water sector. These included the building and rehabilitation of dams and barrages, the promotion of land reclamation, and centralized planning. This official graduated as an engineer in 1962, and spent the following five years working for the Aswan High Dam Authority, first at Aswan and then in Libya on a technical cooperation project. Transferred to the Ministry of Irrigation with the dissolution of the authority, he worked in the section responsible for renovations of Nile barrages and then in the land reclamation division. He then served in the technical office of the minister, as the director of the minister's office, and as director of the ministry's planning sector, before retiring and returning as a consultant on IWRM.[12]

## Implementing IWRM

Applying the general principles of integrated water resource management to the actual conduct of work within the Ministry of Irrigation's core tasks poses a serious challenge. In 2004, the ministry employed 97,000 permanent employees, mostly distributed in the provinces, and 26,000 temporary staff. The ministry is composed of four main departments, responsible for irrigation, drainage, groundwater, and mechanical operations (i.e. pumped water), respectively. Each of these departments are spatially decentralized to the provinces, and the boundaries are not coterminous across different ministerial departments; for instance, the boundaries of irrigation districts are not the same as those of drainage districts (Institutional Reform Unit *et al.*, 2005: 29). Nor do they correspond to the boundaries of villages and municipalities used by the central government for purposes of central planning and financial transfers from the capital to provincial governments. With the restructuring of the ministry envisioned by managerial networks, leading irrigation officials said that they would need large-scale training programs for thousands of employees (International Resources Group *et al.*, 2002b: 20).

By 2001, USAID and Egyptian irrigation experts began focusing on creating "integrated water management districts" as the most practical means of implementing IWRM within Egypt. The integrated district would, in theory, combine the functions performed by the three ministry departments (irrigation, drainage, and mechanical/electrical) operating at the lowest official level—the district—into one local administrative unit. This unit would aggregate information and take decisions on how best to combine water from different sources and of varying quality. The problem, as seen by consultants working for USAID, was that "the District Engineer focuses solely on irrigation issues, and has little or no management coordination authority to integrate the other aspects of delivery and use, i.e. drainage, groundwater, and rainfall" (International Resources Group *et al.*, 2001: E-1).

The lack of horizontal coordination across district offices for irrigation, drainage, groundwater, and mechanical pumping was compounded by the fact that district employees were primarily supposed to channel information upwards in the irrigation bureaucracy, but did not have autonomy to take local-level decisions. Thus, managerial networks viewed creating integrated districts as an integral step in moving the central ministry towards more decentralized and integrated resource decision-making, by granting district irrigation officials the authority to incorporate non-conventional sources (such as groundwater pumping and drainage reuse) into water balances and deliveries (ibid.). More decentralized yet integrated control of water resources was supposed to increase equity in irrigation deliveries and help alleviate chronic water shortages experienced at the tail end of canals, particularly in summer.

These visions of integrated water reform were predicated on the ministry—whether at the district or the central level—having sufficient control over water resources to make proactive decisions about who receives water. At the national level, this was to take place through inter-ministerial coordination, planning, and consultation; at the district level by empowering and consolidating local-level functions of irrigation employees.

### Attempts at inter-ministerial coordination

Implementing IWRM across government ministries at the national level was predictably difficult. To prepare the National Water Resources Plan, adopted in 2005 with project planning to last until 2017, water officials convened a number of inter-ministerial meetings to compile and compare sectoral development plans (International Resources Group and Development Alternatives Inc., 2003). The goal was specifically to involve other major government entities in water planning, including the Ministry of Housing, Utilities, and Urban Communities, which supplies and manages domestic municipal water and sanitation networks; the Ministry of Agriculture and Land Reclamation, which deals with agricultural demand and consumption; and the Ministry of Defense and Military Production, which exerts a *de facto* first claim over land use and planning. Several participants recalled the process as the first instance where central ministries responsible for various aspects of water supply and water quality engaged in joint agenda setting.[13]

The resulting national plans emphasized four key pillars of IWRM (Kandil, 2003). The plan emphasized managing and coordinating water supply and water demand across sectors, rather than simply within sectors. In practice, this dictum meant coordinating action across central government ministries and within established ministries responsible for resource management. The second principle invoked was decentralizing water management and devolving it to the lowest appropriate level (often termed the principle of subsidiarity), while the related third goal was to incorporate participation by stakeholders. Fourth, national planning documents highlighted the need for financial sustainability, through increased cost recovery, increased role of the private sector in the water sector, and marketization of water where possible.

An inter-ministerial committee and national planning, however, proved inadequate legal mechanisms to foster coordination among ministries accustomed to administering separate planning, budgets, and operations. The creation of high-level inter-ministerial committees had not worked to control industrial pollution (Chapter 3) or establish land use plans for coastal development (Chapter 5). The water sector proved little different. As one water official recalled:

> We encountered several obstacles once we tried to implement the National Water Resources Plan (NWRP). With a change in ministers, some ministries said they were not aware of the plan. Some sectors simply pursued their own plans without referencing the NWRP.[14]

## The limits of IWRM: large land reclamation projects

During the late 1990s and early 2000s, as water experts introduced IWRM into Egypt's national planning documents, leading officials also publicly promoted large-scale state land reclamation projects in the desert. The Mubarak government embraced several new large-scale Nile water diversion projects with much fanfare, including the al-Salam Canal (Peace Canal) in northern Sinai, and the Toshka (New Valley) project in the southwestern desert. The regime invoked a Malthusian crisis narrative in which overpopulation and pollution in the Nile Valley and Delta necessitated the creation of new arable land in the desert for settlement purposes. The government confidently predicted that these projects would increase Egypt's habitable area from 4 percent to 25 percent of the country's total.

Given that Egypt already fully used (and reused) its share of Nile water, water experts were tasked with explaining how Egypt could spare more water for crops without tapping more Nile water. Egypt's then-Minister of Irrigation, Mahmoud Abu-Zeid, became the Mubarak regime's designated spokesperson for the New Valley project, appearing repeatedly in state-owned media TV and newspaper accounts.

If IWRM is predicated on increasing efficiency of water use, and evaluating tradeoffs between different uses, why did some of Egypt's leading water technocrats support expansion in irrigation when they had long argued that the agricultural sector needed to conserve water? Most outside hydrologists and social scientists considered these mega-projects a costly and inefficient use of Egypt's water resources and its limited budgetary resources (Allan, 2001; Ayeb, 2002; Mitchell, 2002).[15] Political scientists speculated that Egypt was maximizing its claim to Nile water by creating facts on the ground (Waterbury, 2002) or that the project was the last-ditch effort of an aging President Mubarak to create a monumental legacy (Mitchell, 2002). As I have detailed elsewhere, critiques within Egypt were also numerous, articulated by hydrologists, engineers, investors, independent journalists, opposition party members, officials, and agrobusiness managers (Sowers, 2011). Many water experts believed, usually off the record, that these mega-projects were unsustainable and would exacerbate distributional conflicts over water. Even the national IWRM reports produced by reform units within the Ministry of Irrigation cautioned against further land reclamation projects. The 2005 Integrated Water Resources Management Plan, for instance, argued that, "by implementing all these measures, *in particular all of the planned horizontal expansion projects*, the water resources systems has reached its limits of what it can support" (Ministry of Water Resources and Irrigation, 2005a: 20; italics added).

The Mubarak-era mega-projects were excessively grandiose in scope, but the underlying rationales for land reclamation had long been a feature of water discourses and water management institutions in Egypt (Sowers, 2011). In the late nineteenth and early twentieth centuries, British irrigation engineers advocated for basin-wide systems of dams designed primarily to increase irrigated land and agricultural production (particularly cotton) in downstream Egypt (Collins, 1990). Proponents of the Aswan High Dam argued that the stored floodwaters at Lake Nasser would allow large-scale land reclamation in the desert. Over time, the emphasis on distributing water to grow crops was supplemented with the strategic goal of redistributing Egypt's population away from the "crowded" and "polluted" Nile Valley and into sparsely populated frontier zones (see Chapter 5 for a discussion of the Sinai Peninsula).

### Land reclamation and discourses of water conservation

Officials such as Abu Zeid argued for land reclamation schemes through yet another framing, that of water conservation. Egypt could conserve sufficient water in the "old" agricultural lands of the Nile Delta and Valley to free up water for land reclamation. This would be accomplished by upgrading the existing irrigation system through projects such as USAID's IIP, limiting the cultivation of water-intensive crops such as rice, and shifting from traditional irrigation techniques to water-saving drip and sprinkler technologies. Less publicly, some water experts pointed out that the rapid and largely informal urbanization of the Nile Delta was freeing up irrigation water. The most rapid loss of arable land was around greater Cairo, where approximately 1,040 acres annually were converted from agricultural to urban uses between 1972 and 2003 (Hereher, 2006).

In the name of conserving water and allocating it to higher-value uses, many water experts inside and outside the government thus supported shifting to modern drip and sprinkler technologies. Yet few of Egypt's numerous small and medium-sized farmers located in the old cultivated lands could afford such capital-intensive, imported irrigation systems. The government thus offered an array of incentives to attract large, capital-rich investors to undertake land reclamation. These incentives included government-financed construction of the irrigation infrastructure to the borders of newly allocated lands, a twenty-year tax holiday, long-term concessions on land ownership, tax exemptions on imported equipment, and guaranteed allocations of irrigation water.

This attempt to conserve water by supporting capital-intensive agrobusiness in land reclamation, however, did not play out as scripted in official speeches and media coverage touting the advantages of mega-projects. In the New Valley, few agrobusiness investors proved willing to invest in areas far from centers of population, transport, and distribution.[16] The few who did so, most notably Prince al-Waleed Bin Talal's Kingdom Agricultural Development Company (KADCO), encountered an array of practical and political difficulties in creating a profitable agricultural operation. These included insecure property rights, political scrutiny, and problems in growing crops cost-effectively given high temperatures, wind, sand, and other environmental factors (Sowers, 2011).

As noted by many critics of the land reclamation mega-projects, private investors preferred to reclaim land at the fringes of the Nile Delta or Valley. By offering a range of incentives for agrobusiness to engage in capital-intensive irrigation practices, state policy contributed directly towards shifting distributions of land and water to agrobusiness, even as private investors avoided the mega-project lands in favor of lands adjacent to the Nile Delta. Yet these ongoing land reclamation activities, primarily using modern irrigation technologies, created new problems in water consumption and water pollution.

For instance, private land reclamation along the western Delta, using wells to tap groundwater, was extensive enough to draw down aquifers unsustainably and contaminate groundwater. With the creation of a new agrobusiness constituency, the Ministry of Irrigation was requested to extend the Nile irrigation network to these newly reclaimed lands to avoid further groundwater contamination (Ministry of Water Resources and Irrigation, 2007). The ministry, in turn, sought World Bank assistance to finance the infrastructure costs. Thus, the spread of new irrigation technologies supposed to conserve water merely accelerated depletion and contamination of groundwater, requiring further diversions of Nile water to meet newly created agricultural demands for water. As seen in the western Delta, the role of governmental management institutions for water is often reactive— that is, finding water for activities already undertaken.

## Infrastructural authority and agricultural producers

As we have seen, managerial networks in Egypt helped create and disseminate new norms of water management regionally and transnationally. They drew up extensive plans for moving towards integrated water management and reframed long-standing state goals for land reclamation in terms of novel discourses of water conservation. Yet they were unable to promote significant inter-govern-mental coordination around sectoral water planning. Attempts to implement integrated management remained a top-down process that overlooked existing systems of water use and reuse, and the needs and interests of many of Egypt's small cultivators. In other words, managerial networks lacked the kinds of legal and infrastructural authority necessary to "reach" end-users and incorporate their perspectives effectively into water reform initiatives. In the following sections, we explore several instances where long-standing mistrust and lack of infrastruc-tural authority troubled water reform initiatives.

### *Informational distortions, cropping patterns, and irrigation supplies*

As the agricultural sector liberalized during the 1980s and 1990s, the Ministry of Irrigation could no longer rely on central directives and crop quotas from the Ministry of Agriculture to calculate water demand for different areas. The irriga-tion ministry calculated water discharges for the main canals based on planning targets supplied by the Ministry of Agriculture. In turn, the ministry's district engi-neer (*muhandis al-rayy*) and local water gatekeeper (*bahhar*) allocated discharges at pre-set levels to lower-level canals on a fixed rotation schedule (Radwan, 1997: 80–1). With free cropping, however, calculations for irrigation releases depended upon agricultural extension agents acquiring information on cropping patterns from farmers, by direct observation, or by other means. To complicate matters, such information had to be compiled at least two weeks in advance of irrigation needs for releases at the Aswan High Dam to flow through the system.

Farmers typically mistrusted local officials, given the history of command-and-control policies in agriculture, which minimized their incentives to provide reliable information. In addition, each cultivator has an interest in maximizing claims to irrigation allocations under conditions of uncertainty. In field studies, researchers thus found that farmers selectively provided information on cropping patterns to government extension agents, or simply provided inaccurate information. Farmers overestimated the amount under cultivation, reported only a narrow range of principal crops still subject to mandatory quotas from the Ministry of Agriculture, omitted vegetable and fodder crops, and provided no data for the location of crops along canals (ibid.).

These problems in collecting information on actual patterns of cultivation were magnified at the national level through errors in aggregation and inaccurate simplifying assumptions employed at the central offices of the Ministry of Irrigation. For instance, the ministry assumed that canal efficiency in delivering water was 80 percent, whereas field studies conducted by Lutfi Radwan in the late 1990s found a figure closer to 65 percent (ibid.: 83).

Ministry employees recognized that their estimates of local demand and the efficiency of the supply system as a whole were unreliable. At both national and local levels, irrigation officials compensated for informational shortcomings by releasing more water than their estimates predicted. The result was significant flows of excess water through the system. Based on actual patterns of crop cultivation and water consumption in one Delta province, Radwan found that the ministry discharged water 64 percent in excess of crop requirements during the late 1990s (ibid.). Thus, the principal source of "over-irrigation" and excess water flows stemmed from the ministry's supply practices.

To address this persistent mismatch between irrigation supply and crop demand for water, donors and water experts focused on developing systems to promote information sharing between farmers, the district irrigation engineer, and agricultural extension agents. One such project, for instance, put in place a physical reporting system in pilot areas where agricultural extension agents delivered cropping information to the district irrigation engineer on a bi-weekly basis (International Resources Group *et al.*, 2002b: 12–13).

Alongside efforts to increase direct communication, projects in the water sector supported the deployment of increasingly sophisticated technologies to match irrigation deliveries with actual crop demand for irrigation authorities at various levels. These included funding and training to measure water flow (through installing and calibrating meters to measure flow at key inflow/outflow locations), the expanded use of telemetry, digital mapping, and real-time data gathering systems in project areas, and installing computer and database systems in all project areas to store and access data (International Resources Group, 2008: 67). This use of complex data systems in turn required upgrading the skills of local irrigation employees and the budgetary requirements to maintain and upgrade these systems as needed. Retaining staff, many hired on public-sector temporary contracts and at low wages, posed an ongoing challenge even in the areas targeted by donors. These interventions, however, did not address the disconnect between the technologies and forms of knowledge increasingly employed by ministry employees and those used in practice by small cultivators.

### Restricting rice cultivation

A lack of infrastructural authority between small-scale irrigators and expert networks has similarly plagued attempts to conserve water by restricting the cultivation of water-intensive crops, particularly rice. Rice is a staple food item in Egypt and a significant source of export revenue. It is also a large consumer of water. In efforts to limit acreage under rice cultivation, the government maintains a host of administrative controls, including a centralized target for the total geographical area under rice production, the imposition of fines for excess cultivation, and export taxes and restrictions. Rice production is banned altogether in areas north of Cairo, and irrigation engineers are entitled to cut off water to areas where they observe excessive rice cultivation, regardless of disruptions to the agricultural sector (Ahmed, 2010).

With renewed investment in the agricultural sector as a consequence of market reforms, and rising prices for rice, the amount of acreage cultivated with rice has expanded rapidly in Egypt in recent decades. Rice is a staple food for most Egyptians, with per capita consumption at 40 kilograms per year (Foreign Agricultural Service, 2010). Rice cultivation provides an important source of rural income, consumption, and export revenue for many Egyptian farmers and companies. Labor-intensive in both the planting and harvesting phases, Egyptian rice commands premium prices in global markets.

Compiling estimates from various government agencies, one study estimated that the area under rice cultivation had risen from approximately 1.40 million *feddans* in 1995 to 1.77 million *feddans* in 2008, over a quarter percent increase in acreage for that period (Arafat *et al.*, 2010). Total rice production increased from approximately 4.79 million tons in 1995 to 7.24 million tons in 2008, with yields per *feddan* increasing from 3.4 tons per *feddan* to 4.1 tons, making Egypt's rice producers among the most productive in the world (Othman *et al.*, 2011: 1935).

While seeking to restrict rice cultivation to conserve water, the government also supports keeping domestic rice prices low for domestic consumers and for the state's food ration programs (Foreign Agricultural Service, 2010: 2). In addition, enough rice must be cultivated in the Delta to control soil salinity and limit saltwater intrusion. Particularly in the northern areas of the Delta, and in old reclaimed lands on the outskirts of the Delta, where seawater intrusion and soil salinization are important issues, rice leaches salt from upper soil layers, enabling farmers to continue cultivation. The government's total goal for rice cultivation, including the reclaimed lands, is approximately 1.1 million *feddans* (Arafat *et al.*, 2010).

Since the late 1980s, farmers have faced fines levied by local officials for exceeding their quotas of rice production. These fines, however, were nominal; rural parliamentarians consistently opposed attempts by the Ministry of Agriculture to raise the monetary amounts of the fines. Farmers with all sizes of landholdings have thus consistently flouted these quotas, preferring to pay fines and plant rice. Similarly, when faced with sporadic restrictions on buying domestic rice, Egyptian milling operations have sought to stay afloat by importing cheaper varieties of rice to mill for re-export (Foreign Agricultural Service, 2010).

Periodically, state officials have employed draconian measures to limit rice production. In 1997, as the state's investment in large-scale land reclamation projects escalated, the then-Minister of Agriculture, Yusuf Wali, informed governors that they were responsible for limiting rice production. That year, growing rice in the governorate of Qalyubiyya fetched LE2,000 per *feddan* in profit for farmers, while cultivating corn brought a loss of LE500 per *feddan*. The governor of Qalyubiyya took these directives literally, ordering governorate employees to destroy rice nurseries using bulldozers. As one farmer recalled, the machinery sank in swampy fields, and the local government reportedly did not have the funds to hire enough workers to pull out the rice by hand.[17] The governorate therefore moved to using herbicides to destroy rice nurseries. Approximately eighty *feddans* of rice nurseries, which would have supplied 800 *feddans* of rice paddies, were treated before the Minister of State for Environmental Affairs personally intervened.

The passage below is an account of this incident, as recounted by a modest landowner and journalist from Qalyubiyya. The landowner argues that centralized directives ("the paper targets" of bureaucrats) are not informed by knowledge of local conditions. The passage further highlights how even modest landowners draw on personal connections and threats of court action to contest coercive state actions. The landowner recalled:

> I sent my foreman to where the government officials were spraying to see what they were using before they came to my fields. Right on the bottle, for those who can't read, is a picture of a fish and water, with a big X over it. And here they were, spraying it on land that the farmers will then flood with fresh irrigation water to save the rice nurseries. This herbicide flows into drainage canals, some of which carry water to treatment plants to be reused. People wash in these canals, water buffalo drink from them, and some of the herbicide probably seeps into the underground water table, which is close to the surface around here.
>
> On Wednesday, when they came for my fields, I was waiting for them. Several trucks came along the road towards my rice nurseries. In front was a truck full of soldiers carrying Kalashnikovs from the Amn al-Markazi (Central Security Forces), then a group from the Ministry of Agriculture and the governorate, carrying the herbicide on their backs. The trucks stopped, and the soldiers leapt out. I began shouting at them, all of them, that if they stepped foot on my land I would see all of them in prison. That to destroy crops was against the law, that stepping foot on my property without a court judgment was against the law. I was very angry and didn't care if I went to prison. It was my crop!
>
> The head engineer came over and said, "Calm down, let's talk about this. I know what we are doing is illegal, but I have an order from the governor.

I must do this. But you are from a good family, you have an education, you must have connections. I give you two days: if you get me a paper from the minister [of agriculture], then I can exempt you."

I said, "I will not get a paper. It is illegal to do this."

He laughed, and just kept telling me I had to get a paper from the minister.

All the soldiers got back in their trucks, and I went back to the farm and called a friend, who gave me the number of the Minister of Environment's office. I called her secretary, and explained the use of the herbicide and the consequences. She said, "I will contact the minister, wait by the phone." I waited, and then the governor of Qalyubiyya called me, and said, "What do you want exactly?" I said, "I want you to stop spraying the rice nurseries." He said, "But I have an order from the Minister of Agriculture." I told him that he was destroying the *fellahin* (peasants) and their livelihoods. He was very angry and so was I.

Then a miracle happened. The Nile flooded, the village flooded, and there was no way the ministry could go to a judge and say, "We don't have enough water." The judge would throw it out, of course. So they left my fields, I planted the rice and paid the fine.

This was all because these bureaucrats work by paper; they have paper targets, and don't understand anything about local conditions. They have centralized targets, and so they say, we need more water, and then they try to make you grow what they want. They should fix the irrigation system, in which lots of water goes to waste because the government hasn't maintained it properly. Instead, they tell us you can't grow rice.[18]

The same year that the governor of Qalyubiyya tried to destroy rice nurseries with an herbicide, the Ministry of Agriculture formally approved five new types of rice for cultivation in newly reclaimed lands. These varieties, trumpeted the state-owned media, could be grown with modern drip and sprinkler technologies, thereby consuming less water ("Rice Varieties Approved for Toshka," 1999). State endorsement of rice cultivation in the lands proffered by the new mega-projects, for agrobusiness investors using modern irrigation technologies, acknowledged farmers' principal contentions: that rice was one of the few crops to tolerate high salinity, cleanse salts from surface soil layers, and produce a profit at the same time.

Recurrent conflicts between agricultural producers and the state over the production of water-intensive crops illustrate well how expert attempts to "conserve" water were often seen as inimical to the interests of many cultivators. Managerial networks based in irrigation institutions lacked infrastructural forms of authority that could have provided avenues for local-level information and cooperation from agricultural producers. The question that has emerged in Egypt's rice policies—as in its water policies more generally—is not whether to cultivate rice, but who will cultivate it, where, and how.

Managerial water networks have proposed a few alternative "win–win" solutions that would sustain farm income from rice and yet limit water consumption.

Several donor-state projects successfully promoted substituting short-duration rice varieties for long-duration strains. Short-duration rice varieties mature more quickly, thereby using less water but attaining similar yields. Farmers used the extra month following the rice harvest to cultivate winter crops, resulting in higher farm incomes. As one USAID report noted, however, the change in cultivation also required that the Ministry of Irrigation shift the timing of water rotations accordingly. "The failure to implement any part of the package," cautioned the authors, "will result in the absence of measurable water savings" (International Resources Group and Development Alternatives Inc., 2003: 8). Implementing adequate water rotations again brought water experts back to the problem of accurate reporting of cropping patterns.

Government agencies remain unable to gather reliable information on the actual patterns of rice cultivation at different points in time and in different places and, by extension, have only limited knowledge of the amount of water consumed in rice production. One study found that figures for rice acreage varied by 30–40 percent between the Ministries of Irrigation and Agriculture, with the Ministry of Agriculture consistently underestimating cultivation in line with its preferred targets (Hoogland, 2002: 45).

To improve the accuracy of this data, government ministries have sought to use new technologies that bypass the need for communication and direct linkages with agricultural producers. Increasingly, the Ministries of Agriculture and Irrigation have sought to use remote sensing and satellite imagery to determine rice acreage. The findings highlight the gap between official targets and actual rice cultivation. A 2010 remote sensing study of the Delta governorates, conducted at the "urgent request from the Ministry of Agriculture," found that actual rice acreage exceeded the government's quotas by 46 percent on average (Arafat *et al.*, 2010).

### *User associations and participatory management*

Water experts sought to manage water consumption not only by restricting rice cultivation and promoting the use of new, capital-intensive irrigation technologies, but also by restructuring decision-making at the lower levels of the irrigation system through the creation of user associations.[19] User associations at the lowest level of the irrigation distribution system emerged in USAID's Irrigation Improvement Project in the 1980s, primarily to increase farmer participation in the maintenance and operation of small primary canals. By 1994, the Ministry of Irrigation and donors began experimenting with expanding user associations to the branch or secondary canals, which serve large, heterogeneous communities of users, ranging from 1,000 to 10,000 persons. Donor-funded projects focused on holding elections to create "water boards" that would include industrial and municipal representatives as well as agricultural interests. Donor-funded projects at the ministry established hundreds of elected water boards at the branch canal level during the 1990s and 2000s.

These reform efforts focused on creating new participatory institutions, but little attention had been given to how these would mesh with informal systems of gaining access to resources or existing forms of participation. In response to shortages and pollution, cultivators already petitioned local officials, made visits to and conducted sit-ins at local irrigation offices, and sought the intercession of locally influential individuals. Farmers also tried to cope with water scarcity by directly modifying the canals supplying their fields, through expanding offtake canals, installing additional pipes, and other means (Barnes, forthcoming). While most of these measures were formally illegal, farmers preferred to pay the nominal fines imposed by the Ministry of Irrigation rather than let their crops perish. As one official affiliated with the Institute for National Planning observed, "People have informal ways of getting water and other services that they need, and penalties for violations are usually dropped… They can always go through back doors."[20]

Incorporating branch canal associations (or water boards) into irrigation decision-making encountered another set of obstacles as well. The first wave of donor projects supporting user associations focused on enabling a central ministry department, the Irrigation Advisory Service, to organize associations, conduct elections, and sign memoranda of understanding between the associations and the Ministry of Irrigation. While managerial networks focused primarily on creating associations, the roles of the local-level employees of the Ministry of Irrigation were not similarly restructured. Elected water boards and district engineers frequently expressed mistrust of the other's capacities and intentions (Radwan *et al.*, 2006: 18). In surveys and workshops, local officials reported that the role of user associations was primarily to serve the ministry by carrying out mundane, labor-intensive tasks. They argued that user associations lacked technical expertise and, worse, sometimes organized against actions and decisions taken by the ministry itself (ibid.). These actions were viewed as "irresponsible, indicative of users' ignorance, inexperience, and particularistic interests, rather than as a legitimate function for representatives of community-based organizations."[21] As a result, local irrigation officials offered associations almost no opportunity to participate in irrigation decisions, even though the associations had been present in some areas for a decade (ibid.: 12). These findings held across all areas of irrigation decision-making, including maintenance, operation and water distribution, and finance and administration.

State mistrust and suspicion of the branch canal user associations also derived from their formally representative character. While elected members were often from well-connected, wealthy families, ongoing elections produced significant rotations of power. In some branch canals, elections resulted in turnover of two-thirds of the delegates and the leadership.[22] Moreover, women sometimes won the seats reserved for municipal representation. These delegates raised issues of water quality that had been considered outside the customary purview of local irrigation officials, and included the accumulation of trash in canals and lack of alternative disposal sites for solid waste and sewage discharge directly to drainage canals.

Commonly, these delegates requested funds to repair septic tanks, finance hand pumps, and dig deeper wells to avoid contaminated water supplies.[23]

The irony of rotating power in branch canal associations while the Mubarak regime manipulated national and local elections in order to prevent any real rotation of power did not escape either the consultants involved in organizing water user associations or the representatives themselves. As one consultant recalled, "There were lots of sly jokes contrasting the water boards elections with the lack of true elections at the local, parliamentary, and national levels."[24]

As a result, attempts to legalize the participatory role of user associations encountered further difficulties at the highest levels of the government. The creation of user associations at the *masqa* and branch levels was initially authorized by an administrative decree issued by the Minister of Irrigation, and later ratified through changes in law (World Bank, 2004).[25] Donors and the Minister of Irrigation sought similar amendments in Law 12 for 1984 to recognize branch canal associations as legal entities, grant them authority to collect fees, and allow them to sanction violators.[26] Although work on these legislative amendments began in 1998, they had still not been adopted by Parliament over a decade later.

Thus, while managerial networks regarded user associations as an essential step in moving the irrigation system toward an idealized farmer-managed and demand-driven system, these networks did not initially succeed in endowing associations with sufficient legal or infrastructural authority to facilitate significant participation in water management decisions.

### *Integrated water management districts: building infrastructural authority?*

Water experts and consultants faced similar challenges in establishing integrated water management districts. As with most interventions in the water sector, the idea of an integrated district was tried first in two pilot areas, carefully selected to maximize the chances of success. Project documents noted that the pilot areas should have such desirable qualities as well-trained staff in sufficient numbers, closely coinciding boundaries between existing irrigation and drainage districts, easily monitored in-flow and out-flow points for water flowing through the district, functioning water user associations at *masqa* and branch canal levels, and the improved *masqa* infrastructure associated with the Irrigation Improvement Project (International Resources Group *et al.*, 2001: 2–4). Inversing these ideal attributes suggests challenges that managerial networks encountered as they sought to replicate the integrated district outwards from the two chosen pilot districts.

Field surveys of the pilot districts brought to light the extent to which local agricultural producers had already intervened to address water scarcity and inequity in supply, one of the primary rationales for creating integrated districts. These surveys found that many farmers, particularly at the tail ends of canals, had invested in shallow groundwater wells to supplement inadequate surface-water flows in canals, dug illicitly without permits from the Ministry of Irrigation (ibid.). These were in addition to deeper wells operated by the ministry to supplement canal deliveries at peak demand times.

As in the agricultural policy reform projects, Egyptian and American water experts convened working groups and ongoing workshops with leading ministerial officials and water experts to find mutually agreeable blueprints for a new integrated district. This "*markaz* water resources office" was to combine irrigation, drainage, and pumping functions in a district office employing an estimated 270 staff (ibid.: 4–6). Experts also drafted the text of ministerial decrees to legally authorize the creation of the district entities.[27] As of 2008, twenty-seven integrated water management districts had been established with 600 branch canal user associations, covering 15 percent of Egypt's arable land (United States Agency for International Development, 2011).

A 2008 USAID assessment report attributed the relatively rapid spread of integrated districts to lessons learned from previous interventions. Bypassing the central Irrigation Advisory Service (itself created as part of the original Irrigation Improvement Project), the USAID-funded LIFE Integrated Water Resources Management project (2004–8) worked directly with district employees in the newly formed integrated districts. These district-level officials were trained to establish branch canal user associations and then undertake a phased process of participatory irrigation management. That is, rather than overlooking the employees of the local state, later donor-governmental projects incorporated them as the main conduits to "reach" local users.

The decision to focus on district-level linkages between the irrigation authorities and agricultural users allowed managerial networks to shift their focus from intensive investment in a few pilot areas that represented ideal but unrepresentative features. Instead, later phases of the project provided technical assistance to all integrated districts and user associations but without direct financial transfers. The 2008 assessment argued that this approach allowed "the water users to partner with ministry staff to provide improvements in water delivery services, system maintenance, water quality, conflict resolution, and communications and information exchange" (International Resources Group, 2008: 59). The branch canal user associations and integrated districts jointly planned the rotation schedule for water deliveries. The involvement of the elected association in planning irrigation schedules provided farmers an incentive to provide more accurate information on cropping patterns. Because the user associations took part in substantive irrigation decisions, they were better able to serve as intermediaries between agricultural producers and the Ministry of Irrigation. The ministry also authorized the elected councils of the water boards to deal directly with farmer complaints and conflicts, seeking to diminish the practice of irrigators directly petitioning district engineers. By taking their concerns to the water boards, farmers could also bypass the mistrusted and often hated local police presence (ibid.).

The measures required to build infrastructural authority between branch canal associations and local-level ministry staff also highlighted the difficulties in sustaining these linkages. USAID provided extensive financing to train and upgrade the skills of employees in the integrated district. Retaining qualified personnel at the project's conclusion thus faced the same obstacles as encountered elsewhere in Egypt's sprawling public sector. Many competent district engineers were hired on temporary contracts, resulting in frequent turnover of trained staff and shortages of trained employees. As discussed in previous chapters, similar problems emerged in retaining experienced rangers in protected areas and keeping environmental experts at the environmental affairs agency (ibid.: 64).

Similarly, the Ministry of Irrigation had no provisions to meet the increased financial requirements of operating integrated districts, inspectorates, and directorates. As in dealing with pollution control issues at state-owned factories, the *de facto* stance of the Egyptian government was that these issues of financial sustainability would continue to be met through injections of external assistance on a project-by-project basis. In 2009, USAID met these expectations, starting funding for the LIFE Integrated Water Resources Management II project. The project, funded for 2009–12, was to expand the model of the integrated water resource district throughout the eastern portion of the Nile Delta.[28]

## Conclusion

Managerial networks have remade the constellation of key ideas and practices that constitute the "nature" of Egypt's water-agricultural sector, promoting new technologies and practices (the irrigation improvement project), new forms of social organization (user associations), and new administrative routines and organizations (the integrated water district). Since the 1980s, these initiatives have been implemented by quasi-autonomous reform units within the Ministry of Irrigation or through donor-funded projects staffed by Egyptian water experts and external consultants. Discursively, these interventions have been framed in terms of decentralization, efficiency, participation, demand management, and integrated resource management.

While these efforts improved water delivery, established water user associations, and upgraded the physical infrastructure across some of Egypt's agricultural lands, only recently have some of these initiatives begun to establish forms of infrastructural and legal authority that may prove to be substantively more participatory, decentralized, and integrated. These efforts to build cooperative linkages with cultivators in selected areas contrast with other ongoing state initiatives, such as coercively limiting rice cultivation.

Most expert initiatives have focused on intervening, often quite directly, in the communities of cultivators that are widely held to constitute the major source of water demands. Policy initiatives that restructure who receives water, who can cultivate which crops, and where and how water will be conserved have often been designed and implemented without sufficient knowledge of existing, informal systems for accessing and distributing water, and in the absence of infrastructural authority that would provide the kinds of local-level information and cooperation needed to address these gaps in knowledge and practice.

Interventions focused solely on agricultural producers tend to downplay water demands from a host of other actors and sectors that generate water demand in addition to small-scale agriculture. Government policies on trade, energy, industrialization, and land markets, which shape patterns of water consumption, have been largely left unaddressed (World Bank, 2007). As we saw in the case of the western Delta, agrobusiness interests have been largely shielded from problems of water quality or scarcity.

Instead, experiences of shortages and poor water quality have been decentralized and disaggregated, in villages with water shortages and inadequate sanitation, in poor agricultural households, and in peri-urban areas without adequate water and sanitation networks. Localized experiences with scarcity and water pollution are not communicated upward in any systematic fashion, and there has been no systemic crisis or institutional breakdown that would prompt more serious policy reforms from the political elite. Despite the assertions of water experts that widespread institutional reform is necessary, political leaderships, government authorities, and provincial officeholders do not see that such reforms are critical. Water reform initiatives have thus been relegated to donor-state projects staffed by managerial networks.

IWRM is a hegemonic discourse of these managerial networks, yet as Conca noted, it is only one of several competing "proto-norms" emerging around water management globally (Conca, 2006). Conca identified the marketization of water (i.e. the pricing of water resources) and the notion of water as a human right as two alternative framings of water issues. Neither of these emerging paradigms for water management has made much headway among managerial water networks in Egypt.

There are several ways in which this situation may change, however. The first is rapid and unexpected resource scarcity, such as the record-low Nile flows from drought that occurred in the late 1980s. Sustained drought in Israel and rapid drawdown of Saudi Arabia's fossil aquifers sparked significant policy interventions to limit agricultural consumption of water. In Egypt, however, far larger numbers of people depend directly upon the agricultural sector for consumption, livelihoods, and income, which makes the stakes for adapting to natural fluctuations in water flows very high. For precisely this reason, the existing water infrastructure helps mitigate the variability of flood and drought relatively effectively, dampening the feedback from physical resource change.

Perhaps more likely in the wake of the 2011 uprising is the amplification of demands for more accountability and equity in the provision of public goods in the water sector. The idea of water as a fundamental right, with implications for equity and justice, is the norm in use by the vast majority of Egypt's water users, particularly those in the agricultural sector. While this widely shared norm is often lamented by donors who promote marketization (particularly pricing) of water supplies, it also offers a different basis on which to think about integrated water management. In other words, IWRM's notions of water efficiency, demand management, and participation would benefit from being grounded in a framework of social rights to water. This shift in discursive authority would suggest greater attention in identifying ways in which actual users are deprived of water and suffer from water pollution. A focus on water rights, then, suggests different kinds of interventions in constructing legal and infrastructural authority around water. A shift toward thinking about—and managing—water as a social right, however, will most likely not be proposed from above, but demanded from below.

# 7 Environmental politics in revolutionary times

> The extraordinary sense of liberation, urge for self-realization, the dream of a new and just order—in short the desire for "all that is new" are what define the very spirit of these revolutions. In these turning points, these societies have moved far ahead of their political elites, exposing albeit the major anomaly of these revolutions—the discrepancy between a revolutionary desire for the "new," and a reformist trajectory that may lead to harboring the "old."
>
> (Bayat, 2011)

In early 2011, mass street protests across Egypt forced Hosni Mubarak out of office after three decades in power. The revolution or *thawra*, as it was termed in Egypt, broke the regime's ability to instill fear and suppress dissent, as the internal security forces were unable to contain or control collective disobedience in multiple cities simultaneously, while the army chose not to intervene. With Mubarak placed under hospital arrest in Sharm el-Sheikh, the senior security and military generals took control of the country in the form of the Supreme Council of the Armed Forces (SCAF). This rapid shift in government but not in regime initially left intact much of the hierarchies of the internal security services and the military.

In the subsequent year, as protesters continued to demand fundamental political change, the ruling military junta increasingly employed lethal violence against activists in several Egyptian cities, using snipers as well as beatings and detentions. Over 12,000 civilians were subjected to military trials. The SCAF, several Mubarak-era ministers, and the state-owned media also employed many bitterly familiar tactics to intimidate and harass civil society organizations, including mobilizing the media to portray a diverse array of protesters as threats to national security and economic stability. These trends prompted some commentators to observe that these were the actions of an unaccountable "deep state" in Egypt, illustrating the limits of what the military–security apparatus would tolerate in a new political order (El Amrani, 2012).

Yet as in Turkey, where the notion of the "deep state" has been widely employed by political scientists, the retrenchment of the military–security apparatus is only part of the unfolding political transformation unleashed by mass protest. Parliamentary elections for the Majlis al-Sha'b, the lower parliamentary house, in the fall of 2011 saw Egypt's largest and oldest organized movement, the Muslim Brotherhood, banned from formal political participation for decades, compete as the Freedom and Justice Party, winning 47 percent of the seats. The more conservative Islamist party Al-Nour and its affiliated parties won roughly 25 percent of the seats, and the old liberal party Wafd Party took close to 9 percent ("Egypt's Brotherhood Wins 47% of Parliament Seats," 2012).

Prior to the election, new political parties proliferated rapidly, particularly those organized by youth and liberal activists. Many candidates stood for each seat, as individuals or on party lists. In the third, concluding electoral round, for instance, 2,754 candidates competed for 150 parliamentary seats ("Citing JFP Violations, Judge in Qalyubiya Halts Voting," 2012). Most of these aspiring politicians and political currents lacked an organized infrastructure and constituency to support their political campaigns and, not surprisingly, could not compete in getting out voters compared with the grassroots infrastructural capacities that the Islamists had long cultivated. After three decades of electoral fraud and manipulation to ensure that the government's ruling party dominated even a weak Parliament, the autumn 2011 elections were historic. For supporters of parliamentary politics, the challenge remains of revising the constitution to grant Parliament more authority vis-à-vis the executive branch.

The impacts of Egypt's revolutionary year, however, have gone far beyond changes in electoral politics and repeated bouts of repression and accommodation from the SCAF. Instead, the uprising transformed how many Egyptians think about, and engage in, the everyday conduct of politics. As Bayat suggested in the quote that opens this chapter, there has been a revolution in expectations and an explosion in social mobilization. The importance of the activist networks analyzed in this book is now abundantly clear in light of the repeated popular marches, protests, sit-ins, and strikes. But the tactics and claims once employed primarily by relatively small activist networks and organized groups in the years before the uprising—from striking textile workers to demonstrating judges to petitioning lawyers—have been adopted by a much broader array of groups and communities across the country (Figure 7.1).

The SCAF presumes to govern a more mobilized society than before the 2011 uprising. Many Egyptians have been willing to engage in direct action that directly impacts official business and economic activity despite the risks. These actions— blockades of transport routes and infrastructure, sit-ins at government offices, railway tracks, highways, subway stations, and public squares—did not start with the January 25 uprising, but have by most accounts intensified as a result. The Egyptian National Railways, for instance, reported that, during 2011, railroads were blocked 1,720 times by protests, sit-ins, and demonstrations ("Railways Authority Estimates 2011 Losses at LE70 Million," 2012).

Contentious politics around many issues, including environmental ones, is thus no longer the exception but the norm in Egypt. As a result, many policy arenas formerly closed to public input and monopolized by governmental authorities now have to respond to the claims and tactics of a deeply mobilized public. While repression makes headlines, these proliferating protest campaigns

*Figure 7.1* Bedouin protest on the anniversary of the January 25 uprising,
Martyr's Square, Sheikh Zoweid City, North Sinai, January 25, 2012
Mohamed Sabry, 2012

regularly win concessions from governmental authorities, even as these same authorities often employ force to disperse, detain, and injure those engaged in direct action.

Since the 2011 *thawra*, environmental issues and policies are thus increasingly contested by a broader array of actors taking a variety of direct actions in the public sphere. These changes have altered the character of environmental networks and signal deeper changes in the landscape of popular participation and political decision-making. This chapter explores how changes in political institutions and popular mobilization have already begun to impact the politics of the environment in Egypt, marked by intensified social protest around pollution issues and increased demand for access to resources, such as agricultural land and fisheries. Activist and managerial networks have sought to adapt to these new political realities. Managerial networks of experts have begun to adopt activist framings more proactively and to make use of emerging infrastructures of protest. Activist and expert networks alike increasingly recognize the need to work with mobilized communities to better address industrial pollution, protection of habitats, and conservation of resources.

## Looking back: continuities amidst change

In analyzing how environmental networks mobilized forms of authority in different places and at multiple scales of governance during more than three decades of Mubarak's rule, this book contributes to a more nuanced understanding of the constraints and possibilities of political change in Egypt more generally. While Egyptians term the events of 2011 a revolution, the restructuring of the political order underway has not led to dramatic rupture in state–society relations, the overturning of old state and business elites, or a protracted period of civil conflict. Indeed, the structures, institutions, and personnel of the central ministries—and their institutions and staff deconcentrated in the provinces—remain intact. This means the design and implementation of all kinds of environmental policies and projects will be to some extent path-dependent, relying on existing institutions of governance. Similarly, the dominant narratives and discursive framings used by state officials, experts, and activists to debate environmental problems and challenges of economic development will change only slowly. Efforts to address Egypt's environmental challenges will build on existing discourses, legal frameworks, and forms of infrastructural authority already elaborated by environmental networks of experts and activists in specific places and around particular policy domains.

By focusing on the agency of networks, this book was written against the grain of conventional accounts of Egypt's environmental problems, which cast the country and its inhabitants as prisoners in a neo-Malthusian scenario. In a grim future marked by increasing population growth, water scarcity, and intensifying urban densities, the severity of environmental problems can seem overwhelming. Yet as the empirical cases in this book illustrate, physical scarcity and population increase do not figure as straightforward "causes" of the environmental problems analyzed in the case studies. Instead, the analysis here calls attention to the complex ways that state policies and business privilege, ranging from allocations of property rights to subsidies and investment incentives, shape environmental problems. Physical resource scarcity and population growth, a lack of financial resources and shortages of human capital, are "real" constraints in developing countries such as Egypt, but ones that are partially constituted by distributions of power, patterns of political inclusion and exclusion, and state policies.

To summarize and revisit some of the key findings from the case studies of industrial pollution, habitat protection, and water management in previous chapters, we can return to the notion that networks have spatial contours (Mann, 1986: 10). That is, different environmental issues located in distinctive places shaped opportunities for managerial and activist networks to build forms of authority. While legal and discursive authority could be constructed and enacted from the center, often by limited numbers of experts, infrastructural authority requires constructing on-the-ground linkages. For managerial networks, this enables project implementation; for activist networks, it is the key to coordinating effective collection action. Thus, some environmental issue areas and places posed greater challenges of coordination for experts and activists than others.

In the case of industrial pollution (Chapter 3), managerial networks focused their efforts on concentrated "hotspots" of severe industrial pollution, produced by old state-owned enterprises and partially privatized firms. These clusters of heavily polluting large firms are relatively few in number, but their emissions and effluents contribute significantly to pollution loads in Cairo and Alexandria as well as other cities. Pollution control experts, working as consultants and staff for international donor-funded projects and at the Industrial Compliance Office of the Egyptian Environmental Affairs Agency (EEAA), sought to induce firms to pursue pollution reduction. Promoting market-based approaches such as pollution prevention and clean production, they sought to build tangible, cooperative linkages with firms—infrastructural authority—by providing managers with pollution inventories and suggested remediation measures ("compliance action plans"), tools that were used to leverage donor assistance and financing.

While the relatively small numbers of large firms would seem to facilitate coordination with pollution control networks, the entrenched, privileged position of large state-owned and quasi-privatized firms in Egypt's political economy instead allowed them to engage in protracted negotiations over compliance with environmental regulations. In the absence of effective enforcement mechanisms and faced with uncertainty about the pace and scope of privatization, managers responded only half-heartedly to market-based approaches to pollution control. Instead, firms bargained with donors and government ministries for more comprehensive, costly assistance packages in order to modernize their plants and upgrade their production lines. In lieu of more systematic enforcement, the Ministry of Environment intermittently undertook highly publicized, targeted campaigns against small groups of firms (as with public sector enterprises discharging directly into the Nile or the cement factories of Helwan), while the Cairo and Alexandria sanitation organizations imposed their own fines on industrial wastewater discharges. Aside from these activities, however, managerial pollution control networks and donors found they had inadequate leverage with large polluting firms, particularly those in the military, state, and hybrid public–private "investment" sectors. The overall result was that firms complied only slowly and partially with environmental regulations, leaving industrial pollution as a significant environmental problem, almost two decades after comprehensive legal standards were imposed.

Inadequate control of industrial pollution had long produced sporadic attempts by local activists to challenge urban pollution, through petitions to local officials, media coverage, demonstrations, and lawsuits. These efforts grew in scale and intensity as the Mubarak regime sought to increase foreign direct investment in chemicals, fertilizers, cement, fossil fuels, steel, and other industrial sectors. The activist networks that emerged in response relied upon the density of urban social linkages, existing state-sanctioned organizations, and coverage by state and private media outlets to publicize their cause and sustain protest.

In Chapter 4, I compared two such activist campaigns, one opposed to sea disposal of sewage in Alexandria, and the other opposed to building yet another fertilizer plant in Damietta. In contrast to most of the literature on "civil society," which focused on the expansion of voluntary organizations under Mubarak and constraints on their activities, these campaigns did not emerge from NGOs or formal organizations. Instead, initially a small network of activists, catalyzed by perceptions of specific environmental threats, launched public campaigns that steadily increased pressure on the central government.

In Alexandria, a relatively narrow circle of middle-class professionals, academics, and public intellectuals were able to keep the question of sea versus land disposal of Alexandria's sewage in the public eye primarily through media coverage, meetings with provincial officials, and framing their criticisms in resonant discourses with wide popular appeal. The eventual endorsement of their position by USAID and American consulting firms was only partly a function of organizational "success," however, as the Mubarak regime and many environmental experts shared the activists' goal of reusing treated wastewater for land reclamation.

The Damietta campaign a decade later, in contrast, drew on a broader social and political coalition, which not only employed mass, sustained street protest but also lawsuits, work stoppages, strikes, and administrative decrees. From a small core of activists, which organized themselves into "popular committees" to coordinate outreach and protest, opposition rapidly spread to participants from a number of state-sanctioned institutions. These organizations provided an infrastructure to legalize the concerns of activists, mobilize broader constituencies, and undertake direct action. Participants from universities, professional syndicates, unions, chambers of commerce, business federations, and municipal and provincial public employees took actions that directly affected the routine work of the city. These forms of "infrastructural authority" or power had concrete effects. For instance, strikes and work stoppages blocked construction work at the proposed fertilizer site long before the Mubarak regime annulled the investment agreement with the Canadian firm Agrium.

While the immediate target of the campaigns seemed to be foreign donors (USAID in Alexandria) and foreign firms (the multinational firm Agrium in Damietta), the campaigns were just as clearly trenchant criticisms of the centralization, neglect, and corruption of the government. In their condemnation of the dismal performance of *al-masuleen*, the "responsibles," local activists in Damietta and Alexandria castigated the regime in Cairo even as they appealed to Mubarak and appointed provincial governors to bring pressure to bear on USAID and Agrium. Discursively, they framed their criticisms of sea disposal for sewage and new fertilizer factories as threats to public health and economic livelihoods. Both campaigns highlighted that their cities were *masayif*, summer coastal destinations for many middle- and lower-middle-class Egyptians, where pollution would destroy an important part of the local economy.

For the creation and management of protected areas (Chapter 5), a small network of conservation scientists and protected area managers used a strong legal framework to build some infrastructural authority in the South Sinai protected areas. They sought to build linkages with leading figures in the military, provincial governors, tourism investors, and tribal communities located in and around protected areas. Discursively, the conservation network successfully marketed the idea of protected areas to the Sadat and Mubarak regimes by framing conservation in terms of its contributions to preserving heritage, promoting tourism development and facilitating population settlement in frontier border regions. To leverage international support, however, conservation experts employed a different discourse, emphasizing the global significance of Egypt's marine and terrestrial protected areas to safeguarding biodiversity and preserving rare habitats.

When the Mubarak regime enacted new laws and created new governmental agencies to promote rapid tourism development during the 1990s, the challenges of building infrastructural authority became more complex. With an explosion of land claims along the Red Sea coast as well as South Sinai, the challenges of negotiating with such powerful actors as Egypt's military, the Tourism Development Authority (TDA), and ever larger and more politically influential real estate firms deepened. Protected areas located in sensitive border or frontier areas remained in the first instance the domain of the state's military and security complex. The regime also increasingly extended ownership rights to coastal land along the Red Sea to the TDA, undermining the reach and effectiveness of conservation experts working on donor projects and in the Nature Conservation Sector at the environmental agency. Consequent environmental damage to reefs, shorelines, and local communities from untrammeled tourism development in turn prompted the formation of activist networks such as HEPCA, the small group of activists and experts pursuing on-the-ground conservation efforts in Hurghada and along the Red Sea coast.

As the politics of protected areas has unfolded largely along Egypt's coastlines, where lucrative land speculation and resort development clashed with conservation goals, interventions by expert environmental networks in the water-agricultural sector have also had a specific spatial focus, in the "old" lands of the Nile Valley and Delta. Managerial water networks, based in donor projects and in new administrative enclaves within the Ministries of Irrigation and Agriculture, have sought to reshape the physical infrastructures of the irrigation and drainage systems, create new communities of users, and implant new technologies and practices of water management in ever-expanding pilot areas. Within these areas, these interventions have thus restructured roles and responsibilities of cultivators and the thousands of public sector workers employed by the Ministry of Irrigation in the provinces. At the same time, however, the ambitious scope and high costs of these irrigation and drainage improvement packages have meant that geographic expansion in the old lands has been gradual. In addition, these interventions have been complicated by contentions over changing legal jurisdictions for water and land. Proposed changes in law by experts, such as legislation to legitimate the roles of user associations in participatory irrigation management, have faced protracted delays at the national level. Expert discourses framing water reforms in terms of urgent needs for decentralization, participation, and resource conservation have found limited support in national political institutions.

Consistently, managerial water networks encountered significant difficulties in building infrastructural authority and "reaching" small-scale cultivators. Entrenched mistrust and avoidance of state institutions from decades of command-and-control policies in agriculture are reinforced by coercively applied rules, such as fines for cultivating rice. Small agricultural producers remain adversely affected by national policies favoring large-scale agrobusiness, whether in the new land reclamation areas or in the "old" lands of the Nile Valley and Delta.

For many cultivators, expert discourses about integrated water resource management (IWRM), decentralization, and participation have only limited bearing on their day-to-day challenges. As managerial networks and international donors promote such interventions as "integrated water management districts," which combine the establishment of formal user associations and the redrawing of irrigation and drainage boundaries with investments in infrastructure, it is possible that cultivators will be more actively involved in setting irrigation rotations and other water management decisions. That is, the discourses of integrated, participatory, and decentralized water management may eventually have an infrastructural grounding in institutions.

## Environmental issues in a democratizing polity

Popular concern with environmental issues has already emerged as a politically salient issue in Egypt's emerging system of competitive politics. In 2011, environmental issues appeared in electoral party platforms and campaign speeches of candidates for Parliament from across the political spectrum (Baraka, 2011).

Parties ranging from the liberal party Free Egypt to the Salafi Al-Nour Party, which headed a coalition of fourteen Islamist parties as the Islamist Alliance, incorporated environmental issues into their electoral platforms. The Islamist Alliance platform listed their top environmental priorities as the relocation of industries outside densely populated areas, enforcing mandates for pollution control equipment in urban industries, controls on the use of dangerous pesticides, and the promotion of clean energy to lower pollution levels (ibid.). With the seating of a new, emboldened Parliament, activist networks may find new opportunities to work with sympathetic parliamentarians on environmental issues.

The Muslim Brotherhood's Freedom and Justice Party (FJP) is no exception. The FJP includes some members with direct experience with urban pollution issues. One such parliamentarian is Ali Fath al-Bab, recently elected speaker of the Shura Council, Egypt's upper parliamentary chamber, in early spring 2012. In 1995, Fath al-Bab had been elected to the Majlis al-Sha'b, the lower house of Parliament, as an independent candidate affiliated with the Muslim Brotherhood for the industrial district of Helwan. Fath al-Bab served on the Parliament's Environment and Health Committee during this period. He has long argued that environmental issues affecting public health merit immediate governmental attention, including health threats from air pollution, sewage, clean drinking water, and soil pollution from adjacent polluting industries.[1]

Fath al-Bab's interest in environmental issues stemmed from his work with the state-owned Iron and Steel Company in Helwan. Helwan had long been considered a pollution hotspot given the large number of state- and military-owned industries in the area, and Helwan Iron and Steel has been one of the worst offenders. In his view, state-owned enterprises pollute intensively because they employ antiquated technologies (*model bit'ahu adeem*), sustain excessive numbers of workers, and lack funds for inadequate reinvestment.[2] His views thus correspond fairly closely to those of Egypt's pollution control experts about the causes of pollution in state-owned firms, as explored in Chapter 3.

As Fath al-Bab and others in Helwan recall, concrete improvements in air quality only began in the late 1990s. The environmental agency targeted Helwan's cement plants specifically, installing devices to deliver real-time monitoring of emissions directly to the office of the environmental minister (or so the agency claimed). In ensuing years, revenues from privatization of some cement plants, such as Tora Cement, were combined with donor aid to finance some improvements in production lines and pollution control equipment.

## Industrial pollution, privatization, and state-owned enterprises

The Helwan cement factories provide a good example of how gravely polluting firms improved performance only when the costs of pollution became politically unacceptable at the highest levels of the government. Most firms continue to pursue delayed, soft compliance with environmental laws, as argued in Chapter 3.

The challenges of addressing industrial pollution in an effective and timely manner in state-owned enterprises and quasi-privatized firms remain significant. Even before the 2011 uprising, Egypt's privatization program had been halted amidst mounting worker protest and criticism that only the wealthy and well connected had reaped the benefits. As government officials admitted openly in 2010, privatization was stopped primarily because the remaining state-owned firms were unlikely to find private buyers. Deeply indebted, these firms were thought to require comprehensive restructuring and upgrading in order to become profitable. Despite the sobering environmental as well as economic performance of state-owned enterprises, a significant proportion of industrial production remains under state ownership.

### *Continuities in the military-industrial sector*

Military-owned firms were never among the initial 314 state-owned enterprises targeted for privatization. Since the 1970s, the military has not only operated its own handful of large firms, but also pursued a number of joint ventures with foreign and domestic capital. Investment by military and state-owned firms and their multinational partners in sectors such as fertilizers and chemicals has only increased in recent years given ample natural gas reserves and attractive export revenues. The SCAF's approach toward private capital thus represents continuity with much of the Mubarak period, reinforcing what Waterbury aptly termed "a public–private symbiosis" (Waterbury, 1993).

This symbiosis has been particularly apparent in lucrative sectors such as fossil fuels and associated industries. The military-owned Nasr Company for Chemicals, for instance, inaugurated three new factories to produce fertilizers and sulfuric acid in Fayoum in 2010. Farmers living nearby complained to the local governor about the effects of air pollution on their date palms, olive trees, and crops (Osman, 2011). The governor, according to one press account, responded that the military sector simply was not under his jurisdiction. While farmers had discussed undertaking more direct action—such as blocking a main road leading into the area—an activist network working to sustain a coordinated campaign is not yet evident. "We are poor people," one farmer told the press, "and most of us are not educated. People still fear the authorities. We are not in Damietta" (ibid.).

## Industrial facilities, direct action, and activist networks

As this farmer noted, the city of Damietta emerged again as a leading site of environmental activism in 2011. While the activist campaign in 2008 called for the relocation of the proposed plant outside of Damietta, the Mubarak regime quietly made other plans. While the government cancelled approvals for Agrium to build on the proposed site, the Mubarak regime offered the company a 26 percent stake in the state-owned enterprise MOPCO, located directly across a small canal from the original site. The government pledged to build two additional production lines at MOPCO, making the plant's total production similar to that planned for EAgrium. It was thus predictable that renewed protest would break out once residents realized that the MOPCO–Agrium expansion was underway and that they had, in effect, gained very little from their 2008 campaign.

In late November 2011, angry residents from the village of Senaniya, near MOPCO, took direct action. They staged a sit-in, blocking the main roads leading into Ras al-Barr and the industrial port, and cut off power to the port from the main power station (El-Kashef *et al.*, 2011). They issued a statement saying that the government had deceived them, since the plant had not been relocated. In the early hours of the morning, the military attacked protesters camping out in the road, injuring a number of them and shooting dead twenty-one-year-old Islam Amin Abu Abdullah ("One Killed, 12 Injured…," 2011). Several hours after Islam's death, Field Marshal Mohamed Hussein Tantawi, the head of the SCAF, ordered the factory closed pending an environmental investigation on November 13.

Several prominent figures, including the provincial governor, local politician Essam Sultan, and well-known engineer Mamdouh Hamza, negotiated with the villagers to open the port. The protesters agreed to allow the port to open, and in doing so sought to counteract attempts by the SCAF and other state agencies to depict them as lawless hooligans disrupting the local economy. As one activist told Reuters, "unblocking the road does not mean that our protest is over. This is merely a goodwill gesture to prove we are not thugs or a mob, just people fighting for their right to live" (Reuters, 2011b). The protesters wanted the plant immediately dismantled; as a middle-aged furniture worker told the press, "We don't trust the government. They never responded to our demands or cared about our environment and health. They attacked us with live ammunition rather than listening to our complaints" (Sabry, 2011).

MOPCO demanded that the government allow the factory to resume production. In a memo to the prime minister, MOPCO claimed that the plant was losing US$3.2 million daily in lost production, and that if the company was forced to move, it would not be able to pay back US$1.05 billion in debt borrowed from twenty international and Egyptian banks to finance the expansion (Aref, 2011; Reuters, 2011a). MOPCO filed a lawsuit arguing that the prime minister had incorrectly ordered the firm to suspend the expansion of production lines, and that the Damietta governor and the SCAF had illegally halted company operations pending environmental review ("Administrative Court Rules in Favor of Mopco…," 2012). MOPCO and Uhde, the German firm that had built eight similar plants in Egypt already, also embarked on various attempts to improve their public image in Egypt. MOPCO created a Facebook page ("Yes Mopco"), while Uhde representatives gave presentations showing that their fertilizer plants were built in close proximity to residential areas in developed countries, including the Netherlands, Austria, and Belgium. In its 2011 annual report to shareholders, Agrium noted it fully expected that MOPCO would move ahead with its expanded production lines.

In the midst of these developments, residents of Damietta went to the polls in the fall to elect parliamentary representatives. Similar to returns elsewhere in Egypt, the Muslim Brotherhood's Freedom and Justice Party won a majority, with 86,608 votes, followed closely by the Salafi Al-Nour Party with 80,936. However, in Damietta the moderate Islamist Al-Wasat Party did reasonably well, with 60,814 votes. A leading Al-Wasat candidate elected to Parliament was the lawyer Essam Sultan. Sultan had filed several lawsuits challenging the government's contract with EAgrium in 2008, and emerged as one of the principal figures negotiating between the armed forces and emboldened villagers during the street clashes in November 2011.

A year after Mubarak was deposed, in January 2012, the SCAF-appointed environmental inspection committee declared that MOPCO met Egyptian and international environmental regulations and was not significantly polluting the local water or air ("Damietta's Controversial Mopco Factory…," 2012). In stark contrast to the 2008 parliamentary committee of inquiry's report, the 2012 report focused narrowly on actual pollutant loads, rather than the risks of siting fertilizer plants next to urban areas. The composition of the committee also differed significantly. While the parliamentary committee sought out nationally respected environmental scientists, the SCAF-commissioned committee was delegated to the syndicate of scientific professions and chaired by an administrator from Mansoura University (ibid.).

In a further blow to the protesters, the Administrative Court in Mansoura found in favor of MOPCO in March 2012. The judge ordered that the plant be allowed to resume production immediately and complete work on the expanded production lines. It further imposed legal fees on the state, and dismissed a lawsuit filed by civil society organizations in Damietta. According to press accounts, while the verdict was delivered central security forces cordoned off the courthouse, admitting only MOPCO workers and select journalists inside, while citizens and lawyers from Damietta were shut out (ibid.).

The second environmental fact-finding committee focused on the question of whether MOPCO and the expansion in production posed a direct public health threat. This emphasis echoed the activist claims that the plants were directly polluting local air and water. Yet this pollution framing serves to obscure some of the key issues at stake for the activists. Environmental and social protest in Damietta can be understood more broadly as a question of center–local relations. Under Mubarak, the Cabinet in Cairo designated a new industrial zone, a large cargo port, and approved a number of large-scale petrochemical and fertilizer plants in Damietta without local consultation, compensation, or upgraded investment in public services. Damietta's activist network has challenged the monopoly of central governmental ministries and the Cabinet to promote concentrated industrial investment without local consultation.

The government's centralized approach to land use and industrial siting is exemplified in the National Plan for Petrochemical Industry, adopted by the Ministry of Petroleum and Mineral Resources, for the period 2002–20. The plan "reserved" lands for petrochemical facilities totaling 33 million square meters in Alexandria, Damietta, Gulf of Suez, Ismailia, Kafr El-Sheikh, and other coastal cities. The government selected these cities for their port, transport, and industrial infrastructures, continuing a long tradition of fostering greater industrial concentration on the peripheries of expanding and densely settled urban areas near ports, waterways, and transport lines. These patterns of investment are contrary to the government's formal commitments calling for decentralization of industrial investment to "greenfield" desert areas.

In effect, the Damietta activist networks took on the impunity of the state-owned industrial sector and its close ties with foreign investors. The emerging coalition of protesting villagers, civil society organizations, sympathetic journalists, and parliamentarians thus face an uphill battle in trying to relocate a lucrative state-owned enterprise backed by foreign investors and heavily indebted to Egypt's banks. With such stakes, the more civic, civil, and inclusive style of environmental campaign waged in 2008 might simply have encountered endless delays and prevarications, while MOPCO completed construction on additional production lines. Instead, angry workers and villagers sought to capture governmental attention directly, by closing the port, the roads, and the power plant.

Direct action by environmental activist networks has diffused to other campaigns against industrial facilities in several Egyptian cities. In Idku, east of Alexandria, activists organized against a proposed natural gas processing plant owned by British Petroleum (BP), demanding a full review by the environmental agency (Marroushi, 2011a). The BP project had been approved by the SCAF, but other agencies had not yet completed their reviews. As in Damietta, the city already contained several fossil fuel operations jointly owned by state and foreign companies. These included Rashpetco, a joint venture between the state-owned Egyptian General Petroleum Company (EGPC), the UK's BG Group, and Italian power company Edison, and the Burullus Gas Company, a joint venture between EGPC, BG Group, and Malaysia's state-owned petroleum company Petronas. As in Damietta, the emerging activist network in Idku included middle-class professionals, particularly lawyers, and local residents concerned about the impact on agricultural land and fisheries. The campaigners blocked roads, raided BP's office in Idku, conducted a sit-in at the site, submitted legal complaints to the SCAF, and met with the governor (ibid.).

In another instance of locals taking direct action around central plans for land use, residents displaced from the proposed site of Egypt's first nuclear reactor reoccupied the site in January 2012. The residents dismantled existing buildings, built new houses, and announced that not only would they reoccupy their land, but also that they would distribute some to those who could not afford housing ("Protests at Nuclear Power Station…," 2012).

## Contested coastal lands and corruption charges

Just as at the center of the conflict in Damietta is a dispute over who determines land use, conflicting land use claims on Egypt's coastlines have lost none of their salience in the post-Mubarak era. As we saw in Chapter 5, rapid development of Egypt's coastlines for tourism and luxury housing under Mubarak largely benefitted leading Egyptian business conglomerates and well-placed officials. Popular outrage against these privileged relationships and corruption prompted the SCAF to review some of the more controversial land acquisition deals shortly after it took power in early 2011. The anti-corruption campaign has been selective, however; it has been unclear why some businessmen were charged with corruption, price-fixing, and suspect business dealings, while others were exempted from scrutiny. In some cases, the junta simply quietly re-negotiated land deals with influential foreign investors, such as Saudi prince Al Waleed bin Talal's stake in the New Valley (Toshka) land reclamation project. But others were not so fortunate.

A previously moribund agency, the Illicit Gains Authority, as well as public prosecutors, began systematically investigating some of Mubarak's associates, their private fortunes, and their acquisition of lucrative real estate on the Red Sea and Sinai coastlines (El-Din, 2011). The legal dossiers held at the Ministries of Environment and Tourism documenting land acquisition on the Red Sea and Sinai coasts were suddenly of great interest to public prosecutors.[3] One of the first members of the old regime to be charged was Zuhayr Garrana, the last Minister of Tourism under Mubarak, sentenced to five years in prison in May 2011 pending an appeal. Public prosecutors also charged businessmen known for being close to the Mubarak family, such as Hussein Salem and Kamal Shazly, with illicit acquisition and development of coastal land. Noticeably lacking from these prosecutions, however, were cases against the many military, police, and internal security officers who had acquired and often resold large tracts of coastal land.

To classify these land transactions as illicit, state prosecutors invoked an obscure 1998 legal provision that required all state land to be sold through competitive bidding. This rule had never been applied to tourism land previously. As a result, decision-making on land transfers ground to a halt in many governmental authorities after the spring 2011 uprising, amidst fears of corruption charges.[4] This included the TDA, which temporarily stopped allocating land for tourism development along the Red Sea altogether. In an interview with Reuters, Samih Suweiris, the owner of Orascom Development Holdings, one of the largest tourism development companies in Egypt, accurately captured the ramifications of invoking this little-known legal requirement for all land transactions in the country: "The biggest problem the state is facing now is the lack of clarity on the legal status of all of Egypt's land," he observed. "The problem is the rule can apply to any land which has been sold in Egypt" (Zayed, 2011).

Suweiris and his firm were particularly concerned with the criminalization of land transactions conducted by the TDA and other governmental agencies under Mubarak. Orascom had built a niche market in creating new luxury towns, featuring villas, apartments, and hotel rooms integrated with leisure offerings, such as marinas, sailing, diving, and shopping. The first two such towns built—Taba Heights on the Gulf of 'Aqaba and El Gouna on the northern Red Sea—were successful enough that the company had built integrated resort towns in additional Middle Eastern and European countries, including Switzerland. According to the firm's own promotional material, Orascom's success was built upon acquisition of a "land bank of 127 million square meters" in "some of the most breathtaking locales in the region" (Orascom Development Holdings, undated).

## Tourism development and protected areas clash in Lake Qarun

In 2008, Suweiris' Orascom Development Holdings had announced it would build a luxury resort on the northern shores of Lake Qarun in the Fayoum oasis. The company had obtained 1.3 million square meters in the protected area a decade earlier from the TDA, and planned on developing 400,000 square meters into a new resort, the Byoum Residence.[5] Marketed with a Western theme and the logo of a shotgun, the Byoum Residence was to include 158 villas, a marina, a four-star hotel, and a hunting lodge, all located within the boundaries of the Lake Qarun protected area (Kasinof, 2008).

Located only a few hours by car from Cairo, the Lake Qarun protected area is one of two protected areas in the Fayoum depression. Declared by prime ministerial decree in 1989, Lake Qarun and Wadi al-Rayan protected areas include several manmade saline lakes (fed primarily by agricultural drainage water), unique marine and primate fossil remains, Pharaonic basalt quarries, and archaeological sites dating from the Neolithic period forward. The numerous villages and towns in Fayoum, along with three cities, sustain a sizable permanent population of 2.48 million people. The area also includes an industrial area and a large salt extraction factory on the southern shore of the lake.

Popular with artists, resident foreigners, and Egyptians looking to escape Cairo's cacophony, the numbers of visitors to Lake Qarun and Wadi al-Rayan protected areas have steadily increased. In 2005 alone, the Fayoum Tourism Authority recorded that 56,206 Egyptians, 18,288 foreigners, and 879 Arabs (non-Egyptian) visited the Fayoum protected areas, with 32,962 hotel guests (Protected Area Management Unit, 2001: 14). Since the early 2000s, conservation experts had leveraged international assistance to build organizational capacities to cope with rapidly rising numbers of visitors. With support from the Italian government from 1998 through the mid-2000s, conservation experts and staff from the Nature Conservation Sector had developed a management plan, hired and trained rangers, constructed a visitors' center, and began monitoring existing industrial and land reclamation activities within and around the park (ibid.).

These steps in creating infrastructural authority, however, were overtaken by central government plans to market much of the rest of Lake Qarun for mass tourism, along the model of Egypt's coastlines (Hateita, 2010). Orascom's Byoum Residence was thus only one project in a larger "world tourism zone" planned for the Lake Qarun area by the last Mubarak-era Minister of Tourism, Zuhayr Garrana (Werr, 2011). In 2004, the TDA marketed eighteen plots of land on the northern shores of Lake Qarun as the "Qarun Tourism Center" under a twenty-five-year concession. The center included a target of 2,850 hotel rooms and 4,200 secondary housing apartments and villas, covering 2,760 feddans (Environmental Design Group, 2006: 13).

### The No Porto Fayoum campaign

In December 2010, one of the parcels in the Qarun Tourism Center was bought by the Amer Group, another large Egyptian real estate developer. The group announced it would build the "Porto Fayoum" resort on 2.8 million square meters under a ninety-nine-year concession agreement with the TDA (Zayed, 2010).[6] Amer Group had already completed two similar luxury developments, Porto Sukhna in 'Ayn al-Sukhna on the Red Sea coast and Porto Marina on Egypt's north coast. A member of Nature Conservation Egypt wrote that the two completed Porto projects consisted of "towering, endlessly expanding holiday apartment complexes... When viewed from afar, Porto Ain Sokhna's gigantic beehive of holiday homes rises as high as the gigantic mountains behind it" (Gauch, 2011). Indeed, Porto Sukhna is clearly visible across the Gulf of Suez from the main north–south coastal highway in the Sinai Peninsula.

With 2010 net profits of LE557.1 million, the Amer Group had plans for additional "Porto" projects throughout Egypt and the Arab world. These included luxury resorts at Porto Cairo, Porto Pyramids, Porto Aswan, Porto Matrouh on Egypt's north coast, Panoramica North Coast, Porto Tartous in Syria, and Porto Jeddah in Saudi Arabia.[7]

The small network of conservation experts involved in protected areas believed that the Porto Fayoum project set a dangerous precedent. If tourism development continued to proceed unhindered around Lake Qarun, it would set a legal and practical precedent for encroachments on other protected areas. Local conservationists had already sought to intervene, unsuccessfully, to halt Orascom's Byoum Residence on Lake Qarun. In 2011, several met directly with Orascom's director and majority shareholder, Samih Suweiris, who promised to review the project, but few changes in the design of the resort materialized, and it was constructed largely as planned.

The association of conservation professionals, Nature Conservation Egypt, and a local association called Friends of Lake Qarun combined their efforts, launching the "No Porto Fayoum" campaign. Each organization had small, overlapping memberships of conservation experts, birders, and local residents (both Egyptians and resident foreigners). They established a Facebook group, launched an online petition that garnered 2,000 signatures in a few months, wrote blogs, letters, and op-eds for the international and local press, and gave TV and online interviews.[8] The result was a spate of critical media coverage in Egypt and abroad regarding the Porto Fayoum project during the spring and summer of 2011.

With former regime stalwarts and ministers under arrest for corruption, and an increasing number of land deals frozen and under review, the Fayoum activists sought to capitalize on post-revolutionary outrage about cheap allocations of land to wealthy private investors. They framed their campaign to the local newspapers and TV stations in terms of reversing ill-advised land sales approved by the TDA under Mubarak.[9] Their online petition to stop the Porto Fayoum project highlighted that "Amer Group Chairman Mansour Amer is a former member of Mubarak's National Democratic Party and reportedly has close ties to former president Hosni Mubarak."[10]

To the international press and transnational conservation networks, however, these conservation experts invoked long-standing framings of protected areas as safeguarding Egypt's natural heritage and preserving international biodiversity, as explored in Chapter 5. The director of the Friends of Lake Qarun told Reuters that Porto Fayoum represented "the destruction of Egyptian natural heritage for future generations" (Werr, 2011). In their public communications, members of Nature Conservation Egypt also highlighted the global importance of Lake Qarun.

As the spectacular marine reefs and archaeological sites of Sinai had stimulated international interest in their conservation, the extensive, unique fossil remains and archaeological sites in Lake Qarun were of great interest to small transnational networks of researchers interested in archaeology, Egyptology, ancient quarry sites, paleobiology, and paleontology. In 2003, Egypt's conservation network had requested that UNESCO designate part of the northern shore of Lake Qarun, the Gabal Qatrani (Tar Hills), as a World Heritage site. In this escarpment, researchers had uncovered rare primate, mammal, and marine fossils, as well as remains of ancient basalt and gypsum quarries and settlement sites from at least 3000 BC.[11] In 2005, conservation networks successfully applied for Wadi al-Hitan ("valley of the whales"), within the Wadi al-Rayan protected area, to be declared a UNESCO World Heritage Site. This site contains unique and extensive fossil remains of an extinct suborder of whales, in the last evolutionary stages of losing mammalian hind legs, dated to 40 million years ago. Egypt's conservation networks had further arranged for Lake Qarun to be designated an internationally recognized wetland under the Ramsar Convention to Preserve Wetlands, as well as an Important Bird Area (IBA) by Birdlife International. Lake Qarun, like the manmade Lake Nasser to the south, is a significant stopover for bird migrations from Africa to Europe.

These international designations confer no legal or infrastructural authority within Egypt's political system, of course. International designations helped publicize the case of Lake Qarun to an international audience; domestically, however, the conservation network emphasized the economic contributions of protected areas for developing the Fayoum oasis. They repeatedly invoked a 2006 report by the Fayoum Tourism Authority and the Egyptian–Italian Cooperation projects in Fayoum, which critiqued the Ministry of Tourism's focus on cheap, mass-marketed tourism. The report concluded that:

> The product image of Fayoum is based on fossils, bird watching, lake activities, desert safari and rural life... The environmental deterioration caused by mass tourism development demonstrates a pattern of unsustainable resource use that adversely affects both environmental quality, and economic investment.
>
> (Environmental Design Group, 2006: 13)

In 2010, participants in an international conference on the Fayoum adopted a written declaration that embraced an even more expansive notion of "heritage" than that customarily used in Egypt's conservation circles. The conference participants urged immediate intervention to protect Lake Qarun.[12] Moving beyond the prevalent discourses of natural and cultural heritage, the declaration argued that Fayoum's "heritage" included "geological, environmental, archaeological, historical, rural, and traditional resources." In framing heritage as resources, the declaration argued that these should not only be conserved and documented, but also sustainably exploited to promote local economic development. Participants proposed that the Egyptian government allow the formation of a "heritage consortium" to implement a participatory regional development plan.[13]

Such innovative land use planning, however, required finding a government authority or popular constituency to serve as an advocate within the state. As a HEPCA member argued in Chapter 5, activist networks in Egypt are more successful when they enlist support from a governmental authority to intervene against other state entities. In the case of the Lake Qarun protected areas, conservation experts pinned their hopes on Egypt's Supreme Council of Antiquities (SCA), based on its authority to exclusively manage Egypt's cultural heritage and antiquities under Law 215 for 1951.[14] In 2009, the SCA's internationally known, controversial director, Zahi Hawass, ordered the Amer Group's Porto development in Aswan halted, on the heels of complaints from local villagers that they had not been consulted and after an archaeological survey found antiquities. Conservation experts knew that the SCA had already conducted an archaeological impact assessment for Lake Qarun, driven by reports that the Ministry of Tourism intended to develop the area.[15]

In their online petition, the No Porto Fayoum campaign thus called on the SCA to cancel the project on the basis of findings from its recent archaeological excavations. In a telling response posted on his blog on May 20, 2011, Zahi Hawass responded directly, highlighting the fragmented legal jurisdictions governing land use in Egypt more generally:

> Three years ago the Minister of Tourism decided to sell the site of Lake Qarun, which is government property, to the Amer Group to use for touristic purposes. I strongly objected to the project from the beginning because I know that this is an archaeologically rich area... I have told the Ministry of Tourism and other bodies as much. At the same time, however, I will have to wait and see what the opinion of the appointed committee is. This is a decision that is not completely within the jurisdiction of the MSA [Ministry of State for Antiquities].

> (Hawass, 2011)

Hopes that Hawass might personally intervene in the Fayoum dispute were further dashed when he was removed from his position in the post-revolutionary churn of Cabinet shuffles that marked the spring of 2011. Targeted by young activists and ministry employees for perpetuating the closed, centralized, and opaque decision-making that epitomized the Mubarak regime, he was accused of close relations with the Mubarak family and corruption (Lawler, 2011).

In contrast to the environmental campaigns waged in Damietta and Alexandria, the No Porto Fayoum campaign lacked a popular constituency from the cities and villages of Fayoum. It also lacked substantive linkages to the governor, a former general appointed by the SCAF. Despite these limitations, however, the conservation network was clearly more successful in politicizing the Porto Fayoum project in 2011 than it had been in trying to counter Orascom's Byoum Residence in 2010. As one activist blogged, "Within hours of launching our campaign via a press release, Internet petition, and the Facebook site No Porto Fayoum, local and international reaction and outrage began... How different from a year ago, when we launched a similar campaign against Byoum" (Gauch, 2011). By summer 2011, the new tourism minister, Munir Fakhri 'Abd al-Nur, assured the BBC that the Porto Fayoum project had been sent back to the environmental agency for consideration, while Al Hayat TV announced that Egypt's attorney general, Mahmud 'Abd al-Magid, had promised to review the Porto Fayoum project.[16]

## Demanding rights to resources on the periphery

Conflicts over land use and land rights have further intensified as marginalized groups have moved to reassert access to places and resources. Most assertive have been communities directly dependent upon access to natural resources for their livelihoods and systematically marginalized by the regime in Cairo, such as Nubians and villagers in upper Egypt, and the Bedouin in the Sinai.

The Nubians, displaced decades ago when the Aswan High Dam submerged most of their lands, launched a series of protests in 2011 demanding the right to return to the shores of the dam's reservoir, Lake Nasser (Figure 7.2). Development around the lake is supposed to be restricted to ensure Nile water quality, as the reservoir supplies most of downstream Egypt's water. In practice, a number of uses, including fish stocking, fish farming, and land reclamation on the shores of the lake, are tolerated and have already had deleterious impacts on water quality. As in Damietta in 2011, the Nubian protesters took direct action. Activists blockaded roads in Aswan, burned the governorate office building, and launched a sit-in in front of the burned building, while far to the north in Cairo, a simultaneous demonstration was conducted outside the Cabinet building ("Nubians Will Finally Go Home...," 2011).

Protesters employed discursive claims that focused not only on the restitution of property rights, but also invoked the Egyptian revolution's demands for more inclusionary decision-making. The protesters demanded an open meeting with the then-prime minister, Essam Sharaf, who had been scheduled to meet with thirty Nubian delegates hand-picked by governmental authorities (Al-Gaafari, 2011). The protesters refused to participate in the long-standing pattern of Cairo selecting its favored intermediaries on the periphery. After a week of the sit-in, the government promised to grant Nubians access to land around Lake Nasser, though it remains to be seen if such promises will be fulfilled.

*Figure 7.2* A member of the El Salam Nubian village prepares coffee. The Nubians were relocated during the construction of the Aswan High Dam and are seeking to return to adjacent lands
David Degner, 2012

In the Sinai, where Cairo's approach to Bedouin tribes has long been dominated by security concerns, conflicts between Bedouin and the state intensified. As the International Crisis Group warned in 2007, heavy-handed security sweeps, indefinite detentions, and "a development strategy that is deeply discriminatory and largely ineffective at meeting local needs" had produced widespread disaffection in the years before the uprising (International Crisis Group, 2007: i). Years of drought, which affected most of the eastern Mediterranean, had decimated livestock and grazing along the northern coast, prompting greater migration and competition into South Sinai for limited jobs. In addition, the international isolation of Hamas in the Gaza Strip created a black-market economy of tunnels and smuggling in which northern Sinai was the key transit route.

As a result, protest and insecurity escalated in Sinai. Armed tribesmen attacked police stations, where torture and indefinite detention were routine practices, and surrounded courthouses. In May 2011, armed tribesmen shut down the main road leading into Sharm el-Sheikh, the city near Ras Mohamed National Park on the southern tip of the Sinai Peninsula, demanding the release of relatives imprisoned by Egypt's security forces (Aboudi, 2011). The pipeline supplying Egyptian natural gas to Israel and Jordan, which runs through northern Sinai, was sabotaged fourteen times from January to May 2011, amidst mounting public criticism that the government should cancel the sale of gas to Israel.

As in the environmental campaigns in Damietta and Idku, public criticism centered around the claim that the regime in Cairo was selling Egypt's natural resources for the benefit of foreign firms and foreign countries. This criticism gained even greater currency as ordinary Egyptians found that they faced short-ages of locally used fuels—diesel, propane, and butane—in the spring of 2012, leading to long queues at gas stations and bakeries. As a result of public pressure, the Egyptian state-owned petroleum company cancelled its contract supplying gas to the private multinational consortium that supplied gas to Israel in May 2012. By this time, the Egyptian government had already doubled the price of natural gas sold to Jordan.

Protected areas in Sinai were not immune from intensified mobilization among Bedouin communities. In the spring of 2011, sixty Bedouin conducted a sit-in at the South Sinai governor's office, demanding that they be allowed to fish in Ras Mohamed National Park during the spawning period for emperor fish, a valuable and lucrative species for local fishermen. Faced with a mobilized local constituency, the governor capitulated, issuing a decree allowing angling in an important spawning area within the boundaries of Ras Mohamed.

When Ras Mohamed was established in 1983, fishing inside protected areas was legally prohibited, as fish are an integral part of coral ecosystems. In practice, protected area rangers had long allowed small numbers of Bedouin to discreetly fish using lines, at night, to supply the local tourism market.[17] Yet increasing numbers of fishing boats, moving into the Red Sea and Gulf of 'Aqaba from depleted fisheries in the northern lakes and Mediterranean coast, threatened this informal arrangement. These boats often used large nets and dynamite, destroying coral habitat and decimating fish populations. In population surveys of the Red Sea reefs, some fish species had declined precipitously (Charbel, 2011). Net fishing in the Red Sea and Gulf of 'Aqaba was already formally banned during spawning season from May to September, by order of the Ministry of Agriculture's fisheries department (ibid.).

To oppose the governor's unexpected decree legalizing fishing inside the boundaries of the national park, long-standing members of the conservation network working on the Red Sea and Sinai mobilized quickly. These included a few well-known ecotourism and dive operators, representatives from HEPCA, and the Ras Mohamed park manager.[18] As with the No Porto Fayoum campaign, the network started online petitions and alerted domestic and international news outlets and conservation organizations, which ran scathing coverage of the governor's decision (Al-Awami *et al.*, 2011). Conservationists also used their positions in a variety of non-governmental and governmental organizations to issue appeals to the Ministers of Tourism and Environment to intercede. The Egyptian Federation of Tourism's Chamber of Diving and Water Sports, for instance, issued a press release arguing such a decision would hamper protected coral ecosystems and hurt the tourism industry (Chamber of Diving and Water Sports, 2011).

A turning point in the campaign arguably came in a televised debate between Amr Ali, managing director of HEPCA, and the then-governor of South Sinai,

Mohamed Shosha, on the popular talk show "Biladna Bil Masr." The talk show, hosted by well-known TV personality Reem Maged and carried by Orascom Television (OTV), the private satellite TV station owned by the Suweiris family, has become a forum for spirited political debate since the revolution.

Both men cast their positions in terms of scientific expertise and economic development. The governor noted that he had convened an expert committee to investigate the issue. HEPCA's director countered that the consensus of Egypt's conservation community was clear, as the Ras Mohamed Park authority and the environmental agency opposed the governor's decision, while existing laws on fisheries issued by the Ministry of Agriculture clearly banned angling in spawning grounds.[19] Ali also argued that the issue was not simply a local one, but an international one, as negative press would affect Egypt's tourism and diving industry. The next morning, the governor rescinded his decision.

Conservationists knew, however, that efforts by protected area rangers and the coast guard to enforce the ban risked direct confrontation with Bedouin fishermen.[20] Meeting at one of the few Bedouin-owned hotels in Sharm el-Sheikh, conservation experts met with Bedouin leaders to discuss monetary compensation for affected fishermen. They then contacted the Ministry of Tourism, the EEAA, and the South Sinai governorate to establish a compensation fund, and asked local Bedouin to collectively agree upon a list of boats impacted by lost fishing revenue. The Ministry of Tourism quickly paid into the fund, but neither the environmental agency nor the South Sinai governorate were as forthcoming. In interviews, participants indicated that they would continue to pursue the development of a longer-term financial mechanism to compensate local fishermen seasonally excluded from critical spawning areas.[21] They viewed this effort as one step towards incorporating community rights into the management of protected areas and natural resources.

## Integrating rights into water and agricultural policies

Putting inclusiveness and rights as the centerpiece of an environmental agenda has long been championed by a handful of activist networks and voluntary organizations working in Egypt. As discussed in Chapter 4, advocacy organizations persisted in Egypt under Mubarak despite the Emergency Law and legal restrictions on rights of association, as well as raids, detentions, and trials of leading activists and their organizations. These organizations included Markaz al-Ard li Huquq al-Insan (the Land Center for Human Rights), which had filed several legal cases to contest illegal quarrying near protected areas in the late 1990s. The discourses and organizational strategies of the Land Center provide one example of how environmental issues, economic livelihoods, and community mobilization may increasingly fuse with broader campaigns for socioeconomic and environmental justice.

Since 1996, the Land Center has provided legal aid to small agricultural producers, migrant laborers, children, women, and tenant farmers. It was one of the first organizations to try and document the numbers of tenant and smallholding farmers displaced after 1994, when the government lifted legal restrictions on how much rent landlords could charge tenant farmers. The center also documented labor activism among industrial workers, linking problems of agricultural welfare to a broader exploitation of poor laborers, whether industrial or agricultural.

In its research reports, press releases, court cases, and episodically issued magazine, *Al-Ard*, the Land Center's discourse drew on its roots in leftist politics and middle-class activist networks. The center's legal advocates recast neo-Marxist arguments about labor exploitation and inequality into the context of rural Egypt's small producers. "Egyptian history...will remain for the foreseeable future a history of struggle for the soil of agricultural land and a drop of water for irrigation," noted a summary of one report issued in June 2011 (Land Center for Human Rights, 2011c). The plight of small and landless agricultural producers was caused by corrupt land deals and government policies, particularly neoliberal agricultural reforms, which took the country back to the "worst eras of poverty and injustice, tyranny and corruption, banditry and looting" (ibid.). The center thus situated agriculture and rural issues as part of the broader struggle of the Egyptian people for a decent livelihood and a just society. These discursive themes thus dovetailed well with the revolutionary claims of 2011 for justice, dignity, and bread, as the Land Center activists were well aware. Most of their press releases and report summaries after January 25 concluded with the taglines "Long live the struggle of the Egyptian people!" and "Glory to the martyrs!"

The center also attempted to build infrastructural authority among small producers, by encouraging them to form unions independent of the Ministry of Manpower's restrictive rules and distinct from existing corporatist structures sanctioned by the central government, such as the Ministry of Agriculture's farmer cooperatives. In workshops and training sessions, the lawyers and handful of researchers who staff the center laid out the practical and legal steps required for small-holding farmers, fishermen, and squatters on government-owned land to form independent associations. These included obtaining legal recognition, conducting elections for boards of directors and assemblies, collecting dues, and establishing qualifications for membership.

The Land Center's efforts to create independent small producer organizations drew upon intensified union organizing among workers in public sector firms and employees in government ministries during the 2000s. One lead article in the September 2010 issue of *Al-Ard*, for instance, highlighted the achievements of the real estate tax collectors, among the first such groups to successfully establish a union outside of government control.[22] The ability to establish independent political parties and trade unions, along with abolishing the Emergency Law and ensuring rights of association and expression, were among the central demands of the January 25 revolution. Despite assurances from post-Mubarak Cabinets that independent unions were to be allowed, attempts to legally register such unions encountered numerous delays and obstacles. For instance, the governmental authority designated to receive such registrations, the Ministry of Manpower and its local provincial offices, simply refused to accept many of the registration papers.

Workshops and meetings held to form independent unions illuminated the concerns of small agricultural producers. For small farmers from villages in Fayoum and in the Beheira governorate, these included gaining ownership of land farmed for years but owned by large landlords, improved support of production and marketing of agricultural crops, and improved public services for irrigation and drinking water (Land Center for Human Rights, 2011b). For the fishermen of Lake Edku and other lakes, large fish farms had deprived small fishermen of their fishing grounds. They also called for halting land reclamation and other activities that destroyed aquatic habitat, and demanded that water police stop arresting and fining small fishermen (Land Center for Human Rights, 2011a).

Other NGOs, including Sons of the Soil (*Awlad al-Ard*), are undertaking similar organizing efforts among agricultural producers. As in the Sinai and Nubia, a focus on redistribution and rights thus figures prominently in emerging bottom-up mobilizations for land, water, and resources in the Nile Valley and Delta.

In the wake of the 2011 uprising, activist networks have thus proliferated and diversified in terms of the participants that they attract, the issues that they tackle, and the geographical spaces in which they emerge. Many activist networks working on environmental issues still draw upon the infrastructure of contestation and legal advocacy channels established by state-sanctioned organizations, universities, labor and human rights associations, and the courts. Yet as the numerous examples of direct action show, activist campaigns and collective protest draw in much greater numbers of ordinary people, from villagers blockading roads and conducting sit-ins at governorate and ministerial offices, to Nubians seeking compensation for lost land, to urban residents protesting in Idku and Damietta.

Managerial networks of experts, moreover, have begun to play a more autonomous role as environmental advocates, outside the confines of donor-state projects and private consultancies. In doing so, they have begun to adopt the discourses, tactics, and organizational forms of activist networks, as shown in the No Porto Fayoum campaign. In the case of the Bedouin claims to fish in Ras Mohamed National Park, the local conservation network sought to mediate between mobilized local communities and the executive institutions of the state, including the governor, the Ministry of Tourism, and the environmental agency.

Environmental networks will likely build upon the variety of new political openings and increased social mobilization, adapting their discursive framings and organizational tactics to reach broader constituencies. As a result, they may build more effective forms of infrastructural authority, which had been difficult in a broader authoritarian context of sustained mistrust and avoidance of state authorities, particularly in rural areas. Environmental networks will continue to participate in a more vibrant public sphere and lively media scene, to seek alliances with elected parliamentarians and advocacy organizations, and to file lawsuits with the relatively autonomous judiciary.

It is unclear whether the intensified popular mobilization and willingness to take direct action chronicled in this chapter will be sustained. Many of the legal restrictions and institutions designed to contain and coopt dissent have not yet been dismantled, and proposed revisions to many laws provide inadequate protection of civil liberties. Yet in light of Egypt's ongoing political transformation, we can expect further democratization and contestation in Egypt's environmental politics. The advent of this more mobilized, participatory, and dynamic phase in Egyptian environmental politics does not stem from the calculations of political elites or the pressures of international donors. Instead, it is the product of ongoing, sustained political engagement by environmental networks of activists and experts—and by thousands of ordinary citizens participating in Egypt's revolutionary moment.

# Appendix

## Transliteration note, document collections, and organizational affiliations of interview participants

### Transliteration note

For ease of recognition and cross-referencing, the text and figures render names of persons, places, and organizations as these commonly appear in English-language publications, online sources, and reports by international organizations. For example, Muhammed al-Qassas appears as Mohamed Kassas.

### Document collections and press archives in Cairo

*Al-Ahram* Library

Cairo University, Department of Botany, Papers of Mohamed Kassas

Centre d'Etudes et de Documentation Economiques, Juridiques, et Sociales (CEDEJ)

Library of the Majlis al-Sha'b

Library of the Majlis al-Shura

Middle East Library for Economic Services

USAID Library (now closed)

### Interviews

From September 1997 to June 1998, January–June 1999, May–June 2007, Fall 2008, and May–June 2011, I conducted open-ended, confidential interviews with local and national government officials, public and private sector managers, journalists, former officials, environmental activists, academics, consultants, donor staff, and representatives of non-governmental organizations and political parties. Interviews typically ran for one to two hours and, despite this fact, a number of people have graciously met with me repeatedly over the years. I am grateful to individuals affiliated with the following organizations and companies for their help. Unfortunately, this list does not include environmental activists without formal organizational affiliations, to whom I am also very grateful.

Where a government ministry is listed, I have listed the relevant department, research center, or donor project with which the interviewee was associated. In private sector companies, I most often interviewed the production manager, the environmental manager if one existed, and managers assigned to work with donor projects.

Abu Qir Fertilizers

*Al-Masry Al-Youm*, Cairo

Alexandria Businessmen's Association

Alexandria Carbon Black Company

Alexandria Governorate Environment Office

Alexandria Metals Company

Alexandria National Preservation Trust

Alexandria University

    Department of Environmental Sciences

    Faculty of Agriculture

    High Institute of Public Health

    Institute for Graduate Studies and Research

    Institute of Oceanography

American Chamber of Commerce, Environment Committee

American University in Cairo

Amriyah Cement

The Arab Contractors (Osman Ahmed Osman)

Arab Organization for Youth and Environment, Cairo

Association for the Protection of the Environment, Cairo

Association of Enterprises for Environmental Conservation, Cairo

Cairo University

    Botany Department

    Center for the Study of Developing Countries

    Center for Environmental Research Studies

    Faculty of Economic and Political Studies

Centre d'Etudes et de Documentation Economiques, Juridiques, et Sociales (CEDEJ), Cairo

Center for Environment and Development for the Arab Region and Europe (CEDARE), Cairo

Chemonics Egypt, Cairo

Ecoconserve, Cairo

Egyptian Association for Industry and Environment, Alexandria

Egyptian Center for Economic Studies (ECES), Cairo

Egyptian Environmental Affairs Agency

    Cairo Air Improvement Project (USAID)

    Nature Conservation Sector (NCS) (European Union, Italian Cooperation)

    Environment Fund (Danida)

Greater Cairo Governorate Office

Industrial Compliance Unit/Industrial Pollution Abatement Project (World Bank)

Legal Unit

Minister of State for the Environment Office

Organizational Support Program

Technical Cooperation Office

Egyptian Federation of Tourism

Chamber of Diving and Water Sports, Sharm el-Sheikh

Egyptian Financial and Industrial Co. (EFIC), Cairo

Egyptian Plastics and Electrical Industries, Alexandria

Electroplating Factory, Alexandria

European Union, Privatization Management Unit, Cairo

Exact Battery Company, Alexandria

Federation of Egyptian Industries, Cairo

Environmental Compliance Office (ECO)

Friends of the Environment (*Asdiqa' al-Bi'a*), Alexandria

*In memoriam*, 'Adil Abu Zahra

General Organization for Physical Planning, Cairo

Glue Factory, Alexandria

Greenpeace Middle East, Beirut, Lebanon

Hurghada Environmental Protection and Conservation Association (HEPCA), Hurghada

International Center for Environment and Development, Cairo

Jamiyyat Qanoun al-Tib, Cairo

The Land Center for Human Rights/Markaz Al-Ard, Cairo

Metcalf and Eddy, Alexandria Wastewater Project, Phase II (USAID)

The Ministry of Agriculture

Agricultural Extension Training

Integrated Pest Management Project (GtZ)

The Minister's Office

Pest Control Division

The Ministry of Industry

Chemical Industries Holding Company

Egyptian Pollution Prevention Project (EP3)

Metallurgical Holding Company

Mining and Quarries Holding Company

Public Enterprise Office

The Ministry of Irrigation and Water Resources
    Institutional Reform Unit
    Integrated Water Resources Management Project (USAID)
    The Minister's Office
    National Water Research Center
    Water Resources Division
The Ministry of Tourism
    LIFE Project (Livelihoods and Income from the Environment), USAID
    Red Sea Sustainable Tourism Project (USAID)
    Tourism Development Authority
Misr Beida Dyers Co., Kafr Dawar
Misr Chemical Industries, Alexandria
Misr International Bank (MIBank), Cairo
Muslim Brotherhood
    Environment Committee, Cairo
Nature Conservation Egypt (NCE), Cairo
Osman Group, Cairo
Popular Committee for the Protection of the Environment, Damietta
Principal Bank for Agricultural Development and Credit (PBADC), Cairo
Ragab Group, Alexandria
Rakta Paper Company, Abu Qir
Red Sea Diving Safari, Marsa Allam
Sadat Academy for Management Science, Cairo
Sharks Bay Umbi Diving Village, Sharm el-Sheikh
Sidi Krir Petrochemicals, Alexandria
SIMO Paper Company
Sinai Environment and Development Organization (SEDO), Sharm el-Sheikh
South Sinai Protected Areas (European Union)
    Nabq Multiple Use Area
    Ras Mohamed National Park
    St. Catherine's Protected Area
Shell Oil Ltd, Egypt
Sixth of October Investors Association
Tenth of Ramadan Investors Association
Terra Incorporated, Cairo
United States Agency for International Development (USAID), Cairo Mission
World Health Organization, Alexandria and Cairo
Young Entrepreneurs, Alexandria

# Notes

## 1 Networks, authority, and environmental politics in Egypt

1 Although I do not employ the same typology, Clapp and Fuchs' (2009) work on the "three faces" of corporate power was helpful in clarifying my thinking about forms of environmental authority.
2 For climate change and challenges of adaptation in the water sector for the Middle East and North Africa, see Sowers *et al.* (2010).
3 For the increasingly important role that courts and the judiciary more generally played in contesting executive power in the late Mubarak period, see Moustafa (2007).
4 While Mann and subsequent authors largely discussed infrastructural authority in the context of elaborating the nature of state power, he was fully aware that these logistical techniques and "inventions" were equally available to social groups. See Mann (1984).
5 As Janos Kornai argued in his now-classic study of state socialism (1992: 13), the use of qualitative, diverse forms of evidence "often leads much closer to an understanding of the truth than many more ambitious analyses on a higher plane that rest upon distorted official data."
6 Interview with the author, Cairo, May 31, 1998.

## 2 Managerial networks

1 Kassas' regional reputation was reflected in receiving the UAE's first "Zayed International Prize for the Environment" for scientific achievement in the field of environment, awarded in 2001.
2 Interview with the author, Cairo, June 10, 1998.
3 Interview with the author, M. Kassas, Cairo, June 2, 1998.
4 For an overview of the MAB program under UNESCO, see http://portal.unesco.org/science/en/ev.php-URL_ID=6784&URL_DO=DO_TOPIC&URL_SECTION=201.html (accessed March 21, 2010).
5 Interview with the author, Cairo, June 5, 1998.
6 Interview with the author, Cairo, June 5, 1998.
7 Although many other incidents of pesticide poisoning did not receive international press coverage, the US press reported this incident in 1976–7, as the American chemical company Velsicol came under scrutiny for misleading federal regulators at EPA and OSHA about the dangers posed by the pesticide. Velsicol manufactured leptophos, trade-named Phosvel, from 1971 until January 1976, when it was deregistered on the basis of the Egyptian experience, as well as documented illness among workers at the US-based production plant.

8  Interview with the author, High Institute for Public Health, Alexandria, Egypt, June 1, 1998.
9  Interview with the author, Cairo, January 28, 1999.
10 Interview with the author, Cairo, June 2, 1998.
11 Interview with the author, Egyptian Environmental Affairs Agency, Cairo, February 3, 1998.
12 Interview with the author, Cairo, June 3, 1998.
13 Interview with the author, Alexandria, April 27, 1999.
14 Interview with the author, Cairo, May 6, 1998.
15 Interview with the author, Cairo, May 6, 1998.
16 Interview with the author, Egyptian Environmental Affairs Agency, Cairo, May 20, 1998.
17 Bilateral donors working in Egypt included the United States (USAID), Canada (CIDA), Denmark (Danida), Finland (Finnida), Germany (KfW, GTZ, FES), Italy, Japan (JICA), the Netherlands, Sweden, Switzerland, and the United Kingdom (DFID). Multilateral donors included the European Union, the Food and Agriculture Organization (FAO), the Arab Fund for Economic and Social Development (AFESD), the United Nations Development Programme (UNDP), the World Bank, the Mediterranean Technical Assistance Program (METAP), the Global Environment Facility (GEF), and the Ozone Multilateral Fund (El Baradei, 2001).
18 European Commission/ODI database, 1999.
19 Interview with the author, Egyptian Environmental Affairs Agency, Cairo, February 26, 1998; interview with the author, USAID EP3 Project, October 29, 1997; interview with the author, Ministry of State for Environmental Affairs, January 15, 1999.
20 Educated Egyptians disproportionately have the opportunity to leave the country to find work relative to the rest of the population. Permanent migration to OECD countries is attainable to only about 1 percent of the Egyptian labor force as a whole and opportunities to move abroad are significantly biased in favor of Egyptians with university education; see Özden (2006).
21 The number of Egyptians working abroad fluctuates significantly in any given year, primarily due to wars and economic crises that limit demand for labor in the Gulf.
22 Since Gulf countries regulate immigration by issuing work contracts, the compilation of these contracts by Egypt's Ministry of Manpower and Emigration serves as the primary empirical dataset for tracking temporary migration to these countries. The Gulf countries themselves restrict information on expatriate labor, in part because of the politically charged nature of immigration in countries where citizens are far outnumbered by foreign workers (Zohry, 2003).
23 Interview with the author, Alexandria, February 7, 1998.
24 Interview with the author, Nature Conservation Sector, Egyptian Environmental Affairs Agency, Cairo, June 6, 2007.
25 The PLAID database constructed by Hicks *et al.* classifies environmental aid as either "brown" aid, for projects that focus primarily on local environmental issues and outcomes in a given country, or "green" aid, meant to address global or regional environmental problems (Hicks *et al.*, 2008: 31). For all donors, the amount of "brown" aid allocated was significantly larger than that for "green" aid. Environmental aid accounted for between 10 and 12 percent of all international assistance during the 1980s and 1990s (ibid.).
26 Interview with the author, director, environmental consulting firm, Cairo, May 30, 2007; interview with the author, project manager, Egyptian Environmental Affairs Agency, Cairo, June 6, 2007; interview with the author, consultant, Egyptian Environmental Affairs Agency, Cairo, June 12, 2007.
27 Interview with the author, Egyptian Environmental Affairs Agency, Cairo, June 6, 2007; interview with the author, environmental consultant, May 30, 2007.

28  Interview with the author, consultant, environmental consulting firm, Cairo, May 30, 2007; interview with the author, project manager, Cairo, June 6, 2007; interview with the author, consultant, Egyptian Environmental Affairs Agency, Cairo, June 12, 2007.
29  Interview with the author, Cairo, June 30, 2007.
30  Interview with the author, Cairo, June 12, 2007.

## 3  Persistent hotspots of industrial pollution

1  Interview with the author, Misr International Bank, Cairo, January 20, 1999.
2  Industrial Development Authority, Arab Republic of Egypt, http://www.ida.gov.eg/egmaly_ro5as_seglen.html (accessed August 15, 2010).
3  Figures from the Industrial Development Authority, Arab Republic of Egypt, http://www.ida.gov.eg/Egmaly_en.html (accessed February 2, 2009).
4  Food processing was the single greatest source of solid soluble substances, suspended matter, oils and lubricants, and bio-organic loads in industrial drainage water, particularly from the sugar industry in upper Egypt. The chemical, metals, and engineering industries were the second largest consumers of water in production processes, and dispersed an estimated 2,272 tons per year of toxic waste and heavy metals to waterways (Egyptian Environmental Affairs Agency and Ministry of Industry, 1995: 26).
5  Interview with the author, EP3 Project Consultant, Cairo, February 26, 1998.
6  Interview with the author, US Embassy, Cairo, June 15, 1998.
7  Interview with the author, Senior Technical Advisor, Egyptian Pollution Abatement Project, Cairo, February 7, 1998.
8  Interview with the author, EEAA Industrial Compliance Office, Cairo, February 7, 1998.
9  Interviews with the author, Egyptian consultants, USAID Egyptian Pollution Prevention Project (EP3), Cairo and Alexandria, September 16, 23, and 28, and October 23, 1997.
10  Interview with the author, production manager, *Misr Chemiwiyyat* (Misr Chemicals), Alexandria, June 14, 1998.
11  Interview with the author, Metallurgical Holding Company, Cairo, March 3, 1999.
12  Emerging Markets Information Service (accessed June 18, 2010).
13  Ibid.
14  Interview with the author, production manager, Rakta Pulp and Paper Company, Abu Qir, October 27, 1997.
15  See Article 17, Executive Statutes of the Law 4/1994, issued by Decree of the Prime Minister 338, 1995.
16  Legal provisions for environmental impact assessments (EIAs) for new industrial facilities were similarly fragmented among various administrative authorities. Law 4 required new plants to submit EIAs to the "competent authority," which was to forward these for review to the EEAA. If the EEAA did not respond within sixty days, the project received automatic approval. One of the principal problems was ensuring that the "competent authority" actually forwarded such assessments to the environmental agency. For the sake of expediting review, the environmental agency later classified projects into simple color-coded categories, and a substantial review was triggered only for industrial enterprises deemed high-risk or extremely polluting.
17  Data compiled at author's request by EP3 staff, Cairo and Alexandria, 1999.
18  Interview with the author, High Institute for Public Health, Alexandria, February 7, 1998.
19  Interview with the author, Project Manager, World Bank Pollution Abatement Project, Cairo, February 3, 1998.

## 4  Activist networks and anti-pollution campaigns in the provinces

1  An array of governmental authorities controls internal elections, leadership, agendas, and financing of the organizations that ostensibly represent labor, education, and the press. These state organs include the Ministry of Social Affairs, which monitors voluntary associations, the Egyptian Trade Union Federation, which claims to represent industrial and other workers, the Ministry of Information, which oversees media outlets, and the Ministry of Education, which runs public universities and schools.
2  The CDM report noted that urban disease rates, however, were generally higher than in rural areas because of better access to health care by urban residents, resulting in higher reporting rates for diseases, such as typhoid, dysentery, and cholera (termed "acute enteric summer disease" by Egypt's Ministry of Health).
3  Decree 28, issued by the president of the Academy for Scientific Research and Technology, January 14, 1982, in Arabic.
4  Other committee members included the professors Abu al-Futuh 'Abd al-Latif, Tharwat Fahmi, Hasan Farid Zaghlul, 'Uthman 'Adli Badran, Fahmi Muhammad Ramadan, and Muhammad al-Khatir.
5  Interview with Professor of Environmental Engineering, High Institute of Public Health, Alexandria, January 22, 1998.
6  Interview with project manager, Metcalf and Eddy, Alexandria, May 15, 1998.
7  In 1981, a presidential decree merged the two government authorities responsible for potable water and sanitation into one national authority, under the Ministry of Housing, but did not devolve responsibility for revenue collection, expenditures, or planning to the governorates or utilities.
8  Interview with the author, Metcalf and Eddy, Alexandria, May 10, 1998.
9  This account draws on research conducted with Sharif Elmusa; some of our findings were published in "Damietta Mobilizes for Its Environment," *Middle East Report Online*, October 21, 2009.
10  Interview by the author and Sharif Elmusa with residents in Damietta, November 22, 2008.
11  For a sample of the satellite coverage, see Al Jazeera Talk, "Agrium: al-Tala'ub bi Masir Watan," broadcast on June 17, 2008, http://www.aljazeeratalk.net/portal/content/view/2861/1/ (accessed September 10, 2008).
12  Hoda Baraka interview with Nasser al-Kashif, Cairo, June 1, 2009.
13  The port was subject to Crusader raids several times; for example, in 1169 a fleet from the kingdom of Jerusalem with support from the Byzantines attacked the city, but it was defeated by Saladin.
14  See http://www.oilnergy.com/1gnymex.htm#year (accessed September 12, 2008).
15  The specific shares in the consortium included the following state-owned firms: Egas (Egyptian Natural Gas Holding Company) and Echem (Egyptian Company for Petrochemicals) (24 percent) and GASCO (9 percent). The remaining 7 percent was held by Arab Petroleum Investment Corporation (APICORP), an inter-Arab joint stock company owned by the governments of ten member states of the Organization of Arab Petroleum Exporting Countries (OAPEC).
16  Slogans translated and rhymed by Sharif Elmusa.

## 5  Natural heritage, mass tourism

1  The next three sections are adapted from Sowers (2007).
2  Interview with the author, CEO, Tourism Development Authority, Cairo, March 7, 1999.
3  Interview with the author, M. Kassas, Cairo, June 2, 1998.

4  Ibid.
5  Interview with the author, Michael Pearson, South Sinai Protectorates Project Director, Cairo, June 15, 1998.
6  Interview with the author, Alaa D'Grissac, Cairo, June 12, 1998.
7  Author's communication with John Grainger, October 19, 2011.
8  Interview with the author, Ranger, Ras Mohamed National Park, June 5, 1998.
9  Interview with the author, Cairo, May 4, 1998.
10  Interview with the author, South Sinai Sector Manager, Cairo, January 12, 1998.
11  Interview with the author, Cairo, June 5, 2007.
12  Interview with the author, Ranger, Department of Planning, Nature Conservation Sector, Egyptian Environmental Affairs Agency, Cairo, June 8, 2011.
13  Ibid.
14  Land designated for tourism inside municipal boundaries was to be allocated by the governorate, or provincial government. Prominent line ministries, such as Agriculture and Housing and New Communities, could also propose zones to be included within their jurisdiction, which were subject to approval by the Ministry of Defense and the Council of Ministers. See Ministerial Decree 933/1988 and Law 7/1991.
15  See Law 142/1981, "Concerning Desert Land."
16  Investment Law 8 for 1997.
17  Interview with the author, Consultant, Ministry of Tourism, Cairo, February 14, 1999.
18  Interview with the author, Member, Alexandria Businessmen's Association, Alexandria, June 8, 1998.
19  Interview with the author, Professor, University of Alexandria, San Diego, CA, July 26, 1999.
20  Interview with the author, Sharm el-Sheikh, May 25, 2011.
21  Interview with the author, Program Manager, Gulf of 'Aqaba Protectorates, Cairo, May 4, 1998.
22  Interview with the author, CEO, Tourism Development Authority, Cairo, March 7, 1999.
23  Ibid.
24  Interview with the author, South Sinai Sector Manager, Cairo, January 12, 1998.
25  Interview with the author, South Sinai Protectorates Program Manager, Cairo, June 15, 1998.
26  Ibid.
27  Interview with the author, Legal Department, Egyptian Environmental Affairs Agency, Cairo, December 27, 1998.
28  Ships that ran aground or moored illegally on the reefs were fined through a fixed formula that calculated damage as a function of: the area damaged multiplied by the severity of damage multiplied by the time for recovery (which varies by coral species) and the fine per meter. The formula was later updated in consultation with international experts to take account of the fact that recovery times for corals were longer than originally estimated.
29  Interview with the author, Sharm el-Sheikh, June 15, 1998.
30  Interview with the author, Consultant, LIFE Red Sea Project, Egyptian Environmental Affairs Agency, Cairo, June 13, 2007.
31  Interview with the author, USAID LIFE Project, Cairo, June 13, 2007; interview with the author, USAID LIFE Project, Cairo, June 17, 2007.
32  Details about the resort can be found at http://www.gorgoniabeach.com (accessed October 22, 2011).
33  See http://www.hepca.com/about/supporters (accessed October 15, 2011).
34  Interview with the author, Member, Hurghada Environmental Protection and Conservation Association, Cairo, May 30, 2011.
35  Ibid.

36   Ibid.
37   Interview with the author, Land Center for Human Rights, Cairo, February 18, 1999.
38   Interview with the author, Protected Area Consultant, Cairo, January 17, 1999.
39   Interview with the author, Consultant, Nature Conservation Sector, Cairo, June 3, 2007.
40   Interview with the author, Consultant, Nature Conservation Sector, Cairo, May 31, 2011.
41   Ibid.

# 6   From *masqa* to ministry

1   Barnes highlights this contrast, and analyzes the production of excess and scarce water at different levels of Egypt's irrigation system, in her forthcoming book *Cultivating the Nile*.
2   Like most Egyptian ministries, the Ministry of Irrigation has had several formal name changes. These have included the Ministry of Public Works and Water Resources, the Ministry of Irrigation and Water Resources, and others.
3   Guenther Meyer, email communication with the author, August 13, 2003.
4   These estimates encompass the "low" and "high" ranges for population growth provided by the UN Population Bureau, Annual Statistics, 2007.
5   Interview with the author, Institutional Reform Unit, Ministry of Irrigation, May 27, 2007.
6   Interview with the author, Cairo, May 20, 2007.
7   Interview with the author, Center for Environment and Development in the Arab World (CEDARE), Cairo, May 17, 2007.
8   See http://www.worldwatercouncil.org/index.php?id=88&L=0 (accessed December 12, 2011).
9   See http://www.arabwatercouncil.org/index.php?CMS_P=35 (accessed December 16, 2011).
10   See http://www.awacademy.ae (accessed December 17, 2011).
11   See http://www.arabwatercouncil.org/index.php?CMS_P=33 (accessed December 16, 2011).
12   Interview with the author, Institutional Reform Unit, Ministry of Irrigation and Water Resources, Cairo, May 27, 2007.
13   Interviews with the author, Egyptian water experts, May 2007.
14   Interview with the author, Cairo, May 10, 2007.
15   Several leading expatriate Egyptian hydrologists and geologists have been particularly critical of the government's mega-projects, arguing that the government should continue to create new cities and communities in the desert and save valuable agricultural land in the Delta, rather than invest in costly land reclamation with uncertain economic returns. There is no doubt that this solution would be the most efficient in terms of scarce water resources. Yet it is also completely impractical. Agricultural land in the Nile Delta, owned largely in tiny-to-small plots, produces some of the highest yields and cropping intensities in the world; however, it is still more valuable, in local market terms, when converted to housing or other urban uses.
16   In contrast to the difficulties faced in attracting investments in land reclamation, however, the government found eager bidders for the state-financed infrastructure contracts to build the large-scale canals and pumping stations required to divert Nile water to large-scale land reclamation schemes. Lucrative construction contracts were awarded to consortiums of international, Arab, and Egyptian contracting firms. The construction of Toshka's Mubarak Pumping Station was awarded to a consortium led by Swedish/UK Skanska/Cementation International, while excavation of

the Branch 3 canal in Toshka went to Abu Dhabi's Al-Jaber Transport and General Contracting Establishment.

17 Interview with the author, Cairo, January 27, 1999.
18 Ibid.
19 This section includes material adapted from Sowers (2012).
20 Interview with the author, Cairo, June 13, 2007.
21 Interview with the author, Consultant, Branch Canal Water Boards Project, the Ministry of Irrigation and Water Resources, Cairo, June 5, 2007.
22 Interview with the author, Consultant, Branch Canal Water Boards Project, the Ministry of Public Works and Water Resources, Cairo, June 8, 2007.
23 Interview with the author, Project Manager, Branch Canal Water Boards Project, Ministry of Public Works and Water Resources, Cairo, June 6, 2007.
24 Interview with the author, Consultant, Branch Canal Water Boards Project, the Ministry of Public Works and Water Resources, Cairo, June 5, 2007.
25 Branch canal user associations were legally ratified by Ministerial Decree 28, January 28, 1999.
26 The two primary laws concerned with irrigation and drainage are Law 12 of 1984 and Law 312 of 1994.
27 Ministerial Decree 506 for 2001, Ministry of Water Resources and Irrigation, December 10, 2001.
28 See http://www.iwrm2eg.org (accessed April 15, 2012).

## 7 Environmental politics in revolutionary times

1 Interview with the author, FJP Member Ali Fath al-Bab, Cairo, December 2, 2008.
2 Ibid.
3 Interview with the author, Legal Department, Egyptian Environmental Affairs Agency, Cairo, June 7, 2011.
4 Interview with the author, Tourism Development Authority, Cairo, May 30, 2011.
5 Orascom Development Holdings, Projects, http://www.orascomdh.com/en/projects/projects-under-development/el-fayoum-oasis.html (accessed October 30, 2011).
6 In an unusual if not outright irregular pricing scheme, the firm paid only US$28,000, a penny per square meter for the first year of the contract, increasing a penny per square meter every four years, and then from the eleventh until the ninety-ninth year increasing at 2 percent per year.
7 In May 2011, Amer Group gave land in Marsa Matrouh back to the Tourism Development Authority, citing lack of demand for secondary luxury homes in Egypt after the January 25 uprising, and halted its development in Syria with the uprising (Gunn, 2011).
8 As of November 2011, the Facebook group was available at http://www.facebook.com/groups/noportofayoum/. The petition was online at http://www.petitiononline.com/nce3/petition.html, linked to a number of websites concerned with Egyptian conservation and archaeology.
9 Interview with the author, organizer, No Porto Fayoum Campaign, Cairo, May 30, 2011.
10 See http://www.petitiononline.com/nce3/petition.html (accessed October 15, 2011).
11 As of November 2011, Gabal Qatrani remained on the list of tentative World Heritage Sites, while Wadi al-Hitan was approved in 2005 (World Heritage Convention, 2011).
12 Conference information is available at http://www.archaeogate.org/papirologia/event/1202/international-fayum-colloquium-natural-and-cultural-lan.html (accessed February 2, 2012).

13  The full text of the declaration is available at http://www.e-c-h-o.org/fayoum.htm (accessed February 10, 2012).

14  Law 215 asserts that all antiquities "either known or concealed" are state property and subject to expropriation. It defined antiquities as "all movable and immovable objects, which are produced by the arts, sciences, literatures, customs, religions, etc. from prehistorical times to the reign of Ismail." Law 215 was revised in Law 529 for 1953, Law 24 for 1965, and Law 117 for 1983. The central provisions for defining antiquities and asserting state ownership remained intact, however. The Egyptian Cultural Heritage Association provides a useful summary of Egypt's laws governing antiquities at http://www.e-c-h-o.org/CHLaw.htm (accessed February 10, 2012).

15  In January 2011, the Supreme Council of Antiquities was made a Ministry of State, similar to the Ministry of Environment. By the fall of 2011, however, it had been restored to its original name, while maintaining a direct line of reporting to the Cabinet. For consistency, the organization is referred to in the text throughout as the Supreme Council of Antiquities (SCA), although it may be found in some of the source material as the Ministry of State for Antiquities.

16  No Porto Fayoum Facebook Page, posting by Rebecca Porteous, June 5, 2011, https://facebook.com/groups/noportofayoum (accessed June 10, 2011).

17  Interview with the author, Sharm el-Sheikh, May 19, 2011.

18  Interviews with the author, Sharm el-Sheikh, May 17–20, 2011.

19  The relevant segment (in Arabic) of the TV show is available in two parts on HEPCA's Facebook page, http://www.facebook.com/video/video. php?v=10150237566320095#!/video/?id=245765842108436 (accessed February 15, 2012).

20  Interview with the author, Sharks Bay, Sharm el-Sheikh, May 18, 2011.

21  Interview with the author, Sharm el-Sheikh, May 19, 2011.

22  The periodical is available at http://www.lchr-eg.org/index.htm (accessed February 20, 2012).

# References

Abaza, H., Saab, N., and Zeitoon, B. (eds) (2011) "Green Economy: Sustainable Transition in a Changing Arab World." Beirut: The Arab Forum for Environment and Development. http://afedonline.org/Report2011/main2011.html (accessed December 10, 2011).

Abdel-Malek, A. (1968) *Egypt, Military Society: The Army Regime, the Left, and Social Change under Nasser*, New York: Vintage Books.

Abdelrahman, M. (2004) *Civil Society Exposed: The Politics of NGOs in Egypt*, London: Tauris Academic Studies.

Abdel Razek, S. (2003) "Institutional Analysis of EEAA/NCS and the Red Sea Rangers." Cairo: Program Support Unit, Egyptian Environmental Policy Program, March 2003.

Aboudi, S. (2011) "Armed Bedouins Cut Road to Egypt's Sharm El-Sheikh." *Reuters*, May 28, 2011. http://in.reuters.com/article/2011/05/28/idINIndia-57344220110528 (accessed January 9, 2012).

Abu-Zeid, M. (1995) "Major Policies and Programs for Irrigation Drainage and Water Resources Development in Egypt." *Options Méditerranéennes*, Sér. B, No. 9, Egyptian Agriculture Profile. http://ressources.ciheam.org/om/pdf/b09/CI950934.pdf (accessed January 15, 2010).

Academy of Scientific Research and Technology (1979) "Towards the Requirements for Development in Sinai." Cairo: unpublished mimeograph, December 18–19. In Arabic.

Academy of Scientific Research and Technology (1986) "Summary of the Economic and Social Development Plan for 1987–88 to 1991–92 for the North Sinai Governorate." Cairo: Technical Department, Research Agency for the Development and Reconstruction of Sinai. In Arabic.

Academy of Scientific Research and Technology (undated) "Development Possibilities of the Marine Environment and Fish Resources in South Sinai." Cairo: Institute for Marine Sciences and Fisheries.

"Administrative Court Rules in Favor of Mopco Plant in Damietta." *Egypt Independent*, March 20, 2012. http://www.egyptindependent.com/news/administrative-court-rules-favor-mopco-plant-damietta (accessed April 15, 2012).

Agati, M. (2007) "Undermining Standards of Good Governance: Egypt's NGO Law and its Impact on the Transparency and Accountability of CSOs." *The International Journal of Not-for-Profit Law*, 9. http://www.icnl.org/knowledge/ijnl/vol9iss2/special_4.htm (accessed September 10, 2010).

Ahmad, Y. J., Keckes, S., Dregne, H., Liseth, P., and Parry, G. (1986) "Report on Alexandria Wastewater Management." Nairobi: United Nations Environment Programme, August 6, 1986.

Ahmed, F. (2010) "Rice Production Withers as Egypt Diverts Water Supply." *AFP*, November 22, 2010. http://www.google.com/hostednews/afp/article/ALeqM5jAScH9 VJdsR1L9NLbixexahS2Gbg?docId=CNG.b4ced9ea800e7eb0772fd5b6b038bf9a.3d1 (accessed January 2, 2012).

Al-Awami, Y., Abu Zeid, A., and Al-Qadi, Y. (2011) "International Organizations Criticize Decision of the South Sinai Governor Regarding Fishing in the Protectorate Ras Mohamed." *Al-Masry Al-Youm*, May 17, 2011. In Arabic. http://www.almasryalyoum.com/node/441018 (accessed September 14, 2011).

Al-Gaafari, M. (2011) "Angry Nubians Set Fire to Aswan Governorate Building." *Al-Masry Al-Youm*, September 4, 2011. http://www.almasryalyoum.com/en/node/492252 (accessed October 15, 2011).

Al-Gazar, A. A.-A. (1989) "Letter to 'Adil Al-Baltagi." Washington, DC: Agricultural Bureau, Embassy of the Arab Republic of Egypt, Ref No. 89–27, March 14, 1989. In Arabic.

Al-Said, M. (2006) "Political Reform Tops Agenda." *Al-Ahram Weekly*, March 16–22, 2006. http://weekly.ahram.org.eg/2006/786/eg6.htm (accessed January 14, 2007).

Allan, T. (2001) *The Middle East Water Question: Hydropolitics and the Global Economy*, London: I.B. Tauris.

Alpern, D. M. (1976) "The Phosvel Zombies." *Newsweek*, December 13, 1976.

Alvarez, M. G. and Beevers, L. (2009) "Ecological Modelling for Lake Maryut." UNESCO, Institute for Water Education.

Arab Water Council, CEDARE (Center for Environment and Development for the Arab Region and Europe), and United Nations Development Programme (2005) "Status of Integrated Water Resources Management (IWRM) Plans in the Arab World." Cairo: Arab Water Council, CEDARE, and UNDP.

Arafat, S., Afify, A., Aboelghar, M., and Belal, A. (2010) "Rice Crop Monitoring in Egyptian Nile Delta Using Egyptsat-1 Data." Presented at Joint US–Egypt Workshop for Space Technology and Geoinformation for Sustainable Development, Cairo.

Arden, H. (1982) "Eternal Sinai." *National Geographic*, April: 420–61.

Aref, A. (2011) "Damietta Factory on the Defensive." *Business Today*, December 13, 2011. http://businesstodayegypt.com/news/display/article/artId:235/Damietta-Factory-on-the-Defensive/secId:3 (accessed January 2, 2012).

Ascher, W. (1999) *Why Governments Waste Natural Resources: Policy Failures in Developing Countries*, Baltimore, MD: Johns Hopkins University Press.

Atraqchi, L. (1998) "Sharm El Sheikh II." *Business Monthly*, July 1998.

Awad, H. R. (ed.) (1998) "Working Plan to Diversify Tourism Activities in Egypt." Cairo: Public Administration Research and Consultation Center, Cairo University. In Arabic.

Ayeb, H. (2002) "Hydraulic Politics: The Nile and Egypt's Water Use: A Crisis for the Twenty-First Century?" In Bush, R. (ed.) *Counter-Revolution in Egypt's Countryside*, London: Zed Books.

Ayubi, N. (1995) *Overstating the Arab State*, London: IB Tauris.

Badawi, M. M. (1987) *Modern Arabic Drama in Egypt*, Cambridge: Cambridge University Press.

Baha El Din, S. (2006) *A Guide to the Reptiles and Amphibians of Egypt*, Cairo: American University in Cairo Press.

Baraka, H. (2011) "Environment on the Electoral Agenda." *Al-Masry Al-Youm*, November 27, 2011. http://www.almasryalyoum.com/en/node/521026 (accessed January 16, 2012).

Barnes, J. (forthcoming) *Cultivating the Nile: The Everyday Politics of Water in Egypt*, Durham, NC: Duke University Press.

Bayat, A. (2009) *Life as Politics*, Stanford: Stanford University Press.

Bayat, A. (2011) "Paradoxes of Arab Ref-ol-Lutions." *Jadaliyya*. March 3, 2011. http://www.jadaliyya.com/pages/index/786/paradoxes-of-arab-refo-lutions (accessed March 15, 2011).

Beinin, J. and Vairel, F. (eds) (2011) *Social Movements, Mobilization, and Contestation in the Middle East and North Africa*, Stanford: Stanford University Press.

Ben-Nafissa, S. and Kandil, A. (1994) "NGOs in Egypt." Cairo: Al-Ahram Center for Political and Strategic Studies. In Arabic.

Bevir, M. and Richards, D. (2009) "Decentring Policy Networks: A Theoretical Agenda." *Public Administration*, 87(1): 3–14.

Bianchi, R. S. (1989) *Unruly Corporatism: Associational Life in Twentieth-Century Egypt*, Oxford: Oxford University Press.

Bortot, M. S. (1999) "Bulldozers Turn 'Bedouin Dream' into Nightmare." *Middle East Times*, July 23, 1999.

Brown, W. (1977) "EPA Called Careless of Pesticide Safety; Reforms Demanded." *The Washington Post*, January 3, 1977.

Bryner, M. and Alperowicz, N. (2008) "Agrium to Sell Egypt JV Stake; Acquires Share in MOPCO." *Chemical Week*, August 11, 2008.

Bush, R. (2004) "Civil Society and the Uncivil State: Land Tenure Reform in Egypt and the Crisis of Rural Livelihoods." Geneva: United Nations Research Institute for Social Development.

Bush, R. (2007) "Politics, Power and Poverty: Twenty Years of Agricultural Reform and Market Liberalisation in Egypt." *Third World Quarterly*, 28(8): 1599–615.

Bush, R. and Sabri, A. (2012) "Mining for Fish," in J. Sowers and C. Toensing (eds) *The Journey to Tahrir: Revolution, Protest, and Social Change in Egypt*, London: Verso, 242–9.

Camp Dresser & McKee (1978a) "Review of Alexandria Wastewater Master Plan Study: Supplemental Report on Toxic Industrial Wastes." Alexandria: United States Agency for International Development (USAID), October 19, 1978.

Camp Dresser & McKee (1978b) "Initial Environmental Impact Statement for the Alexandria Wastewater Master Plan Study, Volume II, Final Technical Report." United States Agency for International Development and Ministry of Housing and Reconstruction, October 1978.

Canan, P. and Reichman, N. (2001) *Ozone Connections: Expert Networks in Global Environmental Governance*, Sheffield: Greenleaf Press.

Chamber of Diving and Water Sports (2011) "CDWS Call to Stop Fishing in Ras Mohamed National Park." Sharm el-Sheikh: Egyptian Federation of Tourism, May 17, 2011. http://www.cdws.travel/news-article/ras-mohamed-fishing/65 (accessed January 9, 2012).

Charbel, J. (2011) "Ras Mohamed National Park Threatened by Overfishing." *Al-Masry Al-Youm*, May 15, 2011. http://www.almasryalyoum.com/en/node/438224 (accessed June 15, 2011).

Chemonics International (2007a) "Elba Protected Area: Marine Biological Field Survey and Coastal Sensitivity Mapping." LIFE Red Sea Project, United States Agency for International Development.

Chemonics International (2007b) "Wadi Gimel National Park Management Action Plan." LIFE Red Sea Task Order No.: 263-M-00-04-00032-00. LIFE Red Sea Project, United States Agency for International Development, January 28, 2007, 1–35.

Chemonics International (2008) "Livelihoods and Community Development: LIFE Red Sea Final Report." Washington, DC: United States Agency for International Development.

Child, G. (2006) "Suggestions to Strengthen Policy and Institutional Development in Nature Conservation in Egypt." Egyptian–Italian Environmental Cooperation Program and International Union for the Conservation of Nature (IUCN), May 2006.

"Citing JFP Violations, Judge in Qalyubiya Halts Voting." *Egypt Independent*. http://www.almasryalyoum.com/en/node/581196 (accessed January 4, 2012).

Clapp, J. and Fuchs, D. A. (2009) *Corporate Power in Global Agrifood Governance*, Cambridge, MA: MIT Press.

Clark, E. (1975) "The Strangest Sea." *National Geographic*, September: 338–43.

Colby, M. S. (2002) "Red Sea Marine Protectorates: Budget Analysis and Scenarios for 1999–2007." Program Support Unit, Egyptian Environmental Policy Program, December 2002.

Cole, D. and Al-Turki, S. (1998) *Bedouin, Settlers, and Holiday-Makers: Egypt's Changing Northwest Coast*, Cairo: American University in Cairo Press.

Collins, R. O. (1990) *The Waters of the Nile: Hydropolitics and the Jonglei Canal, 1900–1988*, Oxford: Clarendon Press.

Conca, K. (2005) "Growth and Fragmentation in Expert Networks: The Elusive Quest for Integrated Water Resources Management." In Dauvergne, P. (ed.) *Handbook of Global Environmental Politics*, Northampton, MA: Edward Elgar.

Conca, K. (2006) *Governing Water: Contentious Transnational Politics and Global Institution Building*, Cambridge, MA: MIT Press.

"Damietta's Controversial Mopco Factory Found Environmentally Safe: Committee." *Al-Ahram Online*, January 4, 2012. http://english.ahram.org.eg/NewsContentPrint/3/0/30935/Business/0/Damiettas-controversial-MOPCO-factory-found-enviro.aspx (accessed April 20, 2012).

Davis, D. K. (2006) "Neoliberalism, Environmentalism, and Agricultural Restructuring in Morocco." *Geographical Journal*, 172(2): 88–105.

Davis, D. K. and Burke, E. (eds) (2011) *Environmental Imaginaries in the Middle East: History, Policy, Power, and Practice*, Athens: Ohio University Press.

"Disposal of the Sanitary Drainage of Alexandria on Land." *Al-Ahram*, April 30, 1997. In Arabic.

Dorman, W. J. (2007) "The Politics of Neglect: The Egyptian State in Cairo, 1974–1998." Unpublished thesis, University of London.

Ebeid, N. M. and Hamza, A. A. (2001) "Prevention of Industrial Pollution to the Nile: A Success Story." Cairo: Ministry of Public Works and Water Resources: 6.1–6.21.

Egyptian Environmental Affairs Agency (1997) "Towards an Environmental Strategy for Egypt." Cairo: Draft Consultative Report for the National Environmental Action Plan (NEAP).

Egyptian Environmental Affairs Agency (1998) "Regariding Coordination for Inspection of Industrial Facilities." Cairo, unpublished document.

Egyptian Environmental Affairs Agency (2002) *Water Quality Achievements*. Cairo. http://www.eeaa.gov.eg/English/main/accomp3.asp (accessed November 10, 2010).

Egyptian Environmental Affairs Agency and the European Union (1993) "Ras Mohamed National Park Sector Development Project." Cairo: EU/EEAA, May 1993.

Egyptian Environmental Affairs Agency and Ministry of Industry (1995) "Industrial Environmental Map (Al-Kharitah Al-Sina'iyah Al-Bi'ah)." Cairo: Friedrich Ebert Stiftung. In Arabic.

"Egypt's Brotherhood Wins 47% of Parliament Seats." *Egypt Independent*, January 21, 2012. http://www.egyptindependent.com/news/egypts-brotherhood-wins-47-parliament-seats (accessed February 15, 2012).

Eiteiba, M. and Ali, A. K. (1996) "The Youth of Alexandria Witness the Achievements of the Governorate and the Environmental Committee of the National Democratic Party." *Journal News of Alexandria*, August 18, 1996. In Arabic.

El Amrani, I. (2012) "Sightings of the Egyptian Deep State." *Middle East Report Online*, January 1, 2012. http://www.merip.org/mero/mero010112 (accessed January 3, 2012).

El Baradei, L. (2001) "Review of Donor Projects Implemented in Cooperation with EEAA over the Past Ten Years, 1991–2001." Cairo: Egyptian Environmental Affairs Agency, DANIDA, and Danish Environmental Protection Agency, Organizational Support Program. December.

El Maadawy, M. (1999) "Implementing an Integrated Wastewater Treatment Plant: Arab Organization for Industrialization Engine Factory Methodology." Presented at "Efforts of Helwan Industries to Improve the Environment," March 10, 1999. Helwan: Helwan University, College of Engineering.

El-Ashtoukhy, E.-S. Z., Amin, N. K., and Abdelwahab, O. (2009) "Treatment of Paper Mill Effluents in a Batch-Stirred Electrochemical Tank Reactor." *Chemical Engineering Journal*, 146(2): 205–510.

El-Bestawy, E., El-Sokkary, I., Hussein, H., and Keela, A. F. A. (2008) "Pollution Control in Pulp and Paper Industrial Effluents Using Integrated Chemical and Biological Treatment Sequences." *Journal of Industrial Microbiology and Biotechnology*, 35(11): 1517–29.

El-Din, G. E. (1996) "MPs Debate Sewage to Blast US Aid." *Al-Ahram Weekly*, January 18–24, 1996.

El-Din, G. E. (2011) "Networks of Corruption." *Al-Ahram Weekly*, March 10–16, 2011. http://weekly.ahram.org.eg/2011/1038/eg21.htm (accessed October 30, 2011).

El-Gamily, H. I., Nasr, S., and El-Raey, M. (1997) "An Assessment of Natural and Human Induced Changes Along Hurghada." Cairo: Information and Decision Support Center.

El-Ghatrifi, A. and El-Kashef, N. (2008) "Agrium Holds a Conference Tomorrow to Show its Situation and Stresses: We Will Not Leave Damietta." *Al-Masry Al-Youm*, May 13, 2008. In Arabic.

El-Ghatrifi, A., El-Shazly, E., El-Kashef, N., and 'Abas, A. (2008) "Al-Masry Al-Youm Discovers 'Agrium' Did Not Obtain Agreement of the Local Council in Damietta for the Factory." *Al-Masry Al-Youm*, May 18, 2008. In Arabic.

El-Ghatrifi, A., Yassin, M., and El-Kashef, N. (2008) "The Expert Report Presented to the Investigative Committee About Agrium Establishing a Factory in Ras Al Barr: 'Impossible.'" *Al-Masry Al-Youm*, June 8, 2008. In Arabic.

El-Kashef, N. (2008) "Delegation from the People of Damietta Goes to the President of the Republic to Present Communique No. 1 against the Fertilizer Factory." *Al-Masry Al-Youm*, April 13, 2008. In Arabic.

El-Kashef, N. (2008) "'Housing' Accuses Agrium of Perpetrating Violations in Building the Fertilizer Plant...And Reports it Continues." *Al-Masry Al-Youm*, April 19, 2008. In Arabic.

El-Kashef, N. (2008) "Complaint to the Public Prosecutor from the People of Dumyat against the Operation of the Factory MOPCO for Urea without Approvals of 'the Environment' [Ministry]." *Al-Masry Al-Youm*, April 26, 2008. In Arabic.

El-Kashef, N. (2012) "Delegation of Workers from the Project Agrium with Reservations on its Equipment...And a Canadian Delegation Meets Nathif." *Al-Masry Al-Youm*, April 22, 2008, In Arabic.

El-Kashef, N. and El-Shazly, E. (2008) "The Government Suggests Resorting to the Preferred 'Foreign Side' on the Issue of the Fertilizer Factory...Leaders of Dumyat Refuse." *Al-Masry Al-Youm*, April 14, 2008. In Arabic.

El-Kashef, N. and El-Shazly, E. (2008) "March of the Children of Damietta with Balloons and Flowers Protesting against the Failure of the Government in the Case of Agrium." *Al-Masry Al-Youm*, June 10, 2008. In Arabic.

El-Kashef, N. and El-Shazly, E. (2008) "With Flowers and Masks: The Children of Dumyat Protest against Agrium...And Appeal to 'Mama Suzanne' to Intervene." *Al-Masry Al-Youm*, June 11, 2008. In Arabic.

El-Kashef, N. and El-Shazly, E. (2008) "Massive Protests in Damietta to Demand Moving the Factory 'Agrium' and the Governorate Councils Freeze Activities until a Decision to Move is Issued." *Al-Masry Al-Youm*, June 18, 2008. In Arabic.

El-Kashef, N. and El-Shazly, E. (2008) "Carnivals and Fireworks and Popular Marches in Damietta Celebrating the Departure of Agrium." *Al-Masry Al-Youm*, June 21, 2008. In Arabic.

El-Kashef, N., El-Shazly, E., and Abd al-Qadr, M. (2008) "Popular Conference in Dumyat Demands Continuing Efforts against Establishing the Factory 'Agrium' and Calls for the Citizens to Hang Black Banners." *Al-Masry Al-Youm*, April 25, 2008. In Arabic.

El-Kashef, N., El-Shazly, E., and Fekry, A. (2011) "Furious Damietta Protesters Shut Down Main Power Station." *Al-Masry Al-Youm*, November 16, 2011. http://www.egyptindependent.com/news/furious-damietta-protesters-shut-down-main-power-station (accessed November 24, 2011).

El-Kholy, O. A. and Beltagy, D. A. I. (2002) "Revision of Pollution Hotspots in the Mediterranean: Country Report for Egypt." Athens: United Nations Environment Programme and Mediterranean Action Plan.

El-Kilany, M. (1997) "Sanitary Drainage in Alexandria." *6th October Magazine*, May 18, 1997.

El-Sayed, M. (2008) "Local Animosity: The Residents of Damietta Are Beefing up Their Campaign against the Construction of a Huge Fertilizer Plant." *Al-Ahram Weekly*, April 24–30, 2008. http://weekly.ahram.org.eg/2008/894/eg7.htm (accessed November 15, 2011).

El-Shazly, E. (2008) "Housing Cooperative Asks to Buy Land of Agrium for 3 Million Pounds." *Al-Masry Al-Youm*, May 28, 2008. In Arabic.

El-Shazly, E. and El-Kashef, N. (2008) "Experts: Agrium Threatens Fishing Fleet and Drains Damietta's Natural Resources." *Al-Masry Al-Youm*, April 21, 2008. In Arabic.

El-Shazly, E. and El-Kashef, N. (2008) "National Holiday Festivities Suspended in Dumyat in Fear of Protests against Agrium." *Al-Masry Al-Youm*, May 5, 2008. In Arabic.

El-Shazly, E. and El-Kashef, N. (2008) "Signs of a New Crisis in Dumyat Because of the Factory 'MOPCO' for Production of Urea." *Al-Masry Al-Youm*, May 9, 2008. In Arabic.

El-Shazly, E. and El-Kashef, N. (2008) "Dumyat: We Will Prevent Agrium in 'All Ways' and Nathif Tries to End the Crisis before Davos." *Al-Masry Al-Youm*, May 15, 2008. In Arabic.

El-Zayat, H., Ibraheem, G., and Kandil, S. (2006) "The Response of Industry to Environmental Regulations in Alexandria, Egypt." *Journal of Environmental Management*, 79(2): 207–18.

Elarabawy, M. and Tosswell, P. (1998) "An Appraisal of the Southern Valley Development Project in Egypt." *Journal of Water Supply, Research, and Technology – Aqua*, 47(4): 167–85.

Elmusa, S. (2009) "Wadi Degla Protectorate: A Tragedy of the Commons?" In Selim, T. (ed.) *Egypt, Energy and the Environment: Critical Sustainability Perspectives*, London: Adonis and Abbey: 187–98.

Elmusa, S. and Baraka, H. (2009) "Justice for the Environment." *Al-Ahram Weekly*, 9–15 April, 2009. http://weekly.ahram.org.eg/2009/942/en2.htm (accessed June 10, 2010).

Elmusa, S. and Sowers, J. (2009) "Damietta Mobilizes for its Environment." *Middle East Report Online*, October 21, 2009. http://www.merip.org/mero/mero102109.html (accessed February 10, 2012).

Ender, G. (2003) "Policy Reform as a Process: Benefits and Lessons from APRP." In Ender, G. and Holtzman, J. S. (eds) *Does Agricultural Policy Reform Work? The Impact on Egypt's Agriculture, 1996–2002*, Abt Associates Inc. and United States Agency for International Development (USAID): 439–53.

Environmental Design Group (2006) "Fayoum Ecotourism Development Plan, 2005–2015." Italian Cooperation and Fayoum Tourism Authority, December 2006.

European Union and Egyptian Environmental Affairs Agency (1998) "Gulf of 'Aqaba Environmental Action Plan: Egypt." Cairo: European Union–EEAA, April 1998.

Evans, P. (1995) *Embedded Autonomy: States and Industrial Transformation*, Princeton: Princeton University Press.

Evans, P. (ed.) (1996) *State–Society Synergy*, Berkeley: University of California Press.

Farag, M. A. (undated) "Comments on the Project of Liverpool University." Undated mimeograph. Alexandria: Department of Sanitary Engineering, University of Alexandria, and High Institute of Public Health: 1–9.

Fiad, N. (1997) "Treatment of Wastewater to Cultivate 100,000 Feddans at Nubaria." *Al Wafd*, March 8, 1997. In Arabic.

Fiana and Partners (1998) "Tourism Sector Profile." *Kompass Egypt Financial Directory*. Cairo: Al-Ahram Commercial Press: 224–33.

Fikry, A. and Ati, M. A. (2008) "IDA Threatens to Stop Project for Producing Methanol in Damietta." *Al-Masry Al-Youm*, September 3, 2008.

Fikry, A. and Shalabi, A. R. (2008) "CAO's Report on Mopco's Takeover of Agrium." *Al-Masry Al-Youm*, December 17, 2008. http://www.almasryalyoum.com/node/172967 (accessed July 10, 2011).

Foreign Agricultural Service (2010) "Egypt: Rice Update." Washington, DC: United States Department of Agriculture, June 29, 2010: 1–4.

Frihy, O. E., Fanos, A. M., Kafagy, A. A., and Abu Aesha, K. A. (1996) "Human Impacts on the Coastal Zone of Hurghada, Northern Red Sea, Egypt." *Geo-Marine Letters*, 16: 324–9.

Gallagher, N. E. (1990) *Egypt's Other Wars: Epidemics and the Politics of Public Health*, Syracuse, NY: Syracuse University Press.

Gallup, J. and Marcotte, B. (2004) "An Assessment of the Design and Effectiveness of the Environmental Pollution Prevention Project (EP3)." *Journal of Cleaner Production*, 13(12): 214–25.

Gauch, S. (2011) "After the Revolution: An Egyptian Conservation Group Fights to Preserve Nature from Development." *OnEarth: A Survival Guide for the Planet*. http://www.onearth.org/blog/saving-egypts-most-vital-nature-preserves-from-reckless-development (accessed January 15, 2012).

Global Environmental Facility (2010) "Request for CEO Endorsement for Project 3668, Egypt: Strengthening Protected Area Financing and Management Systems." Washington, DC: Global Environmental Facility, April 28, 2010.

Global Environmental Facility Evaluation Office (2009) "Country Portfolio Evaluation: Egypt (1991–2008)." GEF/ME/C.35/Inf2. Cairo: Global Environmental Facility, May 26, 2009.

Goldrup, M. (1998) "Tax Incentives Questioned." *Business Monthly*, August 1998: 30–1.

Goma'a, H., El-Kashef, N., and El-Shazly, E. (2008) "Thousands of Dumyatis Protest in Front of Mosques against Agrium...And Port Said Raises Black Banners." *Al-Masry Al-Youm*, June 7, 2008. In Arabic.

Gomaa, S. (1994) "Environmental Threats in Egypt: Perceptions and Actions." *Cairo Papers in Social Science*, 17(4).

Gomaa, S. (1997) *Environmental Policy-Making in Egypt*, Cairo: The American University in Cairo.

Grantham, G. and Cullivan, D. (1978) "Regarding the Alexandria Wastewater Master Plan." Cairo: Camp Dresser & McKee, report to Dr. Hassan Marie, Chairman, Advisory Committee on Reconstruction, Ministry of Housing and Reconstruction, May 30, 1978.

Guha, R. (2000) *Environmentalism: A Global History*, New York: Longman.

Gulf of 'Aqaba Protectorates Development Programme (1997) "Working Group Meeting to Discuss Institutional Capacity Building of the Nature Conservation Sector of the EEAA." Cairo: Egyptian Environmental Affairs Agency, February 17, 1997.

Gunn, M. (2011) "Amer Group Regroups in Wake of Arab World Unrest." *Al-Ahram Online*, May 6, 2011. http://english.ahram.org.eg/News/11505.aspx (accessed November 1, 2011).

Haas, P. (1990) *Saving the Mediterranean*, New York: Columbia University Press.

Haddad, B. (2004) "The Formation and Development of Economic Networks in Syria: Implications for Economic and Fiscal Reforms, 1986–2000." In Heydemann, S. (ed.) *Networks of Privilege: The Politics of Economic Reform in the Middle East*, New York: Palgrave Macmillan.

Hamed, M. M. and El Mahgary, Y. (2004) "Outline of a National Strategy for Cleaner Production: The Case of Egypt." *Journal of Cleaner Production*, 12(4): 327–36.

Hamza, A. (1991) "Innovative Clean Technology in Alexandria: Issues and Prospects." Alexandria: High Institute of Public Health, University of Alexandria.

Harper, V. (2006) "Structuring for Success: Reforming the Nature Conservation Sector." Cairo: Nature Conservation Sector.

Hassan, O. (1996) "Investigations! Admiral Al Hakah in Dialogue with the Chief Editor Regarding Sanitary Drainage Issues in the City." *News of Alexandria*, November 24, 1996. In Arabic.

Hateita, A. A.-S. (2010) "Egypt: Orascom Reveals the Development of a Tourism Project in Fayoum." *Al Sharq Al Awsat*, May 19, 2010. In Arabic.

Hawass, Z. (2011) "Petition about Lake Qarun," May 20, 2011. http://www.drhawass.com/blog/petition-about-lake-qarun (accessed October 30, 2011).

Hellman, J. S. (1998) "Winners Take All: The Politics of Partial Reform in Postcommunist Transitions." *World Politics*, 50(2): 203–34.

Henry, C. M. and Springborg, R. (2001) *Globalization and the Politics of Development in the Middle East*, Cambridge: Cambridge University Press.

Hereher, M. E.-D. (2006) "Monitoring Spatial and Temporal Changes of Agricultural Lands in the Nile Delta and their Implications of Soil Characteristics Using Remote Sensing." Unpublished thesis, University of Arizona.

Heydemann, S. (2007) "Social Pacts and the Persistence of Authoritarianism in the Middle East." In Schlumberger, O. (ed.) *Debating Arab Authoritarianism: Dynamics and Durability in Nondemocratic Regimes*, Stanford: Stanford University Press.

Hicks, R. L., Parks, B. C., Roberts, J. T., and Tierney, M. J. (2008) *Greening Aid? Understanding the Environmental Impact of Development Assistance*, Oxford: Oxford University Press.

Ho, P. (2005) *Institutions in Transition: Land Ownership, Property Rights, and Social Conflict in China*, Oxford: Oxford University Press.

Ho, P. and Edmonds, R. L. (2008) *China's Embedded Activism: Opportunities and Constraints of a Social Movement*, London: Routledge.

Hobbs, J. J. (1996) "Speaking with People in Egypt's St. Katherine National Park." *Geographical Review*, 86(1): 1.

Hochstetler, K. and Keck, M. (2007) *Greening Brazil: Environmental Activism in State and Society*, Durham, NC: Duke University Press.

Holy Land Conservation Fund (1989) "Sinai Newsletter." New York: Holy Land Conservation Fund, 7(1).

Hoogland, I. (2002) "Dealing with Reality: Water Distribution in Egypt." Unpublished thesis, Wageningen University.

Hopkins, N. (2005) "The Rule of Law and the Rule of Water." Égypte/Monde Arabe, Troisième Série, Le Shaykh et Le Procureur, July 8, 2008. http://ema.revues.org/index1871.html (accessed April 13, 2012).

Hopkins, N. S., Mehanna, S., and Haggar, S. (2001) *People and Pollution: Cultural Constructions and Social Action in Egypt*, Cairo: American University in Cairo Press.

Huband, M. (1998) "Surge in Egypt's Private Sector." *Financial Times*, February 5, 1998.

Hussein, A.-R. (2008) "Protestors Say Agrium Plant is Like Nazi Gas Chambers." *Daily News Egypt*, July 27, 2008.

Hussein, M. F. (1999) "Efforts of the Ministry of War Production in Developing the Environment and Protecting it from Pollution." Presented at "Efforts of Helwan Industries to Improve the Environment," March 10, 1999, Helwan University, College of Engineering, Helwan, Egypt.

Hvidt, M. (1998) *Water, Technology, and Development: Upgrading Egypt's Irrigation System*, New York: I.B. Tauris.

Institutional Reform Unit, Royal Netherlands Embassy, and German Technical Cooperation (2005) "Vision and Strategy for MWRI Institutional Reform." Cairo: Ministry of Water Resources and Irrigation, May 2005: 1–90.

International Bank for Agricultural Development (2005) "Arab Republic of Egypt Country Programme Evaluation." Report No. 1658-EG: 1–106.

International Crisis Group (2007) "Egypt's Sinai Question." Cairo/Brussels, January 30, 2007.

International Finance Corporation (1997) "Orascom Projects and Touristic Enterprises, Project No. 00790." Washington, DC: IFC, January 15, 1997.

International Monetary Fund (1998) "Egypt: Beyond Stabilization." Washington, DC: International Monetary Fund, May 1998.

International Resources Group (2008) "Life Integrated Water Resources Management Final Report." Report No. 63. United States Agency for International Development, September 2008.

International Resources Group and Development Alternatives Inc. (2003) "Inter-Ministerial Water Policy Integration." Report No. 71. United States Agency for International Development, Ministry of Water Resources and Irrigation, June 2003.

International Resources Group, Winrock International, and Nile Consultants (2001) "Integrated Water Management District." Report No. 49. United States Agency for International Development, December 2001.

International Resources Group, Winrock International, and Nile Consultants (2002a) "Assessment of the Impacts of the Water Policy Reform Program." APRP-Water Policy Activity, Contract PCE-1-00-96-00002-00, Report No. 58. Cairo: United States Agency for International Development and the Ministry of Water Resources and Irrigation, June 2002.

International Resources Group, Winrock International, and Nile Consultants (2002b) "Water Policy Review and Integration Study Working Paper." Report No. 65. Cairo: Ministry of Water Resources and Irrigation, September 2002.

Issawi, C. (1963) *Egypt in Revolution: An Economic Analysis*, Oxford: Oxford University Press.

Jønch-Clausen, T. (2004) "Integrated Water Resources Management (IWRM) and Water Efficiency Plans by 2005. What, Why, and How?" TEC Background Papers No. 10.

Joynce, S. (1994) "Alexandria Wastewater Systems Expansion." Washington, DC: United States Agency for International Development and Datex, November 8, 1994.

Kandil, A. (1998) "Civil Society and Social Change." Cairo: Al-Ahram Center for Political and Strategic Studies.

Kandil, H. M. (2003) "Institutional Reform Vision for the Irrigation Sector in Egypt." *Water Resources Development*, 19(2): 221–31.

Kasinof, L. (2008) "Orascom to Turn Fayoum into a Luxury Locale." *Daily News Egypt*, June 20, 2008. http://www.dailystaregypt.com/article.aspx?ArticleID=14561 (accessed August 10, 2009).

Kassas, M. (1984) "Letter to President Hosni Mubarak Regarding Gebel Elba," March 10.

Kassas, M. (1995) *Egypt Country Study on Biological Diversity*, Cairo: National Biodiversity Unit, Nature Conservation Sector, Egyptian Environmental Affairs Agency.

Kassas, M. (undated mimeograph) "Alexandria Wastewater Master Plan Study: Comments on Initial Environmental Impact Statement."

Keck, M. and Sikkink, K. (1998) *Activists Beyond Borders: Advocacy Networks in International Politics*, Ithaca: Cornell University Press.

Keith, J. E. (2003) "Impacts of the Water Policy Reform Program." In Ender, G. and Holtzman, J. S. (eds) *Does Agricultural Policy Reform Work? The Impact on Egypt's Agriculture, 1996–2002*, Abt Associates Inc. and United States Agency for International Development: 163–90.

Keshavarzian, A. (2007) *Bazaar and State in Iran: The Politics of the Tehran Marketplace*, Cambridge: Cambridge University Press.

Khagram, S. (2004) *Dams and Development: Transnational Struggles for Water and Power*, Ithaca: Cornell University Press.

Khouzam, R. (1994) "Strategic Water Planning: An Exercise Case Study of Egypt." Presented at "VIII International Water Resources Association Congress on Water Resources," Cairo, November 21–25, 1994: (T6–S1) 3.1–3.19.

Kienle, E. (2001) *A Grand Delusion: Democracy and Economic Reform in Egypt*, London: I.B. Tauris.

Kornai, J. (1992) *The Socialist System: The Political Economy of Communism*, Oxford: Oxford University Press, 13.

Lager, J., El-Hakeh, H. A. W., and Hanchett, R. W. (undated) "Alexandria Wastewater: The End Solution." Water Federation Environment TEC – Asia.

Lajna al-Khadamat (1992) "Water and Sanitary Drainage." Cairo: Majlis al-Shura. In Arabic.

Land Center for Human Rights (2011a) "Lake Fishermen's Message to the Egyptian Revolution: Corruption Destroyed the Fish Wealth and Ruined Our Right to a Decent Life." February 19, 2011. http://www.lchr-eg.org/index.htm (accessed February 2, 2012). In Arabic.

Land Center for Human Rights (2011b) "Agricultural Unions and the Hope for Change." April 18, 2011. http://www.lchr-eg.org/index.htm (accessed February 2, 2012). In Arabic.

Land Center for Human Rights (2011c) Summary of Report No. 65, "Agricultural Land of Missed Opportunities and Desired Hope," June 2011. http://www.lchr-eg.org/index. htm (accessed February 1, 2012). In Arabic.

Langohr, V. (2005) "Too Much Civil Society, Too Little Politics." In Posusney, M. P. and Angrist, M. P. (eds) *Authoritarianism in the Middle East*, Boulder, CO: Lynne Rienner.

Lawler, A. (2011) "The Fall of Zahi Hawass." *Smithsonian Magazine*, July 18, 2011. http://www.smithsonianmag.com/history-archaeology/The-Fall-of-Zahi-Hawass.html (accessed January 20, 2012).

Lemos, M. C. (1995) "The Politics of Pollution Control in Cubatao: State Actors and Social Movements in the Environmental Policy-Making Process (Brazil)." Unpublished thesis, MIT.

Luong, P. J. and Weinthal, E. (2010) *Oil is Not a Curse: Ownership Structure and Institutions in Soviet Successor States*, Cambridge: Cambridge University Press.

Lust-Okar, E. and Zerhouni, S. (2008) *Political Participation in the Middle East*, Boulder, CO: Lynne Rienner.

Lynch, M. (2006) *Voices of the New Arab Public: Iraq, Al-Jazeera, and Middle East Politics Today*, New York: Columbia University Press.

Mabro, R. and Radwan, S. (1976) *The Industrialization of Egypt 1939–1973: Policy and Performance*, Oxford: Clarendon Press.

Madbouli, M. (2005) "Background Paper on Urban Planning, Management, and Administration." Cairo: UN-Habitat, UN Common Country Assessment in Egypt.

Maksoud, M. A. (1996) "Prohibition of Disposal in the Sea." *Al-Ahram*, August 15, 1996. In Arabic.

Mann, M. (1984) "The Autonomous Power of the State: Its Origins, Mechanisms, and Results." *European Journal of Sociology*, 25: 185–213.

Mann, M. (1986) *The Sources of Social Power*, Cambridge: Cambridge University Press.

Marroushi, N. (2011a) "BP Project in Ikdu Raises Environmental Concerns." *Al-Masry Al-Youm*, September 20, 2011. http://www.almasryalyoum.com/en/node/497501 (accessed January 2, 2012).

Marroushi, N. (2011b) "Warming Red Sea Waters Pose Threat to Ecosystem." *Al-Masry Al-Youm*, September 29, 2011. http://www.almasryalyoum.com/en/print/500399 (accessed October 20, 2011).

Marsh, A. V. (1997) "What Price the Hurghada Boom?" *Cairo Times*, August 7–20, 1997: 14.

Meade, B. and Shaalan, I. (2002) "Red Sea Sustainable Tourism Initiative." Paper presented at the Sustainable Tourism Egypt (STE) Conference and Exhibition, Cairo, December 15–17, 2002.

"Meeting of the National Democratic Party to Survey the Present and Future Sanitary Drainage Projects." *Journal News of Alexandria*, August 18, 1996. In Arabic.

Mehanna, S. R., Huntington, R., and Antonius, R. (1984) "Irrigation and Society in Rural Egypt." *Cairo Papers in Social Science*, 7(4).

Meisami, J. S. and Starkey, P. (1998) *Encyclopedia of Arabic Literature*, London: Routledge.

Mernissi, F. (1997) "Social Capital in Action: The Case of the Ait Iktel Village Association." In Diwan, I. (ed.) *Voices from Marrakech: Towards Competitive and Caring Societies in the Middle East and North Africa*. Washington, DC: World Bank.

Mesahil, M. A. K. (2008) "Lake Maryut Fishermen Threatened by Pollution." *Al-Masry Al-Youm*, June 30, 2008. http://almasry-alyoum.com/article2.aspx?ArticleID=111431 (accessed July 20, 2008).

Metcalf and Eddy International (1995) "Report of Telecon on Public Participation." Alexandria, Memorandum, October 26, 1995.

Metcalf and Eddy International (1996) "Chairman of Alexandria General Organization for Sanitary Drainage Presentation at the High Institute of Public Health." Alexandria, March 19, 1996.

Ministry of State for Environmental Affairs (2001a) "Egyptian Environmental Directory." Cairo: EEAA, October 2001.

Ministry of State for Environmental Affairs (2001b) "National Environmental Action Plan of Egypt, 2002/2017." Cairo, December 25, 2001.

Ministry of State for Environmental Affairs (2006) "Egypt: State of the Environment Report 2005." Cairo: Ministry of State for Environmental Affairs.

Ministry of State for Environmental Affairs (2007) "Annual Report." Cairo: Ministry of State for Environmental Affairs.

Ministry of State for Environmental Affairs (2009) "Egypt: State of the Environment Report 2008." Cairo: Ministry of State for Environmental Affairs, September.

Ministry of State for Environmental Affairs, Entec Ltd, and UK Department of International Development (2005) "Damietta Governorate Environmental Profile." Cairo: SEAM Programme, Egyptian Environmental Affairs Authority: 1–190. http://www.eeaa.gov.eg/arabic/info/report_gov_profiles.asp (accessed August 15, 2009).

Ministry of Tourism (undated) "Memorandum Concerning the Establishment and Competence of the General Authority for Tourism Development." Cairo: Ministry of Tourism.

Ministry of Water Resources and Irrigation (2005a) "Integrated Water Resources Management Plan." Cairo: Ministry of Public Works and Water Resources.

Ministry of Water Resources and Irrigation (2005b) "National Water Resources Plan for Egypt to 2017." Cairo: Planning Sector, Ministry of Irrigation and Water Resources, January 2005.

Ministry of Water Resources and Irrigation (2007) "West Delta Water Conservation and Irrigation Rehabilitation Project: Draft Resettlement Policy Framework." Cairo: Ministry of Water Resources and Irrigation, January 2007.

Mitchell, T. (1991) "America's Egypt: Discourse of the Development Industry." *Middle East Report*, 169: 18–36.

Mitchell, T. (2002) *Rule of Experts: Egypt, Techno-Politics, Modernity*, Berkeley: UC Press.

Mitchell, T. (2009) "Carbon Democracy." *Economy and Society*, 38(3): 399–432.

Montasser, S. (1999) "Black Clouds over Cairo." *Al-Ahram Weekly*, November 18–24, 1999.

Montgomery, R. (1990) "Troubled Waters." *Cairo Today*. Cairo.

Morton, K. (2005) *International Aid and China's Environment: Taming the Yellow Dragon*, London: Routledge.

Moustafa, T. (2007) *The Struggle for Constitutional Power: Law, Politics, and Economic Development in Egypt*, New York: Cambridge University Press.

Muhafaza Dumyat (undated) "Ras Al-Bar: Return to a Beautiful Time." Muhafaza Dumyat, The Mubarak Project for Development and Urban Coordination. In Arabic.

National Biodiversity Unit (1997) "First National Report to the Convention on Biodiversity." Cairo: Egyptian Environmental Affairs Agency, December 1997.

National Biodiversity Unit and Egyptian Environmental Affairs Agency (1998) "Egypt: National Strategy and Action Plan for Biodiversity Conservation." Cairo: Ministry of State for the Environment, January 1998.

National Committee to Preserve Nature and Natural Resources (1981) "National Program to Preserve Nature." Cairo: Egyptian Association to Preserve Natural Resources, February 1981. In Arabic.

Nature Conservation Sector (2006) "Management Effectiveness of Egypt's Protected Area System." Cairo: Egyptian Environmental Affairs Agency.

"New Plant Halted" (2008) *Africa Research Bulletin: Economic, Financial and Technical Series*, 45(7): 17912.

Norton, A. R. (1995) *Civil Society in the Middle East*, Leiden: Brill.

Novy, M. (1999) "Forging Ahead: Privatization and Restructuring of Czech Steel Firms During the Transition to a Market Economy." Unpublished thesis, Princeton University.

"Nubians Will Finally Go Home; A 7-Day Sit-in Pressures the Government to Agree to Repatriate." *Al-Ahram Online*, September 11, 2011. http://english.ahram.org.eg/News/20953.aspx (accessed October 15, 2011).

"OCI Expands Fertiliser Business" (2009) *Middle East Economic Digest*, 53(13): 23.

Ohshita, S. B. and Ortolano, L. (2006) "Effects of Economic and Environmental Reform on the Diffusion of Cleaner Coal Technology in China." *Development and Change*, 37(1): 75–98.

"One Killed, 12 Injured as Protesters Clash with Security Forces in Damietta." *Al-Masry Al-Youm*, November 13, 2011. In Arabic.

Orascom Development Holdings (undated) "Byoum Residence." Real estate promotional brochure.

O'Rourke, D. (2004) *Community-Driven Regulation: Balancing Development and the Environment in Vietnam*, Cambridge, MA: MIT Press.

Osman, A. Z. (2011) "Military-Owned Factories Threaten Farmers' Livelihoods in Fayoum." *Egypt Independent*, December 21, 2011. http://www.almasryalyoum.com/en/node/560936 (accessed January 2, 2012).

Ostrom, E. (1996) "Crossing the Great Divide: Coproduction, Synergy, and Development." *World Development*, 24(6): 1073.

Othman, A. Z., El-Agroudy, M. N., and Hassan, M. B. E.-D. (2011) "Current Situation and Outlook for Egyptian Rice Economics." *Australian Journal of Basic and Applied Sciences*, 5(11): 1934–41.

Özden, Ç. (2006) "Brain Drain in the Middle East and North Africa." Paper presented at United Nations Expert Group Meeting on Migration and Development in the Arab World, May 15–17, 2006, Beirut.

Pearson, M. (1990) "Ras Mohamed National Marine Park Management Project: Progress Report." Cairo: Egyptian Environmental Affairs Agency, January 1990.

Pilcher, N. and Abou Zaid, M. (2000) "The Status of Coral Reefs in Egypt-2000." Cairo: PERSGA (Regional Organization for the Protection of the Environment of the Red Sea and Gulf of Aden).

Pollick, N. (2011) "Irrigation Canals Mismanagement Leads to Health Hazards: The Example of Abu Sir." *Al-Masry Al-Youm*. http://www.almasryalyoum.com/en/node/437523 (accessed December 22, 2011).

Protected Area Management Unit (2001) "Support to Wadi El-Rayan Protected Area: Final Report and Financial Statement." Cairo: Egyptian–Italian Environmental Program.

"Protests at Nuclear Power Station Construction Site Escalate." *Egypt Independent.* http://www.egyptindependent.com/news/protests-nuclear-power-station-construction-site-escalate (accessed April 15, 2012).

Qasim, M. (1993) *Environmental Pollution and Economic Development*, Cairo: al-Dar al-Misriyah al-Lubnaniyah. In Arabic.

Qazamil, A. H. (1990) *The Dead Lake*, Port Said: Dar al-Kitab. In Arabic.

Radwan, L. (1997) "Farmer Responses to Inefficiencies in the Supply and Distribution of Irrigation Requirements in Delta Egypt." *The Geographical Journal*, 163(1): 78–92.

Radwan, L., Bron, J., and Barakat, E. (2006) "Report on Preliminary Field Workshops, Water Boards Project." Cairo: Ministry of Public Works and Water Resources.

"Railways Authority Estimates 2011 Losses at LE70 Million." *Egypt Independent*, January 13, 2012. http://www.almasryalyoum.com/en/node/599066 (accessed January 20, 2012).

Reem, L. (2008) "No Flow: Fresh Potable Water is Becoming a Scarce Commodity." *Al-Ahram Weekly*, September 11–17, 2008. http://weekly.ahram.org.eg/print/2008/914/eg7.htm (accessed December 27, 2011).

Reuters (2011a) "Damietta Plant Chief Suggests Mediation over Protests." *The Daily New Egypt*, November 18, 2011.

Reuters (2011b) "Damietta Port Reopens but Mopco Dispute Far from Resolved." *Al-Ahram Online*, November 18, 2011. http://english.ahram.org.eg/NewsContent/1/64/26869/Egypt/Politics-/Damietta-port-reopens-but-MOPCO-dispute-far-from-r.aspx (accessed November 22, 2011).

"Rice Varieties Approved for Toshka." *Business Today*, November 9, 1999.

Richards, A. and Waterbury, J. (2008) *A Political Economy of the Middle East*, 3rd edition, Boulder, CO: Westview Press.

Richards, B. (1977) "Health Officials Cite Hazards at Pesticide Plant." *The Washington Post*, December 14, 1977.

Richter, T. and Christian, S. (2007) "Sectoral Transformations in Neo-Patrimonial Rentier States: Tourism Development and State Policies in Egypt." *GIGA Working Paper Series*.

Ru, J. and Ortolano, L. (2009) "Development of Citizen-Organized Environmental NGOs in China." *Voluntas: International Journal of Voluntary and Nonprofit Organizations*, 20(2): 141–68.

Rubin, D. (1994) *The World Encyclopedia of Contemporary Theatre*, London: Routledge.

Rutherford, B. K. (2009) *Egypt after Mubarak: Liberalism, Islam, and Democracy in the Arab World*, Princeton: Princeton University Press.

Saber, K. and Abu Zeid, A. (1998) "About the Protective Affairs of Environment in Egypt: Features of a Crime in the Natural Reserve of Wadi Sanur." Cairo: Land Center for Human Rights, April 1998. In Arabic.

Sabry, M. (2011) "Violence in Port City Sparks Worry About Egypt's Military Tactics." *McClatchy Newspapers*, November 17, 2011. http://www.mcclatchydc.com/2011/11/16/130518/violence-in-nile-port-city-sparks.html (accessed November 20, 2011).

Sachs, S. (2003) "Egypt Clears Rights Activist Whose Jailing Drew World Protest." *New York Times*, March 19, 2003. http://www.nytimes.com/2003/03/19/world/egypt-clears-rights-activist-whose-jailing-drew-world-protest.html?ref=saadeddinibrahim (accessed July 9, 2011).

Sadik, A.-K., Nimah, M., and Alaoui, S. B. (2011) "Agriculture." In Abaza, H., Saab, N., and Zeitoon, B. (eds) "Green Economy: Sustainable Transition in a Changing Arab World." Beirut: The Arab Forum for Environment and Development.

Sakr, M., Massoud, N., and Sakr, H. (2009) "Tourism in Egypt: An Unfinished Business." Cairo: Egyptian Center for Economic Studies, May 2009.

Salah Al-Din, L., Yassin, M., and El-Daragli, A. (2008) "The Governor of Dumyat Announces in Front of Five Thousand Protesters: The Factory Agrium Will Move to Suez." *Al-Masry Al-Youm*, April 30, 2008. In Arabic.

Salem, M., Zalat, A., and Farghali, D. (2009) "Farmers to Remove Crops Grown with Sewage Water." *Al-Masry Al-Youm*, August 10, 2009.

Sarant, L. (2011) "Red Sea: Oil Leak Prompts Government to Declare Emergency near Hurghada." *Al-Masry Al-Youm*, September 22, 2011. http://www.almasryalyoum.com/en/node/498245 (accessed September 30, 2011).

Schwedler, J. (1995) *Toward Civil Society in the Middle East? A Primer*, Boulder, CO: Lynne Rienner.

Scott, J. C. (1985) *Weapons of the Weak: Everyday Forms of Peasant Resistance*, New Haven: Yale University Press.

Scott, J. C. (1998) *Seeing Like a State: How Certain Schemes to Improve the Human Condition Have Failed*, New Haven: Yale University Press.

Segura Consulting LLC and the Institute for Public–Private Partnerships (2004) "Water and Wastewater Feasibility Study for PSP (Private Sector Participation) in Alexandria, Egypt." Washington, DC: United States Agency for International Development, March 27, 2004.

Sewelam, M. F. (1992) "Action Plan for Institutional Report." Alexandria: Alexandria General Organization for Sanitary Drainage, December 16, 1992.

Sfakianakis, J. (2004) "The Whales of the Nile: Networks, Businessmen, and Bureaucrats During the Era of Privatization in Egypt." In Heydemann, S. (ed.) *Networks of Privilege in the Middle East: The Politics of Economic Reform Revisited*, New York: Palgrave Macmillan.

Sharif, Y. (1999) "Launching Enforcement Programs Through Compliance Action Plans," unpublished paper.

Shawky, A. "State Accountability for Harmful Impacts on Health Caused by Industrial Pollution in Egypt." *Third World Legal Studies*, 135–57.

Sims, D. (2010) *Understanding Cairo: The Logic of a City out of Control*, Cairo/New York: The American University in Cairo Press.

Soil and Water Ltd (1998) "Egyptian Pollution Abatement Project: Financing Component." Cairo: Egyptian Environmental Affairs Agency, March 22, 1998.

South Asia Human Rights Documentation Network (2002) "Mubarak Plays Pharaoh: Egypt's 'New' NGO Law." New Delhi. http://www.hrdc.net/sahrdc/hrfeatures/HRF61.htm (accessed January 24, 2011).

South Sinai Sector Staff (1998) "Field Survey on Development of Lands Allocated by TDA." Cairo: South Sinai Protectorates Division, Egyptian Environmental Affairs Agency, February 4–12, 1998.

Sowers, J. (2003) "Allocation and Accountability: State–Business Relations and Environmental Politics in Egypt." Unpublished thesis, Princeton University.

Sowers, J. (2007) "Nature Reserves and Authoritarian Rule in Egypt: Embedded Autonomy Revisited." *Journal of Environment and Development*, 16(4): 375–97.

Sowers, J. (2011) "Re-mapping the Nation, Critiquing the State: Environmental Narratives and Desert Land Reclamation in Egypt." In Davis, D. K. and Burke, E. III (eds) *Environmental Imaginaries in the Middle East: History, Policy, Power, and Practice*, Athens: Ohio University Press: 158–91.

Sowers, J. (2012) "Institutional Change in Authoritarian Regimes: Water and the State in Egypt." In Steinberg, P. and VanDeveer, S. (eds) *Comparative Environmental Politics*, Cambridge, MA: MIT Press.

Sowers, J. and Toensing, C. (eds) (2012) *The Journey to Tahrir: Revolution, Protest, and Social Change in Egypt*, London: Verso.

Sowers, J., Vengosh, A., and Weinthal, E. (2010) "Climate Change, Water Resources, and the Politics of Adaptation in the Middle East and North Africa." *Climatic Change*, 104(3–4): 599–627.

Springborg, R. (1989) *Mubarak's Egypt: Fragmentation of the Political Order*, Boulder, CO: Westview Press.

Springborg, R. (2009) "Protest Against a Hybrid State: Words Without Meaning?" In Hopkins, N. (ed.) *Political and Social Protest in Egypt*, Cairo Papers in Social Science, 29(2).

Stanford, D. (1999) "New Protected Area Looks to Expand." *Middle East Times*, January 24–30, 1999.

Stanley, D. J. and Warne, A. (1998) "Nile Delta in its Destruction Phase." *Journal of Coastal Research*, 14(3): 794–825.

Steinberg, P. (2001) *Environmental Leadership in Developing Countries: Transnational Relations and Biodiversity Policy in Costa Rica and Bolivia*, Cambridge, MA: MIT Press.

Strasser, M. (2011) "Egypt Warns of Foreign Meddling as US Pushes on with Democracy Programs." *Al-Masry Al-Youm*, July 5, 2011. http://www.almasryalyoum.com/en/node/474767 (accessed July 6, 2011).

Sullivan, D. J. (1994) *Private Voluntary Organizations in Egypt: Islamic Development, Private Initiative and State Control*, Gainesville: University Press of Florida.

Tadros, M. (2000) "Leviathan Revisited." *Al-Ahram Weekly*, September 21–27, 2000. http://weekly.ahram.org.eg/2000/500/dev1.htm (accessed January 26, 2011).

Tan, J. (2002) "Impact of Ownership Type on Environment–Strategy Linkage and Performance: Evidence from a Transitional Economy." *Journal of Management Studies*, 39(3): 333–54.

Tawfik, R. T. (2004) "Recreational Value of Coral Reefs—An Application to Coral Reefs in Ras Mohamed National Park." Unpublished MA thesis, University of York.

Tczap, A. (2002) "Final Report, Agricultural Policy Reform Program, Water Policy Program." Report No. 66. United States Agency for International Development (USAID), September 2002.

Tendler, J. and Freedheim, S. (1994) "Trust in a Rent-Seeking World: Health and Government Transformed in Northeast Brazil." *World Development*, 22(12): 1771.

The "Green Man" (1998) "Without Anger." *Al-Ahram*, January 8, 1998. In Arabic.

"The Ministers of Tourism and Environment Witness the Establishment of the Tourism Investors' Association for the Protection of the Environment." *Al-Ahram*, December 10, 1998. In Arabic.

Tolba, M. K. (1986) "Letter Regarding UNEP Mission to Alexandria." To Professor Mohamed Kamel, President of the Academy of Scientific Research and Technology, August 14, 1986.

Tolba, M. K. and Saab, N. W. (2008) "Arab Environment: Future Challenges." Beirut: Arab Forum for Environment and Development. http://www.afedonline.org/afedreport (accessed May 1, 2009).

Tourism Development Authority (undated) "Development Plan for the Egyptian Riviera." Cairo: Ministry of Tourism, Promotional Brochure.

Tourism Development Authority and United States Agency for International Development (1998) "Best Practices for Tourism Center Development Along the Red Sea Coast." Cairo: Tourism Development Authority, October 1998.

"Uhde to Build Damietta Fertiliser Plant" (2007) *Middle East Economic Digest*, 52(19): 17.

United Nations Development Programme (2001) *Egypt Human Development Report 2000/2001*, Cairo: United Nations Development Programme.

United Nations Development Programme (2005) *The Arab Human Development Report 2004: Towards Freedom in the Arab World*, New York: United Nations Development Programme.

United Nations Development Programme and Institute of National Planning (2004) *Egypt Human Development Report: Choosing Decentralization for Good Governance*, Cairo: United Nations Development Programme.

United Nations Development Programme and Institute of National Planning (2005) *Egypt Human Development Report 2005: Towards a New Social Contract*, Cairo: United Nations Development Programme.

United Nations Development Programme and Institute of National Planning (2008) *Egypt Human Development Report: Egypt's Social Contract: The Role of Civil Society*, Cairo: United Nations Development Programme.

United States Agency for International Development (2011) "Safeguarding the World's Water: 2011 Report on USAID Fiscal Year 2010 Water Sector Activities." Washington, DC: United States Agency for International Development, July 2011.

United States Energy Information Administration (2010) "Country Analysis Briefs: Egypt." June 2010. http://www.eia.doe.gov/emeu/cabs/Egypt/Background.html (accessed August 15, 2010).

United States General Accounting Office (1993) "Military Aid to Egypt: Tank Coproduction in Egypt." Washington, DC: USGAO.

United States Information Service (1996) "Media Strategy for Alexandria Wastewater Issue." Cairo: Memorandum, February 8, 1996.

Wahba, S. E.-D. (1995) "'Enemy of the People': A Story of Assassinating a City." *Al-Ahram*, September 30, 1995. In Arabic.

Wahba, S. E.-D. (1995) "'Emperor Jones' in Alexandria: The Story of the Assassination of a City (2)." *Al-Ahram*, October 21, 1995. In Arabic.

Wahba, S. E.-D. (1995) "'Public Enemy' in Court." *Al-Ahram*, November 4, 1995. In Arabic.

Wahba, S. E.-D. (1995) "'Public Enemy' and USAID." *Al-Ahram*, November 11, 1995. In Arabic.

Wahba, S. E.-D. (1995) "The Other Aspect of Alexandria." *Al-Ahram*, November 25, 1995. In Arabic.

Wahba, S. E.-D. (1995) "'People's Enemy' and 'Ashmawi [the Hangman]." *Al-Ahram*, December 16, 1995. In Arabic.

Wahba, S. E.-D. (1995) "Enemies of Success." *Al-Ahram*, December 30, 1995. In Arabic.

Wahba, S. E.-D. (1996) "'People's Enemy' in the People's Assembly." *Al-Ahram*, January 20, 1996. In Arabic.

Wahba, S. E.-D. (1996) "The Golden Anniversary of Alexandria's Wastewater." *Al-Ahram*, September 28, 1996. In Arabic.

Wahba, S. E.-D. (1997) "Did the Conspiracy of Alexandria End?" *Al-Ahram*, May 31, 1997. In Arabic.

Wali, Y. (1979) "Letter Regarding Preliminary Studies for Alexandria Wastewater Reuse." To Hasaballah Kafrawi, Minister of Housing and Reconstruction and New Communities, Cairo, May 20, 1979.

Waterbury, J. (1979) *Hydropolitics of the Nile Valley*, Syracuse: Syracuse University Press.

Waterbury, J. (1983) *The Egypt of Nasser and Sadat: The Political Economy of Two Regimes*, Princeton: Princeton University Press.

Waterbury, J. (1993) *Exposed to Innumerable Delusions*, Cambridge: Cambridge University Press.

Waterbury, J. (2002) *The Nile Basin: National Determinants of Collective Action*, New Haven: Yale University Press.

Werr, P. (2011) "Revolution May Save Neolithic Treasure." *Reuters*, June 2, 2011. http://www.msnbc.msn.com/id/43258991/ns/technology_and_science-science/t/egypts-revolution-may-save-neolithic-treasure (accessed October 30, 2011).

Wizarat al-Dawlah li-Shu'un al-Bi'ah (2007) "Taqrir Halat Al-Bi'ah Fi Misr, 2006." Cairo: Ministry of State for Environmental Affairs.

Woertz, E. (2011) "Arab Food, Water, and the Big Landgrab That Wasn't." *Brown Journal of World Affairs*, 18(1): 119–32.

World Bank (2004) "Balancing Productivity and Environmental Pressure in Egypt: Toward an Interdisciplinary and Integrated Approach to Agricultural Drainage." Washington, DC: World Bank, February 2004.

World Bank (2005a) "Arab Republic of Egypt: Country Environmental Analysis, 1992–2002." Report No. 31993-EG. Washington, DC: World Bank.

World Bank (2005b) "Project Information Document: Egyptian Pollution Abatement II." Report No. AB 1869. Washington, DC: World Bank.

World Bank (2007) *Making the Most of Scarcity*, Washington, DC: World Bank.

World Heritage Convention (2011) "Properties on the Tentative List, Submitted by State Parties, Gebel Qatrani Area, Lake Qarun Natural Preserve." http://whc.unesco.org/en/tentativelists/1797 (accessed November 1, 2011).

Yassin, H. (2011) "US Violated Egypt's Sovereignty by Offering Funds to NGOs, Says Minister." *Al-Masry Al-Youm*, July 6, 2011. http://www.almasryalyoum.com/en/node/474963 (accessed July 6, 2011).

Yassin, M., El-Kashef, N., and El-Shazly, E. (2008) "Popular Conference in Dumyat to Support the Communication of 'Sultan' against Agrium." *Al-Masry Al-Youm*, May 24, 2008. In Arabic.

Zakaria, F. (1997) "A Situation of Confusion in the Execution of the Waste Water Project in Alexandria." *Al Wafd*, February 4, 1997. In Arabic.

Zawahri, N., Sowers, J., and Weinthal, E. (2011) "The Politics of Assessment: Water and Sanitation MDGs in the Middle East and North Africa." *Development and Change*, 42(5): 1153–77.

Zayed, D. (2010) "Egypt's Amer Group Wins Bid for Fayoum Project." *Reuters*, December 12, 2010. http://www.reuters.com/article/2010/12/12/egypt-amer-idUSLDE6BB03D20101212 (accessed November 1, 2011).

Zayed, D. (2011) "Egypt's Real Estate Sector Down, Not Out." *Reuters*, May 18, 2011. http://www.reuters.com/article/2011/05/18/us-egypt-property-idUSTRE74H38F20110518 (accessed November 1, 2011).

Zeinobia (2008) "We, the People of Damitta [Sic] Part 2." http://egyptianchronicles.blogspot.com/2008/04/wethe-people-of-damitta-2.html (accessed March 2, 2009).

Zerhouni, S. (2008) "Looking Forward," in E. Lust-Okar and S. Zerhouni (eds) *Political Participation in the Middle East*, Boulder, CO: Lynne Reinner, 259–66.

Zohry, A. (2003) "Contemporary Egyptian Migration 2003." Cairo: International Organization for Migration, Italian Cooperation, and Ministry of Manpower and Emigration.

# Index

building infrastructural authority in protected areas 104–7, 160; corruption and acquisition of real estate on coastline 167; creating legal and infrastructural authority for protected areas 114–15; investment plan for 100; liberalizing tourism and limiting conservation on coastline 107–10; military and protected areas 105–6; provincial governors and protected areas 106; resort development 99–100; social and environmental impacts of coastal tourism 111–13; tourism development 100; water supply and impact of tourism on 113–14

SOEs (state-owned enterprises): and costs of pollution abatement 54–5; and pollution control 40–1, 42; privatization of 46

Sons of the Soil 177

Sorour, Fathi 28

Stanley, D.J. 22

*State of the Environment Report* (2008) 53

Steinberg, P. 10

Stockholm Conference of the Human Environment (1972) 24

Strong, Maurice 24

Sudan-Egypt water sharing agreement (1959) 130

Suez Canal 10; nationalization of by Nasser 22

Suez-Lyonnaise des Eaux 136

Sultan, Essam 165

SUMED pipeline 10

Supreme Council of Antiquities (SCA) 171

Supreme Council of the Armed Forces *see* SCAF

Suweiris, Samih 167, 169

tank production 50

Tantawi, Sheikh Muhammad 93, 105

TDA (Tourism Development Agency) 107–8, 109, 110, 112, 113, 114, 115, 117, 118, 119, 160, 167

Technical Cooperation Office for the Environment 30

temporary migration 20, 33–4, 37

Tolba, Mostafa Kamal 24, 25, 27, 28, 74, 92

tourism 18, 100, 160; clash with protected areas in Lake Qarun 168–72; coastal 98; and 'Egyptian Riviera' marketing campaign 111–12, *112*; growth in 109; importance of to Egyptian economy

100; liberalizing of on coastlines 107–11; and protected areas 102; and protected areas on the Red Sea 115–19; Sinai 100; social and environmental impacts of coastal 111–14; volatility of 100

Tourism Development Agency *see* TDA

Tourism Investors' Association to Protect the Environment 116

transitional economies: challenges of pollution control 40–2

Tree Lovers' Association 121–2

Turkey 154

Uhde 85, 164

al-Ulfi, Galal 87

UN Convention on Biological Diversity 98

UNDP (United Nations Development Programme) 7–8, 30, 104, 136–7; and IWRM 137

UNEP (United Nations Environment Programme) 24, 37, 74

UNESCO 23, 25

UNESCO World Heritage Sites 170

United Nations agencies 23

United Nations Development Programme *see* UNDP

United Nations Environment Programme *see* UNEP

United States, aid to Egypt 31

United States Agency for International Development *see* USAID

uprising (2011) 11, 15, 18, 65, 66, 96, 126, 152, 154–5, 157, 176, 177

urbanization 4

USAID (United States Agency for International Development) 32, 35, 38–9, 49, 79, 81, 82, 104, 134, 151; Agricultural Policy Reform Program 135; and Alexandria Wastewater Systems Expansion Project 70, 73, 159; Egyptian Environmental Policy project 115, 116, 120; Egyptian Pollution Prevention Project (EP3) 53–4, 59; funding of environmental management projects in Red Sea 115–16, 117; and integrated water resource management 138; Irrigation Improvement Project 147; LIFE project 117; 'Red Sea Sustainable Tourism Initiative' 116

user associations, branch canal 147–9, 150, 151